FAT-PROOFING YOUR CHILDREN

THE BESTSELLING BOOKS OF VICKI LANSKY

BOOKS NO PARENT SHOULD BE WITHOUT

THE TAMING OF THE C.A.N.D.Y. MONSTER

FEED ME! I'M YOURS

PRACTICAL PARENTING TIPS FOR THE SCHOOL-AGE YEARS

WELCOMING YOUR SECOND BABY

TOILET TRAINING

GETTING YOUR BABY TO SLEEP (AND BACK TO SLEEP)

TRAVELING WITH YOUR BABY

BIRTHDAY PARTIES

DEAR BABYSITTER HANDBOOK

VICKI LANSKY'S READ-TOGETHER BOOKS FEATURING KOKO BEAR

KOKO BEAR'S NEW POTTY

A NEW BABY AT KOKO BEAR'S HOUSE

KOKO BEAR'S NEW BABYSITTER

KOKO BEAR'S BIG EARACHE

FAT-PROOFING YOUR CHILDREN...

SO THAT THEY NEVER BECOME
DIET-ADDICTED ADULTS

VICKI LANSKY

BANTAM BOOKS

TORONTO • NEW YORK • LONDON • SYDNEY • AUCKLAND

FAT-PROOFING YOUR CHILDREN
A Bantam Book / April 1988

Grateful acknowledgment is made to the following for permission to reprint
these excerpts:
Lewis A. Coffin, M.D., THE GRANDMOTHER CONSPIRACY EXPOSED, Capra
Press, 1974
Kuntzleman, Charles T., Ed. D. "How Fit Are Your Kids?" SHAPE (December
1984). FAMILY LIFE EDUCATOR, Volume 3, Number 2 (Winter 1984),
published by the National Family Life Education Network, Santa Cruz, CA.

Fitness list on page 182 copyright © 1987 by The New York Times Company.
Reprinted by permission.

Library of Congress Cataloging-in-Publication Data
Lansky, Vicki.
    Fat-proofing your children—so that they never become
diet addicted adults.

    Bibliography: p. 239
    Includes index.
    1. Children—Nutrition.   2. Obesity in
children—Prevention.   3. Cookery.   I. Title.
RJ206.L335 1988   649'.6   87-47791
ISBN 0-553-05134-2

Published simultaneously in the United States and Canada

Bantam Books are published by Bantam Books, a division of Bantam
Doubleday Dell Publishing Group, Inc. Its trademark, consisting of the
words "Bantam Books" and the portrayal of a rooster, is Registered in
U.S. Patent and Trademark Office and in other countries. Marca Regis-
trada. Bantam Books, 666 Fifth Avenue, New York, New York 10103.

PRINTED IN THE UNITED STATES OF AMERICA

FG   0 9 8 7 6 5 4 3 2 1

CONTENTS

FAT-PROOFING YOUR CHILDREN

INTRODUCTION

FAT-PROOFING: A BETTER LIFE FOR YOUR KIDS

When was the last time you went on a diet? Be honest. Yesterday? Last week? Last month? How many calories do you think you've counted during your lifetime? Zillions?

No matter what people like (or despise) about diets, there's one point on which everyone agrees: dieting is no fun. And a lifetime of dieting is nothing to look forward to.

Millions of Americans go on diets every year—and fewer than 10 percent actually keep off the weight they lose. That means that the other 90 percent are likely to diet over and over again, while their weight rises and falls like a yo-yo. This is not only frustrating, it's downright dangerous. Radical and frequent weight changes strain the heart and other vital organs.

As a society, we spend billions of dollars annually on weight-control products—protein powders, shakes, special foods and pills (remember starch blockers?). We join Weight Watchers and diet centers and weight-loss clinics in droves. We eagerly buy the latest diet books (at last count, there were 350 in print, each with its own band of disciples). We scan magazines and tabloids in search of the latest "miracle" diet. We agonize if we can pinch an inch. We fret about cellulite (which most medical experts dismiss as a myth). In a word, we're *obsessed*.

Eating disorders have reached nearly epidemic proportions due to our national preoccupation with food. Anorexia and bulimia are on the rise, and food addictions are becoming more common. A study of California fourth-grade girls, reported in *American Family Practitioner* (1986), found that 80%

said they were dieting. This is frightening. Children need quality calories and well rounded diets to develop properly.

Is this the kind of life you imagine for your children? It's not the kind I imagine for mine. And that's why I believe in Fat-Proofing because *no child should grow up to become a diet-addicted adult.*

In the decade since I published my first book, *Feed Me, I'm Yours,* I've learned that kids are having problems with food at increasingly younger ages. Teenagers aren't the only ones who are worried about their weight. It's tough to be a fat kid—and tough to be a fat, weight-conscious, body-hating, perpetually dieting adult.

The good news is, *the circle can be broken.* Despite my own negatively programmed food attitudes, I've produced two slim, active, healthy children. And I'm convinced that Fat-Proofing can help you do the same for your kids.

WHAT FAT-PROOFING ISN'T

Before we get into what Fat-Proofing is, it's important to understand what it *isn't.*

- Fat-Proofing *isn't* a diet for kids. Its success doesn't depend on counting calories or weighing every bite that goes into your children's mouths.

- Fat-Proofing *isn't* a supernutrition, supplement-oriented plan. It doesn't insist that you ban white bread or stock up on vitamins.

There's a movement afoot—I call it the "new puritanism"—that implies that your kids will turn out wrong unless you feed them right. Being *too* concerned about nutrition is just another form of food obsession.

- Fat-Proofing *isn't* a laissez-faire, "eat anything you want" approach. As a parent, you're responsible for what your kids consume. But, as you'll see, this can be a positive, directive role rather than a controlling, stifling one.

- Fat-Proofing *isn't* a cure for true obesity. It can't *correct* a condition that already exists. It can, however, help *prevent* the onset of obesity that is not medically related.

- Finally, Fat-Proofing *isn't* an answer to allergies or behavior problems. If you suspect that your kids are sensitive to certain foods, see their doctor.

WHAT FAT-PROOFING IS

To put it simply, Fat-Proofing is a lifelong health pattern that can fit any lifestyle. It involves raising, feeding, and treating your kids in such a way that eating and weight never become problems. And that doesn't always mean limiting or restricting food intake. Instead, it means giving *enough* of the *right* foods for the *right* reasons.

Fat-Proofing starts by addressing our mixed-up attitudes about what food can and can't do for our children and our relationships with them.

For many people, food is a language. Between mothers and children it's the first language, the first form of intimate communication. It remains a major connector among people—just before or just after sex in importance, depending on whom you talk to—for the rest of their lives. In a very real sense, it's the language of love. Little girls hear from an early age that "the way to a man's heart is through his stomach." We show affection by preparing for our loved ones their favorite dishes. We return affection by eating the dishes our loved ones prepare for us.

There's nothing wrong with that, but it seldom stops there. The language of love becomes layered with hidden meanings and concealed demands. Somehow it all gets tied up with guilt, anxiety, and conflict. It turns into the language of power and control. And that's where most food-related problems begin.

How often have *you* used food as a bartering mechanism? ("Clean up your plate and you can have dessert." "Be good today and I'll take you out for ice cream later." "Watch your little brother for half an hour and I'll give you a candy bar.") How often have you hassled your kids to eat their veggies? Or placated a cranky child with goodies? Have you found yourself sending a misbehaving child to bed without dinner?

Although I believe there are times when it's appropriate for food to be used as a reward—in toilet training, for example, many parents have found this highly effective as a short-term incentive—but it's inappropriate at most other times. If we counted the number of occasions during a day when we use food to get our way with our kids, we'd be amazed.

The misuse of food has nothing to do with our responsibility to feed our children. Love is not equal to the amount of food your child eats. (I first said that in *Feed Me, I'm Yours,* and it's just as appropriate here.) There are plenty of alternatives to food as proof of your affection. Some no-calorie examples: a hug; a kiss; time together spent reading, or walking, or playing; the words, "I love you a lot."

Fat-Proofing is about putting food in its proper place.

ABOUT FAT-PROOFING

There are five steps to Fat-Proofing.

Step 1 helps you identify and reassess your own food attitudes, past and present. Whether or not you realize it, you pass those attitudes on to your children, and they stick—often for a lifetime.

Step 2 pinpoints your family's eating patterns. It teaches you how to de-emphasize food and relax your family's food attitudes.

Step 3 shows you when and how to start Fat-Proofing your kids. The primary focus is on forming good, nutritious eating habits as soon as possible.

Step 4 tells you what to expect at each stage of your children's development—and helps you identify any eating problems they may already have.

Step 5 takes Fat-Proofing beyond the table into *all* areas of your family's lifestyle. Fat-Proofing is more than just eating right for the right reasons. It's also about building self-esteem and getting enough exercise.

Fat-Proofing can help healthy kids to stay that way now and in the future. It can help overweight kids slim down. It may prevent food-related problems that are far more serious than a few excess pounds. In short, it's an easy, commonsense approach to making sure your kids have a better life.

ONE

WHY YOU SHOULD FAT-PROOF YOUR KIDS

Thinking back to my grade-school years, I can barely remember my long-ago classmates' names or looks. I *think* my best girlfriend was taller than I and had brown hair and freckles. I recall how another friend looked when she had one of her front teeth knocked out. But the person who does stand out in my mind was the class fat boy.

I barely knew him, but I can still picture him overflowing his chair, lumbering down the hall, straining the buttons on his shirts. He must have weighed over 200 pounds. We teased him, I'm ashamed to say, and he kept pretty much to himself.

A fat kid is an easy target for gibes, jokes, and ugly names. A fat kid gets a lot of attention—mostly unwelcome. A fat kid is memorable—for all the wrong reasons.

> As reported in the January 1982 issue of *Families*, it's estimated that for every 100 children, 16 (or more) are obese. That's a whopping *1 in 6*. And, according to the August 1984 issue of *American Baby*, these rates are even higher among low-income families.

Even preschoolers believe that a fat child is ugly, stupid, mean, sloppy, and lazy, prone to lying and not to be trusted. In a fascinating study published in the November 1983 issue of *Parents Magazine,* both children and adults were asked to rank an overweight child against other "different" children, and the chubby child received a lower ranking than a child in a wheelchair, a child with a facial disfigurement, and a child with one hand missing. The more aware overweight children become of others' low opinions of them, the more self-conscious they become.

> As reported in the February 1984 issue of *Prevention Magazine,* researchers have discovered that heavy children don't do as well in school as their thinner classmates. When performance in math and reading was tested, the overweight kids were the under-achievers.

Fat kids don't star in class plays or become class presidents or baseball-team captains. Since they're seldom "natural" athletes, they're often left out of sports altogether—which is especially unfortunate, because they usually need the exercise the most.

Overweight children are generally passive and withdrawn. They are nonjoiners and can become "social outcasts" at an early age—or "class clowns," which gives the other kids more excuses to laugh at them. When they make an effort to change those patterns (which they seldom do), they frequently meet with further rejection. Listen to what one woman says about her experience as an overweight youngster:

When I was in seventh grade I finally worked up the courage to try out for the class musical. Even though I was fat, I could sing! I made the chorus and couldn't wait to start rehearsals. I thought looks wouldn't matter. I was wrong. On the first day the director divided us up into two groups. In the first group were all the pretty, popular, thin girls and good-looking boys; they got to stand in front. The rest of us stood in back, where the audience wouldn't see anything but our heads.

Parents of fat kids—even parents who are fat themselves—feel ashamed of their children. One study even showed that parents tend not to include photos of fat children in their family albums. And children remember every slight, every sign of insensitivity. Here's another comment from one who was formerly fat:

I will never buy my clothes from Sears, I don't care if Cheryl Tiegs does design them! Long ago I was a Sears "Chubby Girl." That was the name Sears gave to its whole line of clothes for girls like me who were overweight or even just bigger than other girls their age. It was printed right on the labels. I begged my mother not to order those clothes but she did anyway. She always promised that if I lost weight I could order clothes out of the "regular" part of the catalog.

And another:

My mom was slim and gorgeous. Every hair was always in place, every nail was perfect. I used to fantasize about growing up and wearing her clothes. As the oldest of four daughters, I hoped one day to be married in her antique satin wedding dress. One day (I think I was twelve years old at the time) we were talking about growing up and getting married. I said something about the dress. She told me that I was already too "broad in the beam" to get into it, and I'd better start dieting then and there.

Babies don't mind when adults praise their chunky cheeks and exclaim over their "baby fat." But older children, especially teens, cringe inside at any reference to their weight, however subtle. And they never forget it. As one man related:

Whenever our relatives got together—there were lots of us—a favorite topic of conversation was always who-looks-like-who. My sister had my mother's build, a cousin had our grandmother's nose, and so on. I was "built like a Mack truck"—or, worse yet, compared to one of my grandfathers. I liked him a lot, but he weighed 250 pounds!

Rude strangers encountered in the grocery store or on the street may make comments in passing, not realizing (or not caring) how harmful they can be to a child's self-image. Even adults who ought to know better aren't innocent. Some teachers reject and ridicule the fat children they're supposed to be helping and encouraging. (One of our neighbors told me about an incident that occurred at snack time at her daughter's school. The teacher told the little girl, *in front of the whole class*, "Watch it, Tracy! You know you shouldn't have that cookie.") A friend of mine remembers a similar event:

A photographer came into my third-grade class one day; I don't recall why. Maybe he was taking pictures for a magazine or something. There were over twenty kids in the class, and the photographer told our teacher that he only wanted to shoot a group of ten. Then he stood there while the teacher chose us, one at a time. Not a single overweight child got picked. I know. I was one.

In another study, published in the November 1983 issue of *Parents Magazine,* the majority of children ages 2 to 5 preferred thin dolls to fat dolls. It's amazing how quickly our children take on our values.

Fat children learn to make themselves the butt of jokes. They build elaborate defense systems. This results in poor self-esteem, which carries into their teen and adult years. The teasing they endure in early childhood gives way to outright discrimination later on—at school, at work, in society. One authority compares this to the discrimination experienced by members of racial and ethnic minorities.

According to a 1974 survey conducted by Roger Half Personnel Agencies, fat executives earn thousands of dollars a year less than their thinner associates.

Being fat also causes health problems. Here are some frightening facts:

- Overweight people—kids *and* adults—are clumsier, react more slowly, and are more susceptible than lean people to complications from surgery, infections, and delayed healing of wounds.

- When fat kids and slim kids develop the same illnesses, fat kids stay sicker longer.

- Overweight adults are more accident-prone, according to the June 1983 issue of *Personnel Journal.* They are more likely to die *natural* deaths sooner than their slimmer peers. What the insurance companies call "excess mortality" is 50 percent higher for severely obese adults.

- Obese kids are more likely to develop diabetes and kidney ailments later in life. As reported in the January 1982 issue of *Families,* when a fat kid becomes a fat adult, he or she also has a greater chance of suffering from high blood pressure, heart trouble, diabetes, stroke, arthritis, hypertension, gall bladder disorders, and liver disease.

- Recent studies show that overweight girls may be more prone than others to menstrual problems and eventual infertility.

- For both girls and boys, carrying all that extra weight around may lead to backaches, knee pains and sore feet (*Families*, January 1982).

Dr. Theodore Van Itallie, Medical Chief Advisor of the Obesity Research Program at New York City's St. Luke's Hospital, maintains that "there is little doubt that even moderate obesity is hazardous to health." (The good news is that most of these adverse conditions improve once the excess pounds are taken off *and kept off.*)

It's clear, then, that being fat is a big problem for a kid. It takes both a social and an emotional toll. It paves the way for long-term health problems. And, in many cases, it sets the stage for a lifelong struggle against fat.

WHY KIDS GET FAT

Obesity is a killing disease. According to a National Institutes of Health panel as reported in *The New York Times* of February 14, 1985, it deserves the same medical attention as high blood pressure, smoking, and other factors that result in major illness and early death. Like many diseases, the sooner it starts and the longer it lasts, the harder it is to cure.

Some 24 million obese American adults started out as chubby children. But how did they get that way? Are fat children born, or made?

There are no definitive answers to those questions. However, there are plenty of theories. The Big Three are *overeating, heredity,* and *environment.*

> There are two ways to define obesity. The first puts it in terms of *body weight:* A person who is 40 percent or more above the average median weight for his or her body type, age, and sex is classified as obese. The second definition focuses on *fatty tissue:* A person who carries 30 percent or more of his or her body weight in fatty tissue falls into the obese category.
>
> For children especially, the second definition must take into account such factors as norms for height, weight, age, and sex, and the natural changes that occur in the fatty-to-lean body-tissue ratio from infancy onward. (If the fatty-tissue measure were the only one we used, all newborns would automatically be labeled obese!)

THE OVEREATING THEORY

If you consume more calories than you burn, the excess translates into pounds. (A pound of fat contains 3,500 calories.) On the surface, it seems as if losing weight should involve nothing more than balancing that equation in your favor and consuming fewer calories. It would work that way, *if* we all burned calories at exactly the same rate. The *if* is what makes things difficult.

How slowly or quickly we burn calories depends on our personal BMR, or "basal metabolic rate"—what health writer Jane Brody calls our "idling speed." Some of us simply burn more calories than others when we're doing essentially the same things—and even when we're doing nothing at all. If you could look inside two people who were lying down resting, you might find that their bodies were using calories in completely different ways. One might be burning them up producing body heat, while the other might be storing them as fat.

Researchers have found that the BMR of a fat child may be *more* efficient than that of a slim child, even a sibling. This means that the fat child's body burns calories sparingly, while the thin child's burns them much more quickly. (Have you wondered why some people can overeat and still stay slim? Metabolism is one answer.)

It *sounds* easy. It *sounds* as if we can blame obesity on low metabolism. Not true! Nearly *all* research indicates that it's the other way around—that *a low metabolism is the* **result** *of obesity rather than its cause*. Most fat people, in fact, started out life with perfectly "normal" metabolisms. As they gained weight, they developed metabolic "abnormalities," making it that much easier for them to keep adding pounds and that much harder to take them off.

Is it possible to return our metabolic rate to "normal"? Researchers think so. Eating less, in and of itself, won't do it, though. In fact, if all we do is start cutting down on calories, the body will fight to maintain its weight. The metabolic rate will actually drop as much as 15 to 40 percent to compensate for the "fuel shortage."

There seems only one way to speed up a slow metabolism: regular exercise. That can boost a sluggish metabolism by 20 to 30 percent. But it has to be *regular,* not occasional. A sudden burst of activity will result in the body's overestimating the amount of calories it needs, and you'll end up eating more than you burn.

What you eat or overeat can make a difference too. The age-old complaint about fatty foods going right to the hips seems to have some merit. In the past, scientists believed that all calories were equal no matter what their dietary source. Now a new picture is emerging. Dr. Elliot Danforth's studies at the University of Vermont have indicated that the more fat that is eaten, the less fat gets burned by the body metabolism. Dr. Danforth believes that merely by switching one's diet away from a high-fat menu, most people could continue overeating and still lose weight. It's easier for your body to turn dietary fat into body fat than to turn carbohydrates into fat. Fat is more fattening then than complex carbohydrates such as grains and vegetables.

For an obese child, overeating will of course make matters worse. Even for a thin child, consistent overeating may lead to obesity. However, overeating is seldom the only cause of weight problems. And successful Fat-Proofing requires more than limiting the amounts of food our children eat.

THE HEREDITY THEORY

A number of findings and studies seem to support this theory. Here are the statistics, as reported in the January 1982 issue of *Families:*

- A child with two obese parents has a 70 to 80 percent chance of becoming obese.

- A child with one obese parent has a 40 to 50 percent chance of becoming obese.

But . . .

- A child with two parents of normal weight has only a 7 percent chance of becoming obese.

It's also been suggested that genes may be responsible for bigger-than-average appetites and the tendency to develop more fatty tissue.

We've all seen enough fat families to lend credence to this theory. And it's convenient to use it as an excuse for our own weight problems and those of our children. If fat is a family trait, why fight it?

Because it's the healthy thing to do. People with genetic predispositions to being heavy will have to work harder at keeping weight down than will thin people. And once they do become overweight, they will have to work much harder to lose excess weight.

The happy truth is that the heredity theory doesn't tell the whole story any more than the overeating theory does. In fact, recent evidence indicates that heredity plays a comparatively minor role. And it certainly doesn't explain why the *adopted* children of overweight parents are every bit as likely as biological children to follow in their parents' pudgy footsteps. Or, for that matter, why fat people have fat pets! (Nearly 50 percent of them do.)

THE ENVIRONMENT THEORY

Almost all specialists agree that environment plays a greater role than any other factor in causing obesity. They're talking about the *home* environment, not whether you live in the mountains or the desert, a city or a small town.

Children's first role models are their parents. If they see Mom and Dad equating food with happiness, that's what they learn to do. If no one else in the family exercises, neither will they. If cleaning up their plate earns praise and rewards, then they'll eat far beyond the point of being full.

Since Mom is usually the one who shops for food and prepares the family meals, "environmentalists" tend to point the finger of blame at her more than at Dad. It seems likely that obese mothers pass their poor eating habits on to their kids. But their contribution to family fatness may be more complex.

One theory proposes that Mom's biggest problem may be inconsistency, prompted by mixed feelings about food. On one hand, she wants to withhold food so that her kids won't get fat; on the other, she wants to lavish it on them so that they don't feel the hunger pangs she does whenever she diets (which she does frequently). By sending confused signals, she teaches her kids from an early age to place too much emphasis on food.

For Fat-Proofing to work, it has to be a family affair. And most often the initial responsibility rests with Mom. As the stocker of the fridge and the keeper of the stove, she'll have to be willing to make some changes in her own food attitudes.

Most experts agree that obesity usually results from a *combination* of overeating, heredity, and environment. But in addition to the Big Three there are other theories that attempt to explain why people get fat. Let's look at some of these, too.

THE FAT-CELLS THEORY

The fat-cells theory has recently been the focus of a great deal of study and attention. It's now known that an average healthy baby is born with 5 to 6 billion fat cells. An adult of normal weight has 30 to 40 billion fat cells (four times as many as brain cells, by the way). An obese adult, in contrast, has 80 to 120 billion fat cells.

Fat cells are the body's storage bins for fat. (So-called cellulite is nothing more than bulging fat cells.) Where do fat cells come from? Are we genetically programmed to have a certain number? Scientists aren't yet sure. But they have learned a lot about fat cells that can help us to understand this enemy-from-within. Here are some findings:

- The development of too many fat cells during childhood (not infancy) may signal the beginning of a lifelong weight problem.

- Fat cells are forever.

You can reduce the size of fat cells by restricting calorie intake, but you can never reduce the number of these cells.

Cutting down on calories forces the body to use up the fat stored in the cells. But the fat cells merely shrink; they don't disappear. They wait there like mean little balloons, waiting for the chance to swell up again.

Does an overabundance of fat cells doom us to obesity? Not necessarily. Someone with many fat cells can be of average weight—if those fat cells are very small.

Does a scarcity of fat cells guarantee slimness? Not at all. Someone with few fat cells can be overweight—if those fat cells are very large.

But scientists have also found that the opposite can be true for each case. In other words, someone with lots of small fat cells can be overweight, and someone with few large fat cells can be of average weight.

- Fat-cell production doesn't necessarily stop at any stage of life.

It was once believed that fat cells were like teeth—once we had a full second set, that was it. Now it's known that this isn't true.

There are peak production periods—before birth, during infancy, early childhood (around 18 months), and the mid-teens (particularly the adolescent growth spurt). But even between those times and afterward, the body can continue making fat cells. Although fat-cell production slows down after adulthood, it can start up again during periods of extreme weight gain no matter how old you are. For many women, pregnancy signals the birth of a whole new batch of fat cells.

Not only do fat cells survive diets, they undermine them. They love to be fat and are self-programmed to stuff themselves when they are starving.

What can we learn from the fat-cells theory? Perhaps the most important conclusion to draw is that it's possible to prevent the development of fat cells. Keeping fit and not overeating seem to be the keys.

THE SET-POINT THEORY

Like the fat-cells theory, the set-point theory is discouraging because it implies that we don't have much control over our weight, after a point. Basically, proponents believe that we have an innate mechanism in our bodies—some trace it to the hypothalamus, which is located in the brain—that fixes our weight at a specific level, or "set point." This mechanism refuses to bow to insurance company charts and other indicators of "ideal" weights. Instead, it sends out messages to the body, telling it to stay at the set point.

When we threaten the set point by cutting down on calories, the mechanism increases our appetite, lowers our metabolism (by as much as 50 percent), and may even decrease our energy level. When we increase our calorie consumption over our usual intake, the mechanism compensates by speeding up our metabolism so that we burn off the excess in energy and body-heat production (which may be why it's often hard for thin people to gain weight).

Some specialists have suggested that an enzyme called AT-LPL ("adipose tissue lipoprotein lipase") may be the mechanism's chief weapon in the battle to maintain the set point. It's known that an obese person's body produces more of this enzyme when he or she loses weight, and that production slows down to normal levels when the weight is regained.

Fighting the set point doesn't have to be a losing proposition, however. The key to victory, once again, is regular exercise. That not only boosts the body's metabolic rate but seems also to lower the set point.

The set-point theory affords one explanation of why dieters regain the weight they lose, over and over again. In an interesting experiment, volunteer test subjects were deprived of food almost to the point of starvation. They lost weight—but they also became inactive, irritable, depressed, and obsessed with food. Later, when they were permitted to eat as much as they wanted, they ate far more than they needed, until their bodies' fat stores returned to where they had been at the beginning of the experiment. Only after they reached their set point did they stop complaining of hunger.

Nutritionists and other specialists are still arguing over the validity of this theory. From a Fat-Proofing perspective, it's worth keeping in mind. It's a fact that fat children who manage to lose weight seldom keep it off longer than five years. Some 85 percent end up fat again. Perhaps if we feed our children properly from the beginning and make sure they get enough exercise, we can keep their set points from being set too high.

THE "FATNESS IS BUILT INTO THE SPECIES" THEORY

Prehistoric peoples had hard lives. They took their meals where they found them—searching for edible roots and berries and bagging the occasional mastodon. Because their food supply was so uncertain, they needed to stash away calories as fat to carry them through the periods when food was scarce. And that, according to this theory, is the reason behind today's tendency toward overweight.

On the surface, it sounds pretty convincing. Once upon a time, humans probably *did* need to store up fat for long winters. But we also used to have eyebrow ridges like shelves and hair all over our bodies.

Over the aeons, our species has changed in many ways. We've evolved to the point where we can walk upright; we've also evolved to the point where we no longer need to pad ourselves like bears preparing to hibernate.

Even as recently as the early twentieth century, fat babies were more apt to survive childhood illnesses than were thin babies. But most of these illnesses can now be prevented by immunizations or by treatment with antibiotics. That's why fat babies are no longer considered healthier than lean babies.

It's true that girls must have a certain percentage of body fat in order to begin (and continue) menstruating, and that women should accumulate some excess fat during pregnancy. But we as a species no longer must stay fat in order to survive.

THE DEPRESSION THEORY

When the American Academy of Psychoanalysis evaluated the effects of psychotherapy on a group of obese patients, they got some unexpected results. After 42 months of therapy, nearly 70 percent of the patients studied had lost significant amounts of weight. Almost 20 percent had dropped more than 40 pounds. And a follow-up study conducted four years later revealed no trend toward regaining the weight lost.

These figures seem to suggest that depression may be a cause of obesity. For this particular group of patients, when depression was treated with psychoanalysis, the obesity problem appeared to solve itself.

Most specialists, however, believe that psychological disorders are the *consequences* of obesity rather than the causes.

MEDICAL REASONS FOR OBESITY

We've all heard people blame their chubbiness on "hormones," "low thyroid," or some other glandular malfunction. The fact is, there are almost *no* bona fide medical reasons for obesity.

There are exceptions: physical injury, damage to the hypothalamus, and a few special (and rare) syndromes. By and large, however, the old excuses don't hold anymore.

This is not to say that you shouldn't have your child examined by a doctor if your child is very overweight—or even if the child is only moderately overweight. Any questions you have about your child's health should be answered by your doctor.

I think it's a good idea to discuss Fat-Proofing with your doctor. Although it isn't a diet, it does recommend that you make changes in your family's eating patterns. Getting guidance from your doctor—and support for what you're about to do—can be very helpful.

WHY FAT-PROOFING WORKS

Everything I've just discussed is based on theories. Fat-Proofing, however, is *not* a theory. It's a matter-of-fact, easy-to-use approach that won't turn your household routines upside-down or create turmoil in your family. And, unlike most of the "kids' diets" you may have heard about (and some of which you may even have tried), Fat-Proofing *works*.

It works because it takes a commonsense, no-nonsense approach to changing food habits and attitudes for the better. It works because it shows you how to feed your kids in a healthier way and get them moving their bodies. It works because it teaches you how to send the positive messages your kids will thrive on—not the negative or mixed-up ones you may now be sending, consciously or not. It works because it gives you real things to do together that will help you and your kids achieve your mutual goals. You may think that your children don't care if they're overweight; but studies have shown that they do, deeply.

Fat-Proofing doesn't promise miracles. It won't turn a fat child into a lean child overnight. But it *can* help keep your child from growing up to become a diet-addicted adult.

BEFORE YOU BEGIN . . .

To make Fat-Proofing a success in your home, there are a few very important things you should understand up front.

First, *Fat-Proofing is something you do **for** your kids, not **to** them.* It's something you do because you want what's best for them, not because your image of yourself as a parent is tied up with having slender children. And especially not because it's a way to control them.

Second, *you don't have to let your kids know that you're about to start Fat-Proofing them.* In fact, don't even mention the term. You should discuss any regimen change with your spouse and enlist his or her support, because Fat-Proofing is a family endeavor. But you may even want to hide this book from your children! (Especially from adolescents, who tend to be supersensitive about their weight and resistant to change.)

Third, *you don't have to be fat-free yourself to Fat-Proof your kids.* I've struggled with weight problems my whole life and still do—yet I'm able to pass on healthy food attitudes to my kids. And you don't have to be at home all day whipping up batches of tofu. As a working mother, I can't be in the kitchen to supervise every forkful, nor do I pretend that my great joy in life is to cook.

THE FOUR RULES OF FAT-PROOFING

The Four Rules of Fat-Proofing can make the difference between success and failure.

Rule 1. Don't assume that a heavier-than-average child is a fat child.

You can't see what's under the skin. A child who tips the scales more than one of so-called average weight may have an unusual amount of muscle, or heavy bones, or some combination of the two. (Muscle tissue weighs more per volume than does fat.) The point is not to make their weight conform to statistics. The "norms" aren't necessarily normal for your kids.

There are times in a child's development when what appears to be chubbiness is a sign of good health. Most babies are neckless wonders. All toddlers have protruding tummies. Many children appear heavy just prior to the "growth spurt" that occurs around age 6. In other words, *don't panic.* Later on, I'll tell you exactly what to look for and when.

Rule 2. Realize that your child's body is different from your own.

This sounds obvious, but we do tend to expect our kids to look like us. After all, we produced them!

But our kids are neither extensions nor mirrors of us. When we bring a child to the pediatrician to be weighed and measured, it's not *we* who are being weighed and measured. It's our unique, special, and wholly separate-from-us child.

Rule 3. Don't measure your child's need for food by your own.

Many of us overestimate the amount of food our children need, giving them adult-sized portions and expecting them to clean their plates. Actually, children require far fewer calories to keep them going and growing than we think they do.

Rule 4. Send your child the message, **"You're okay."**

This may be the most important rule of all. Even if your child is seriously overweight, you must let him or her know, loud and clear, by words and actions, that "You're okay whatever your size, and I love you no matter what."

An essential part of Fat-Proofing has to do with helping your child develop self-esteem and a positive self-image. How children feel about themselves often hinges on how their parents feel about them. If we think that they're less than they should be (because they weigh more) or don't come up to our expectations, they can tell. Our disapproval hurts.

When did someone last say to you, "I *like* the way you look," and mean it? How wonderful it would be to get that message daily! How wonderful if you could *give* it to your children.

As my two teens leave for school, I make a special point of telling them just how nice they look. I say it no matter how they are dressed. Teens are especially sensitive to their appearance and are sure they never look good enough. Since they spend a half-hour getting themselves together each morning, I want to reinforce their efforts.

Fat-Proofing begins when you recognize your child as an individual with individual food needs and preferences.

THE FOUR RULES OF FAT-PROOFING

Rule 1. Don't assume that a heavier-than-average child is a fat child.

Rule 2. Realize that your child's body is different from your own.

Rule 3. Don't measure your child's need for food by your own need.

Rule 4. Send your child the message, **"You're okay."**

TWO

WHAT ARE YOUR FOOD ATTITUDES?

Cheese blintzes still remind me of my grandmother. A whiff of chicken soup takes me back thirty years to my mother's cozy kitchen. The sight of apple strudel and I'm careening down memory lane.

Food was (and remains) the focal point of all our family gatherings. When I remember weddings I attended as a child, I can barely recall who married whom, but I can still see the tables full of food and hear my parents' discussion of the spread afterward. My memories of birthday parties center on cakes and ice cream and paper cups loaded with sweets. Even funerals revolved around the lavish suppers afterward.

I'm not alone. As a nation, we've made food central to our lives. Our reputations as hostesses and hosts are made or broken by the kinds of meals we serve. Major get-togethers focus on food—Christmas dinner, Hanukkah, Easter dinner, Fourth of July picnics, Thanksgiving dinner, even Super Bowl dinner. The success of an occasion is measured by the food. And sometimes not by the quality but by the amount!

TV, magazines, and billboards bombard us with inducements to stuff ourselves. The people who produce those ads really know what they're doing. Soft drinks sparkle, casseroles send out clouds of steam, bacon sizzles, cakes are moist and mountainous. We go to a movie to escape this sensory overload and what do we get? Filmed shorts encouraging us to hit the snack counter and load up on popcorn, Coke, and Milk Duds!

Granted, food is essential to our survival. But so are air and water, and not too many people rhapsodize about their most recent breath of fresh air (unless they live in New York or Los Angeles), or their last drink of water. Yet, we not only talk about meals we've had, we talk about meals we plan to have, meals we'd like to have, meals we're in the middle of, even meals we've only heard about.

There are several reasons for our obsession with food. For one, America is supposed to be the land of plenty. We're a country of immigrants who came from places where there often wasn't enough food, and we still eat as if we don't know where our next meal is coming from. The food traditions that were important to our forebears took on even greater significance when whole families were uprooted from their social moorings and dropped into a strange, foreign culture. Large family meals became a sign of continuity and togetherness—not to mention prosperity.

For another, we used to be a rural, manual-labor economy. The way we eat is a throwback to the days when people did physically demanding work. But while we continue to eat like farmers, most of us spend our days sitting at desks. We no longer need all the calories we take in.

These are some of the historic sources of our eating habits. But there's another, newer theme running through why we eat the way we do: We've become a consumer society. From the time we're old enough to listen, we're taught that consumption is good for us and for our country. And it's come to mean quality as well as quantity. *Status consumption* is today's imperative, and it's added an odd twist to eating. Not only are we supposed to consume magnificently, we're also supposed to stay slim.

In the past, portliness was a sign of affluence; now the ideal is to be rich *and* thin (and, for better or worse, athletic!).

No wonder we're confused. The old reasons for eating to excess don't hold true anymore, and the new ones don't make sense.

So, how do we fight our preoccupation with food and put it in its proper place? We start by changing our food attitudes. Most of these have been handed down to us along with the family silver, and they are very hard to shake.

Many of our strongest childhood memories are food-related. We were taught to clean our plates; we were bribed with sweets; we were ordered to finish our vegetables; we were promised goodies if we sat uncomplaining through a haircut, or did our homework, or brought home a good report card. For some of us, rejecting everything our mothers believed about food was—and in some cases still is—the same as rejecting our mothers. (My sister is thin, her normal diet looked like a diet, and my mother never forgave her for it.)

Since food was an issue when I was growing up, it nearly became so for my kids, Doug and Dana. Fortunately, I recognized the problem early and began to reflect on my own food attitudes, where they came from, and how they were affecting my kids.

The following quiz is designed to help you look back at your childhood and the way food was regarded by your family. Take a few moments to read through each of the statements and pencil in a checkmark next to your response.

WHEN I WAS A CHILD:

1. My family followed the "three square meals a day" rule.

_____ TRUE _____ FALSE

2. I was expected to clean my plate before leaving the table.

_____ TRUE _____ FALSE

3. My parents soothed me with trips to the ice-cream store when I was unhappy.

_____ TRUE _____ FALSE

4. Good behavior was rewarded with a "treat" of a favorite food.

_____ TRUE _____ FALSE

5. I was sometimes bribed with food to do something my parents wanted me to do.

_____ TRUE _____ FALSE

6. My mom was responsible for everything having to do with food in our house—meal planning, shopping, preparation, and serving.

_____ TRUE _____ FALSE

7. My mom acted hurt if I didn't eat something she prepared.

_____ TRUE _____ FALSE

8. I felt guilty when I didn't eat something she prepared.

_____ TRUE _____ FALSE

9. I was instructed never to refuse food when visiting someone else's home, for fear of offending the hostess or host.

_____ TRUE _____ FALSE

10. We usually brought gifts of food when we visited friends or relatives.

_____ TRUE _____ FALSE

11. When visitors dropped by unexpectedly, they were immediately offered something to eat and drink.

_____ TRUE _____ FALSE

12. Our family ate most of our meals together.

_____ TRUE _____ FALSE

13. Some of my family's happiest times together were spent around the table.

_____ TRUE _____ FALSE

14. The dining-room table (or the kitchen table) was our family's social center.

_____ TRUE _____ FALSE

15. I never experienced genuine hunger.

_____ TRUE _____ FALSE

16. Our family usually fixed lavish meals for special occasions.

_____ TRUE _____ FALSE

17. There were always sweets around our house—cookies, coffee cakes, candies.

_____ TRUE _____ FALSE

18. Dinner was always followed by dessert.

_____ TRUE _____ FALSE

19. All the kids were served the same amounts of everything.

_____ TRUE _____ FALSE

20. The family larder—cabinets, refrigerator, and freezer—was kept full.

_____ TRUE _____ FALSE

You'll probably end up with more "trues" than "falses"—these are the attitudes and behaviors most of us grew up with.

We know a lot more about food and its effects today than we did then. Yet we still consider these old-fashioned attitudes "normal." And we're continuing to live them, consciously or not.

Let's look at the quiz again, only this time in the present tense, so that we can begin to examine these statements from a Fat-Proofing perspective. Which remain valid? Which need changing? Which are working for—or against—us in our efforts to raise healthy, happy kids who won't end up as diet-addicted adults?

Like the stretching exercises joggers do before running, these thoughts and ideas should "loosen up" some of the attitudes you have toward food.

1. My family follows the "three square meals a day" rule.

_____ TRUE _____ FALSE

Suggesting alternatives to the "three squares" is, to some people's minds, the same as recommending that the red stripes be taken out of the American flag. Admittedly, this time-honored tradition seems the best way to ensure a balanced diet. But the fact is that we may not *need* three meals a day. A better solution may involve fewer meals—or, in some cases, more.

For example, recent studies show that some adults may be able to skip breakfast without doing themselves any harm at all. Babies eat far more than three meals a day. And a number of nutritionally sound (and effective) diets recommend several smaller meals over the course of the day.

One problem with limiting ourselves to three meals a day is that we usually leave the table feeling stuffed. We come to it so hungry that we eat more than we should.

I'm not going to recommend that you stand by to prepare meals for your family whenever and however frequently they want them. We *do* need some order in our lives, and one of the easiest events to order is the family meal. But often we're too rigid about mealtimes. Mom (it's usually Mom) is expected to have the food on the table at certain times regardless of whatever else she may be doing. Everyone in the family is expected to show up ready to eat regardless of whether they're hungry. What often ensues is conflict—over schedules, personal preferences, and individual wants and needs. This is true especially when kids get older and start developing interests of their own.

Believe it or not, *it's no big deal if your family misses a meal.* No child ever starved to death because he or she was playing softball and forgot to go home for lunch. No parent ever went to jail because dinner wasn't ready at six sharp.

Give yourself permission to relax this rule a bit. Parents who do so sometimes find that their whole household tends to relax as a result. Here's what one mother says:

> I spent years trying to plan three full meals every Saturday. But we all got up at different times and followed different schedules. I finally decided that I wasn't going to let it drive me crazy anymore. Now we all get together for brunch sometime in the middle of the morning, and for dinner in the early evening. Two meals seem like plenty for everyone, and we all have the time—and the flexibility—to do the things we want to do. Including me!

Tired of trying to squeeze breakfast in before church on Sundays? Let the kids snack on juice and bran muffins, and come back to a more leisurely Sunday brunch. Weary of big Sunday dinners that leave you feeling comatose (and result in your having to spend Sunday evening scrubbing the kitchen)? Consider what another mother came up with:

> Sunday has turned into our "leftovers' day." For dinner we clean out the refrigerator and eat whatever we find—salad from the day before, soup or stew from earlier in the week, maybe some cold chicken. Then we set up a buffet on the kitchen counter and bring out the paper plates. My children love it and so do I.

These options are easier on the weekends, when the tyranny of work and school schedules doesn't apply. But a change of habit can be welcome at midweek, too. One couple I know likes to take in an early evening movie with their kids every now and then. They dine on cheese sandwiches and fruit in the car on the way.

Now for a few words about between-meals snacks. If your childhood was at all like mine, cries of, "Wait, you'll spoil your appetite!" rang through the air whenever you headed for the kitchen—and it's likely that you say the same thing to your kids. Actually, controlled, healthful snacking can be a good idea.

I know this sounds like heresy, but it can be wise to let a child take the edge off—*not* "spoil"—his or her appetite before sitting down at the table. When we're ravenous, we eat faster and more. A small snack an hour or so before a meal can leave a child hungry enough to eat but not hungry enough to wolf his or her food. (By the way, a snack doesn't have to be something you "serve," like a minimeal. Keep a supply of nutritious munchies around the house and let your kids help themselves, within reason. If they're *really* hungry, they'll more than likely be willing to eat something that's good for them.)

2. I expect my kids to clean their plates before leaving the table.

_____ TRUE _____ FALSE

As you may already have guessed, the Clean Plate Club is not part of Fat-Proofing. There are several reasons why.

First, the food we pile on our kids' plates is often far more than they can reasonably be expected to eat. (We may not think it's a lot, but remember Fat-Proofing rule 3: *Don't measure your child's need for food by your own.*)

Second, this expectation often results in bad feelings all around. This mother's story will probably ring true for almost everyone:

> Once when my son was about 2 years old I found myself screaming at him to finish his supper. If he didn't, I promised, he could sit there until he was old enough to vote. He was crying, I was shouting, and suddenly I realized—wait a minute! This feels familiar! And then I remembered all the dinner-table battles I'd experienced as a child. That's when I vowed it would never happen again.

How often have you heard yourself say, "Eat your supper; there are children starving in _____ (fill in the blank: Africa, China, Appalachia, wherever)"? Strike that sentence from your vocabulary immediately!

A friend tells what happened in her family when her 5-year-old daughter had heard that line once too often. The little girl brought a shoebox to the table. When her parents asked her what she was doing with it, she replied, "I'm going to put my dinner in here so you can send it to the starving children."

Another reason for stopping insisting on clean plates has to do with the fact that eating shouldn't be an achievement per se. With the exception of very young children just learning to handle utensils, nobody should be praised for knowing how to scoop up food and head it toward one's mouth. Good table manners should be applauded; a clean plate—as an end in itself—should not.

What about bite-counting? You know what I mean. A child is full and doesn't want to eat any more and a parent says, "Just two more bites of your vegetables and three more bites of your meat and you'll be done." What difference will those two or three bites make to the child's future? Not a whole lot. But it will turn the remainder of the meal into a command performance—and eating, once more, into an achievement.

1987 even saw the introduction of a feeding spoon in the shape of an airplane—a high-tech force feed. Now really!!

We have two policies around our house that seem to work well for everyone:

- The first is that Doug and Dana serve themselves. They decide how much to put on their plates, and when they err it's usually on the side of taking too little to begin with. Then they can have more if they want it. (Eating out presents a different problem, however. Dana, when hungry, often has "eyes bigger than her stomach," which has proved to be expensive on occasion.)

- The second is that they have to at least *taste* every dish that's been prepared. It's important to expand kids' food horizons. I let them start with a small spoonful—which looks considerably less intimidating than a large scoop. If they don't like it, they don't have to eat any more.

Interestingly, we end up with more clean plates (their decision, not mine) now than we ever did when clean plates were the goal of every meal. And mealtimes are far happier.

A friend of mine put it nicely: "If you want to see a *really* clean plate, pass it down to the dog!"

   3. I soothe my children with trips to the ice-cream store when they're unhappy.

   _____ TRUE _____ FALSE

   4. I reward good behavior with a "treat" of a favorite food.

   _____ TRUE _____ FALSE

   5. I sometimes bribe my kids with food to do something I want them to do.

   _____ TRUE _____ FALSE

I lumped these questions together because they have a common theme: food as a tool.

When we use food as consolation, reward, or incentive, we're not taking into account the main reason for eating: hunger. Conditioning our children to eat for reasons other than hunger and nourishment sets up adult behavior that equates food with reward and solace. How often have you found yourself reaching for food when you're upset? Is that what you want your children to do as they get older?

A big part of successful Fat-Proofing involves coming up with valid and meaningful responses to situations that we're used to addressing with food. For many of us, food has become an easy out (or "in," when we use it to prod or stimulate desired behaviors).

It's less bother to get a child an ice-cream cone than to sit down with him or her and say, "Something's troubling you. Let's talk." It's simpler to cut a slice of cake than to come up with other, more creative (and maybe more time-consuming) types of rewards. A candy bar is a quicker persuader than a conversation. But when did a bribe ever teach responsibility?

If you're serious about Fat-Proofing your kids, start right now by asking yourself, "Why am I doing this?" whenever you're about to offer a child food. When you start answering, "Because the child is hungry," you'll be on your way.

Meanwhile, here are a few suggestions to consider:

- Is your child sad or upset about something? If at all possible, stop whatever you're doing and devote your full attention to the child. Talk (and listen!). Take a walk together. Start a crafts project. Cradle the child in your arms and rock back and forth; there's no food in the world as comforting as that gesture. If stopping what you're doing isn't possible—which is often true— just learning not to reach for the cookie jar is progress enough. We can't always "cure" a child's sadness, but we can say "I'm sorry that you feel sad/mad/bad," and acknowledge their feelings.

- Is your child deserving of a reward? Terrific. Go to a movie on the spur of the moment. Make a banner for the front door saying "THE WORLD'S GREATEST KID LIVES HERE." Stockpile small gifts for such special occasions: coloring books, stickers, buttons to wear. Have a T-shirt made for your child with his or her picture on it. Put a note in your child's lunchbox for him or her to find later in the day.

Most of all, be liberal with words of praise. A cookie, once eaten, is gone. But the feeling that comes from hearing, "You're wonderful, and I'm so proud of you!" will last and last.

- Does your child need persuading to do a task or chore? How about, "If you clean up your room, we can read a story together afterward." Okay, this is a bribe, too, but instead of sugar over-load, your child gets *you* for a while.

Even better is the gradual teaching of responsibility that you do day by day. It's never too early to start teaching a child that *everyone* in the house has certain duties to fulfill. A toddler can lay napkins on the table. A kinder-gartner can dry spoons and put them away. Children love to help out, to feel as if they're making a contribution, to act "grown-up." Promising a candy bar isn't only unnecessary; it's insulting!

> **6.** I'm responsible for everything having to do with food in our house—meal planning, shopping, preparation, and serving.
>
> _____ TRUE _____ FALSE

Times *are* changing, and some fathers are beginning to play a more active role in this area. That's *some* fathers, not all. A study I read not too long ago reports that in many families—even those where both Mom and Dad work full-time outside the home—Mom is still doing most of the grunt work.

But food chores—especially preparation—differ, I believe, from most other household chores in at least one important respect: when we perform them, we expect feedback (no pun!). We want our families to eat what we fix for them. Beyond that, we want them to *enjoy* eating and to *express* their enjoyment.

When you do the laundry, are you hurt or offended if your child doesn't put on a clean shirt immediately and run to you exclaiming, "Wow, Mom, this shirt is really clean! And it smells great!" Never mind the commercials; this simply doesn't happen in real life. But when you put dinner on the table, chances are you *are* hurt and offended if your child says, "Yuck! I hate this stuff!" and pushes his or her plate away.

It's obvious, but I'm going to say it anyway: When your child says, "I don't like the food you fixed," your child is *not* saying, "I don't like you." (Unless, of course, your child has discovered that this is the best of all ways to "get you.") For Fat-Proofing to succeed in your home, you must stop taking such comments personally. You must stop seeing food as an exten-sion of yourself and your love for your kids and start viewing it objectively.

You're not serving your heart on a platter. You're serving vitamins and calories, nutrients and fiber: body fuel. Expecting your kids to praise you for feeding them is like expecting your car to be grateful when you pump it full of gas.

One way to develop a healthier attitude toward food duties is by dividing them among family members. When a task becomes a family affair, it's not only more fun, it's also less apt to get tied up with a single individual's sense of self-worth. Here are some ideas to get you started:

- During meal planning, enlist suggestions from family members. Would someone like a favorite food for dinner Tuesday night? Have the kids been studying nutrition in school and bringing home recipes to try?

- Carting preschoolers through the grocery store is nobody's idea of a good time, but even very small children can "help" with food selection. Perhaps they can choose the breakfast cereal (from among a few different brands you've preselected). Older children can be sent down an aisle in front of you on a "treasure hunt" to search for specific items. If your grocery store is set up to let you weigh produce yourself, take this opportunity to teach your kids what a scale is for. (Dana loved being lifted up so she could but the bananas on the scale.)

Just as you shouldn't go shopping on an empty stomach (you know the kinds of buying decisions you make when you're hungry!), neither should your kids. A small snack at home before departing can eliminate the whining and "I wants" so often heard in grocery stores. Or discuss one preselected choice of treats ahead of time and stick to it. It might be a piece of fruit, such as a banana, that can be eaten in the store. Just let the cashier know so you can be charged for it. It's better for a child to be satisfied *before* hitting the check-out counter, where all the candies are within easy reach. Or save shopping for after lunch on Saturdays or dinner on weekdays.

- Do you regard the kitchen as your exclusive domain? Unless it's two feet square, there's probably room for a few helpers. Younger children can shell peas; older ones can scrape carrots or peel potatoes. And kids of any age enjoy measuring quantities and mixing ingredients in bowls. It may take more time to prepare a meal with short people underfoot, but unless you're in a hurry, so what? Use the time for conversation, for togetherness, for sharing jokes or stories about your day.

- Put the good china away for a few years so your children can set the table. (Plastic can be quite fashionable.) Don't criticize their efforts. If the fork ends up on the wrong side of the plate, people will still be able to find it.

7. I feel hurt if my kids don't eat something I've prepared.

_____ TRUE _____ FALSE

8. My kids act guilty when they don't eat something I prepare.

_____ TRUE _____ FALSE

Now, for a moment, forget everything you've just read and answer these statements honestly. Then remember everything you've just read and consider how you'd like to change those answers. The sooner you can remove guilt from your children's roster of feelings about food, the sooner they'll develop healthier attitudes toward it.

9. I instruct my kids never to refuse food when visiting someone else's home, for fear of offending the hostess or host.

_____ TRUE _____ FALSE

This can be a difficult situation. Because the offering of food is so wrapped up with emotions, there's a good chance that people *will* get offended if your kids say "no." Once again, though, do we want our children to eat because they "should," or because they're hungry?

My advice is this: If the host or hostess is a close friend, you might be able to talk about this together. If you both have children, maybe you can strike a bargain: you won't force food on her kids if she won't force it on yours! Or you can communicate on the types of meals and snacks you will and won't serve.

What if you're not close friends? You can teach your kids that good manners don't necessarily mean accepting everything a host or hostess offers. Saying a polite "no, thank you" is far better behavior than leaving a picked-at plate of food. (As a matter of fact, giving your kids permission to say "no" when they don't want something is wise for many reasons, and this one may be the least important!)

Or maybe your kids go to their friends' houses and stuff themselves on foods you don't allow at home. I stopped worrying about this with Doug and Dana a long time ago. It's not my place—or yours—to tell other people what to eat or to serve. Kids take most of their meals at home, and that's where most of their food attitudes and habits are formed.

This is an appropriate place at which to repeat that *Fat-Proofing is not a diet.* (I'll talk later, in chapter 7, about why most kids shouldn't go on diets.) In other words, unless your kids have allergies or some other medical condition that limits what they can eat, don't worry about what they consume outside your home. If they occasionally gobble cookies at Grandma's or down ice cream at a friend's, it won't have lasting harmful effects.

Grandparents who continue to disregard nutrition concerns are another matter. If they won't change their style after a respectful conversation on the matter, you might do what one family I know did. They sent the grandparents all dental bills.

10. We usually bring gifts of food when we visit friends or relatives.

_____ TRUE _____ FALSE

11. When visitors drop by unexpectedly, I immediately offer them something to eat and drink.

_____ TRUE _____ FALSE

It's still hard for me to imagine a get-together of any kind without food, and I see no reason to make radical changes here. As you get more involved with Fat-Proofing, the kinds of foods you bring and serve will probably become more nourishing and healthful—something for which your friends and relatives may be grateful!

12. Our family eats most of our meals together.

_____ TRUE _____ FALSE

Why? Because it's convenient for everyone, or convenient for you alone? Because it's forced, or because it's natural?

Most of us were raised to believe that mealtimes were family occasions. Most of us were also raised in families where Dad returned from work to find dinner waiting. Today, with more mothers working outside the home, and with more kids becoming involved in afterschool activities and interests of their own, it's gotten harder for everyone to be in the same place at the same time.

I still enjoy having my family around the table with me, but I realize that it's not always possible. So I'm more flexible than I used to be. I *do* like to know when someone isn't planning to join us, since that affects what and how much food I prepare. A suggestion: Keep a family calendar. At a time when everyone is home—say, Sunday evening—spend a few moments finding out their plans for the week and jotting them down.

Another thought: Why not make breakfast your "family meal"? If it works for you, do it! Dinner together is *not* the Eleventh Commandment.

For some families, mealtimes are the *only* occasions on which everyone comes together in one place. What often happens is that the table becomes the arena for all whole-family communication—including scenes and arguments. This can turn into a sort of arms negotiations conference, with every word and gesture loaded with meaning.

A friend tells me that this is the way things were in her family when she was growing up. For a while during her childhood there were so many dinner-table fights that she often lost her appetite before a meal even began. Today she has a husband and children of her own, and she's determined that things will be different. At least twice every week her family gathers in the family room—*not* the dining room, and *not* over food—to discuss what's happening in their lives and air any grievances. These meetings have become an important part of their family dynamic, and more often than not they're warm and happy. Plus, she and her husband try to set aside time each day—maybe it's only ten minutes—to talk, or simply *be*, with each of their three children individually. These times, she reports, are magical.

13. Some of my family's happiest times together are spent around the table.

_____ TRUE _____ FALSE

14. The dining-room table (or the kitchen table) is our family's social center.

_____ TRUE _____ FALSE

When I think back to the best times of my childhood, I often picture my family around the table; we clung to it like iron filings to a magnet. That's where we shared our daily experiences or regaled one another with stories.

If this is true for your family, Fat-Proofing won't require you to change it. As I said earlier, it's a way of life that can fit any lifestyle. If your kids love spending hours at the table chatting, that says something good about you.

Unfortunately, what often happens is that people keep eating for as long as they keep sitting. And there *is* something you can and should change about that. Clear the table, pile the dishes on the kitchen counter, and bring out the Monopoly board, Chinese checkers, Parcheesi, or any other game your family enjoys playing together. Start a jigsaw puzzle. Begin a crafts project. Have your kids read the latest reports they've written in school. In other words, let your table do double or triple duty. It doesn't have to be a place where all you do is eat.

15. My kids have never experienced genuine hunger.

_____ TRUE _____ FALSE

Naturally we want our kids to get enough to eat. Naturally we don't want them to go hungry. *But they should learn at a fairly early age what hunger feels like.*

Many doctors are now recommending that mothers feed their infants on demand rather than on a set schedule. Those mothers whose lifestyles permit this may want to give it serious consideration. Babies' communications skills may be basic, but they're also effective. A hungry baby fusses or cries. If Mom responds by feeding, the baby begins to make the important connection between vocalizing a want and getting it satisfied. Plus, demand feeding helps an infant to tune in to his or her own "inner clock"—which may be different from Mom's.

I'll talk more in chapter 4 about Fat-Proofing babies—infancy isn't too early to start—but for now I want to point out a mistake that a lot of mothers make, especially those who bottle-feed. They continue giving the bottle until the baby finishes it. Even if the baby pushes the bottle away, they keep offering it. What the baby learns from this is that he or she ought to keep eating even after he's full. The baby is literally taught to overeat. The trouble is, the baby who overeats consistently becomes a fat baby, and a fat baby is on his or her way to being a fat child and a fat adult.

We don't hesitate to teach our children bowel and bladder control; instead, we worry if they don't learn it fast enough. They also need to learn appetite control. And one sure way they'll figure it out is by experiencing the physical signs of hunger. If we never let them get hungry—if we constantly push food and insist that they eat when *we* demand it—they'll eat to please us out of habit.

16. We usually fix lavish meals for special occasions.

_____ TRUE _____ FALSE

Does *every* special occasion have to be celebrated with a meal? I don't think so. Consider some alternatives; here are a few to get you started:

- Reward your son's good report card with the new athletic shoes he's been wanting.

- Commemorate your daughter's starring role in the school play with a roller-skating party.

- If you or your spouse gets a raise, spend part of it on a family membership at your local YMCA or YWCA. (Fat-Proofing is a family affair!)

- Have outdoor picnics for summer birthdays instead of indoor sit-down dinners—and make sure that everyone plays plenty of volleyball between courses.

17. There are always sweets around our house—cookies, coffee cakes, candies.

_____ TRUE _____ FALSE

Are caramel rolls on Saturday mornings part of your family's routine? Do you feel like a failed parent if the cookie jar stands empty for longer than a day? Have you permanently reserved a corner of your refrigerator for sugared soft drinks?

When I was young, my mother baked wonderful treats. Today I still feel some pangs of guilt for not filling our home with the delicious smells of goodies in the oven.

This is not to say that we don't eat sweets; we do. But we don't stockpile them. I know families who buy candy bars by the sack, soft drinks by the case, and doughnuts by the dozens for fear of running out. There's usually ice cream in our freezer—but in pints, not gallons—and peanut butter cookies and fig bars in the cookie jar.

If your family is accustomed to consuming large quantities of sweets, don't try to wean them off them overnight or you'll have a revolution on your hands. Instead, start buying smaller quantities. Get rid of the marshmallow, creme-filled cookies in the cookie jar and put out a bowl of fresh fruit. Try a bowl of nuts and a nutcracker. The smell of freshly popped popcorn is a treat.

Good eating habits are as easy to form as bad ones. The trick is in directing kids toward better, more healthful choices. You can't reasonably expect them to make those choices if they're surrounded by temptation. Since you're probably the one who does most of the family shopping, the responsibility rests with you.

18. Dinner is always followed by dessert.

_____ TRUE _____ FALSE

Dessert has long been the ultimate parental bargaining chip. It's used to get kids to clean their plates, to eat two more bites of vegetables, or to sit up straight at the table. For a while when my kids were younger, it was the be-all and end-all of every meal. Dana's first words before dinner were always, "What's for dessert?"

It constantly amazes me that a child who can't be force-fed one more morsel of meat or potatoes will still have room left for a big slice of chocolate cake. A kid who spends an hour staring sullenly at an untouched plate will perk up immediately at the sight of ice cream. Even toddlers will eat things they despise if they know dessert is waiting.

Recall that Fat-Proofing requires you to stop using food as a tool. One way to do this is to cut out habitual desserts as part of your family's lifestyle. Don't attempt to accomplish this overnight; instead, do it gradually. (Incidentally, this may be one area in which your spouse gives you grief. Enlisting his support at the outset will save you headaches later.) Notice I said *habitual* desserts. That doesn't mean you will never serve a sweet dessert again.

Here's one tried-and-true way to slowly dessert-proof your household:

A. If your family currently has dessert every night, change this to every other night. Don't use it as a bribe or a reward. Serve it to everyone regardless of how they "perform" at dinner.

B. After a few weeks, begin making substitutions for the sweets you usually offer. Try a fresh fruit salad, or a section of fresh pineapple, or frozen bananas on a Popsicle stick coated with a bit of honey and rolled in granola.

C. If all goes according to plan, after a month or so you should be able to start incorporating your dessert substitutes into the main meal. If the kids gobble up their fruit salad first and insist that they don't have room for the rest of their dinner, don't argue with them.

19. All the kids are served the same amounts of everything.

_____ TRUE _____ FALSE

Some families follow the practice of having Dad (or Mom) fill the plates and hand them down the table. This ensures that everyone is treated fairly, but it also results in people getting more (or less) of certain foods than they want. And it often runs counter to Fat-Proofing rule 3: *Don't measure your child's need for food by your own.*

What to do? One alternative is simply to pass the serving dishes around the table and let everyone help themselves, with the older family members assisting the younger ones. Another is to serve meals buffet-style. The important thing to remember is that kids shouldn't feel that food is being pushed on them—or held back from them, either.

One thing to watch for is kids' tendency to take much more than they can eat (of the things they like, that is). It's the old "eyes are bigger than the stomach" syndrome. Monitor this until everyone gets accustomed to the new routine. Encourage kids to take small portions at first, with the understanding that they can have seconds if they want them.

Among siblings, letting everyone have the same amounts may be the only way to prevent civil war at the table. Again, smaller is better to start with; those who are still hungry can go back for more.

> **20.** The family larder—cabinets, refrigerator, and freezer—is kept full.
>
> _____ TRUE _____ FALSE

To this day I derive comfort from walking into my mother's kitchen and finding all the cabinets well stocked. (I still check them.) Fortunately, however, I no longer feel compelled to keep my own larder full. With a supermarket half a mile down the road, it isn't necessary. And I've discovered that not only do we eat less, we waste less. My children seldom snack on leftovers. If I don't incorporate them into their food choices, the only one tempted by leftovers is me.

Maybe it's less expensive to buy certain foods in bulk, but ask yourself: Do you end up eating more rich foods than you might otherwise, simply because you have them around the house?

By now you should have some idea of what Fat-Proofing involves. I hope it's obvious that it won't turn your household upside-down. Unlike most diet plans, which force you to concentrate even more on what you're eating and when, Fat-Proofing allows you to *relax* your attitudes toward food.

This isn't the same as becoming permissive and letting your kids eat anything they want. (Remember that Fat-Proofing is *not* a laissez-faire approach. Rather, it's about putting food in its proper place.) In a Fat-Proofed home, food is something people eat when they're hungry. It has no emotional power. It is not used to control. It is not weighed down with feelings or expectations. It is not a tool.

Before we go on to the next step—assessing your family's eating pattern— there's one more bit of introspection left to perform. Specifically, it's time to look more closely at your own personal food attitudes, including some of which you may not be consciously aware.

A few of the following questions may be uncomfortable to answer. Others may require a great deal of thought. *But before you can really help your family, you must come to terms with some important truths about yourself.*

Check "yes" for those statements that are always true for you, "no" for those statements that are never true for you, and "sometimes" for those statements that are occasionally true for you.

1. I eat when I'm depressed.

_____ YES _____ SOMETIMES _____ NO

2. I try out new diets.

_____ YES _____ SOMETIMES _____ NO

3. I work hard to please my family with the meals I prepare.

_____ YES _____ SOMETIMES _____ NO

4. I eat quickly—I "bolt" my food rather than chewing each bite slowly.

_____ YES _____ SOMETIMES _____ NO

5. I feel guilty when I overeat.

_____ YES _____ SOMETIMES _____ NO

6. I think I'd be happier if I were thinner.

_____ YES _____ SOMETIMES _____ NO

7. I can't resist junk food.

_____ YES _____ SOMETIMES _____ NO

8. I count calories.

_____ YES _____ SOMETIMES _____ NO

9. I finish everything on my plate during meals.

_____ YES _____ SOMETIMES _____ NO

10. My spouse wishes I were thinner.

_____ YES _____ SOMETIMES _____ NO

11. I hate to waste food.

_____ YES _____ SOMETIMES _____ NO

12. I'm embarrassed about my body.

_____ YES _____ SOMETIMES _____ NO

13. I pick at leftovers.

_____ YES _____ SOMETIMES _____ NO

14. I eat in private, when there's no one around to see me.

_____ YES _____ SOMETIMES _____ NO

15. I keep supplies of my favorite foods around the house.

_____ YES _____ SOMETIMES _____ NO

16. When I was growing up, I felt pressured to be thin.

_____ YES _____ SOMETIMES _____ NO

17. I eat aimlessly, without being fully conscious of what I'm putting in my mouth.

_____ YES _____ SOMETIMES _____ NO

18. Cooking is an important form of social expression for me.

_____ YES _____ SOMETIMES _____ NO

19. I hate to exercise.

_____ YES _____ SOMETIMES _____ NO

20. I eat when I'm angry.

_____ YES _____ SOMETIMES _____ NO

21. I wish I had more energy.

_____ YES _____ SOMETIMES _____ NO

22. I buy clothes a size too small, promising myself that I'll diet to fit into them.

_____ YES _____ SOMETIMES _____ NO

23. I reward myself with food.

_____ YES _____ SOMETIMES _____ NO

24. Food is one of my greatest pleasures.

_____ YES _____ SOMETIMES _____ NO

25. I eat second helpings—and sometimes thirds—of foods I really like.

_____ YES _____ SOMETIMES _____ NO

26. I eat in front of the TV.

_____ YES _____ SOMETIMES _____ NO

27. I try to keep up with the latest recipes and cooking techniques.

_____ YES _____ SOMETIMES _____ NO

28. I eat something before going to bed at night.

_____ YES _____ SOMETIMES _____ NO

29. Cooking is a primary form of creative expression for me.

_____ YES _____ SOMETIMES _____ NO

30. I feel as if I've spent most of my life dieting.

_____ YES _____ SOMETIMES _____ NO

Scoring:
When you've finished, add up your answers to get your total score for each response category. Then multiply your "yes" answers by 5 and your "sometimes" answers by 3. Write your score here:

_____

INTERPRETING YOUR SCORE

If you scored between 100 and 150:
Food is an issue in your life. In fact, most of your life revolves around food.

Perhaps you were overweight as a child; you may be overweight now. Your parents may have been overweight (recall that a child with two obese parents has a 70 to 80 percent chance of becoming obese).

You'd like to be thin (who wouldn't in a culture like ours, where thinness is the ideal?), but you somehow feel as if that goal will always be out of your reach. Maybe you tell yourself every spring that you'll be 15 pounds thinner by summer; and when summer comes, you push that ahead to fall.

Perhaps you've tried all kinds of diets, including fad diets that seem silly to you. But as soon as you revert to your regular eating habits, the indicator on your bathroom scale starts creeping up again—and often it edges up higher than it's ever been before.

Food is closely tied to your emotions. Eating may be your way of responding to unpleasant feelings and of enhancing pleasant ones. Or you may use it to mask your feelings and avoid dealing with them, period. You may find yourself bingeing—on an entire box of cookies, or a bag of potato chips, or a pint of ice cream. Following a binge, you may feel awful about yourself.

You're proud of the meals you prepare for your family, and you're happy when they express their appreciation, but you don't like what food does to *you*. So you send conflicting messages to your children: "Eat this to please me—but don't end up like me!"

Although your food attitudes affect your relationship with your kids, *don't despair.*

You don't have to be thin to start Fat-Proofing your kids. You don't have to know everything there is to know about diet and nutrition, calorie counts and food groups. In other words, *you don't have to change anything about yourself.* For the time being, your focus should be on your children. Your goal should be helping them to develop sensible eating habits and food attitudes.

The more involved you get in Fat-Proofing, the more it will rub off on you. The more you put food in its proper place in their lives, the less central it will become in your own.

The main point to remember is this: *You're reading this book because you care about your kids.* You've made the decision that you don't want them to become diet-addicted adults. Therefore, you stand an excellent chance of succeeding in your efforts to Fat-Proof them—and maybe, as a bonus, getting yourself in shape along the way.

If you scored between 75 and 100:

You can rate yourself average among Americans today. You have a good idea of what your personal trouble spots are where food is concerned (food is still tied to your emotions), but you're not quite sure how to go about dealing with them.

You don't usually go off the deep end on either a binge or a diet, but you'd like to get a better handle on your eating habits and food attitudes. Perhaps your weight "yo-yos" 10 or 15 pounds every six months to a year. You're able to stick to a diet (which may mean that you often prepare separate meals for yourself and your family—a conflicting message!), but no single diet has worked for you over the long term.

Your children may sense your ambivalent feelings about food. They may wonder why you encourage them to take seconds without ever taking them yourself. Whether or not you know it, they're getting—from you— the idea that self-denial regarding food is "good" while simultaneously unpleasant.

Fat-Proofing will help you alleviate some of your confusion over food. And it should be fairly easy for you to incorporate Fat-Proofing into your life as you make it part of your children's lives.

If you scored below 75:
You don't live to eat—you eat to live. And you know the difference!

You're probably comfortable with the way you look and feel about yourself. Your self-esteem is higher than average. You may watch your weight, but you're not paralyzed with fear at the thought of getting fat, because you know there's little chance of that ever happening.

You eat when you're hungry, and you don't mind saying, "no, thank you" to an offer of food when you're not. You enjoy preparing (and eating) special meals on special occasions, but you don't punish yourself for weeks afterward if you overdo it. You may exercise regularly—partly to keep your weight under control, but mostly because you enjoy the extra energy and strength exercise gives you.

It's likely that you were raised in much the same way as you're raising your kids: to appreciate good food, to eat slowly, and to put other things besides food at the center of their lives. People rarely stuff themselves at your table because they're usually off and running rather than sitting and eating.

In short, you may have been Fat-Proofing your kids from day one without being conscious of it. Congratulations! You'll find this program very easy to follow. Maybe you're already incorporating much of it into your lifestyle. This book will supplement what you know and provide you with strategies that will be helpful as your kids continue to change and grow. It should answer some of the questions you have about food jags and other peculiarities of children—and give you "ammunition" to use against peer pressure, advertising, and related influences that have gotten other families off the track and headed toward fat and diet addiction.

Step 1 of Fat-Proofing has been devoted to you—your past, your food attitudes, your feelings—because you're most likely the one who's responsible for feeding your children. And, even more important, you're probably the person upon whom they'll model their food habits and attitudes. Many of these—good or bad, positive or negative—will last for a lifetime.

THREE

WHAT'S YOUR FAMILY'S EATING PATTERN?

If your family is like most, when and where and how often you eat are well established. What I'll term your "family eating pattern" probably doesn't vary much from day to day.

Step 2 of Fat-Proofing involves examining this pattern—and learning how it can help or hinder your efforts to Fat-Proof your children.

For each of the following questions, circle the description that comes closest to fitting your family:

1. Which of these sounds most like your family at the dinner table?

   A. It's a close-knit, Norman Rockwell–type scene, with Mom serving, Dad carving, and all the children assembled and in their places. Conversation is enjoyable and good table manners are emphasized. Nobody (except the youngest child) is excused until everybody has finished eating.

   B. There's a different cast of characters every night. Sometimes the kids are involved in activities, or call to say they'll be eating at their friends' houses; sometimes they bring their friends home with them. Dinner is served whenever it's ready, and conversation hinges on whether anyone stays around long enough to talk.

C. Usually all family members are present. However, it's not an issue if someone offers a reasonable excuse for being absent. The meal revolves around very lively discussions; it's noisy at the table, and occasionally unpleasant arguments erupt. More often, though, the kids compete with one another to talk about their day or tell the latest jokes. This is the scene of many passionate family discussions— about family accomplishments or concerns, about world events, about whatever family members are interested in.

D. The parents and the children dine separately. They eat at different times (or in different rooms—the kids in the kitchen, the parents in the dining room) and are served different meals.

2. Generally speaking, what kinds of dinners do you serve?

A. Meals are elaborate and feature at least three courses, including dessert. Most of the dishes are made from scratch, or as close to it as time allows; there are seldom any "instant" or frozen items. Everyone is expected to eat the same food.

B. Meals are usually light and dependent on people's schedules. The focus tends to be on the day's events or on family matters, not on the food itself, so what is served isn't all that important. Offerings range from pot luck to leftovers and even TV dinners. People eat more or less what they want out of what's available.

C. There are ten (or twenty, or thirty) "stock" dinners that can be prepared by almost anyone, and these are what meals revolve around. Mom, Dad, and the kids all have their specialties, and everyone is expected to help out or contribute in some way. Family togetherness at mealtimes is valued more than gourmet cooking.

D. The kids are given "kid foods" while the adults get "adult foods." The meals are planned, conceived, and prepared separately, just as they are eaten separately. Eventually a child "graduates" to the grown-ups' table.

3. What time of day are meals usually served?

A. Dinner is held over the "dinner hour," which may be moved forward or backward only in emergencies or on special occasions. Everyone is expected to be present and ready to eat on time. On weekends, even lunch is served on schedule.

B. It depends on the day and family members' schedules. Dinner might be served as early as 5:30 or as late as 9:00; sometimes (although rarely) it isn't served at all, and family members are expected to fend for themselves. The kids do a juggling act, fitting meals in between baseball practice, swim meets, and piano lessons; parents may work late or attend evening meetings or classes. Lunch on weekends is almost always catch-as-catch-can.

C. They're usually served at a set time, but some flexibility exists to allow people to pursue their own interests and lives. To make sure that dinner is held as close to the "dinner hour" as possible, family schedules are often juggled to coincide with meal schedules. The focus is on bringing the family together, even if the time varies somewhat from night to night. Lunch on weekends is announced an hour or so in advance to give everyone the chance to get ready.

D. The kids eat at the same time every night (and usually during the day as well). Mom and Dad, on the other hand, eat meals on the run and are rarely at the table during the day. They take a late supper after the kids are in bed.

4. Where is dinner usually served?

A. It's always in the dining room, with the table set attractively (although the best china is reserved for special occasions). Everyone comes to the table when they're called, or when the dinner bell is rung.

B. Dinner may be served in the kitchen or even in front of the TV. Often eating accompanies some other activity. If the kids are involved in their homework, they may be allowed to take their meals to their rooms.

C. It's usually at the dining-room table (unless the dining room is "formal" and the kitchen is roomy, in which case most meals are taken in the kitchen). The kids normally participate in serving and clearing and often in meal preparation. Things can get hectic in the kitchen just prior to bringing the food to the table.

D. The kids always eat in the kitchen; Mom and Dad may eat there later, or they may take their meals in the dining room. In general, however, the only time the whole family gathers around the dining-room table is on special or formal occasions, and then the kids are expected to behave.

5. Which best describes a typical family breakfast at your house?

A. It's usually eaten together, especially on weekends (work schedules during the week may make this difficult or impossible). The baby's high-chair is brought to the table so he or she can be with the rest of the family. Although it's not as formal as dinner, breakfast is served at a set time and everyone is expected to be in attendance.

B. This meals is *always* catch-as-catch-can, with each family member grabbing food (or being fed) whenever he or she arises or requests food. Whole-family breakfasts are rare. Some family members skip breakfast altogether; it's hard to tell who does and who doesn't, since nobody keeps track.

C. An attempt is made to eat breakfast as a family, but it's not always possible. The family does eat together on weekends, but sometimes these breakfasts are tense for everyone involved, and their effects are felt throughout the day.

D. Separate breakfasts are prepared for everyone as they're called for, and Mom (or sometimes Dad) ends up feeling like a short-order cook in the process. An attempt is made to ensure that each family member eats a "good" breakfast.

6. How are meals usually prepared in your family?

A. Mom prepares all (or most) of the meals, often planning menus a week in advance. She always knows exactly what she will be serving. Changes in this routine are unwelcome and perceived as disruptive.

B. Family members often fend for themselves, though Mom (or sometimes Dad) helps the younger ones. Last-minute decisions about what to prepare are common. Meals are frequently patched together with whatever foods happen to be around the house, or someone makes a quick run to the local supermarket.

C. Everyone participates in some way. The kitchen functions as a family center. The family also works together to set and clear the table and clean up the kitchen afterward.

D. Mom prepares and serves most of the children's meals, although the kids sometimes help out in the kitchen. Their assistance is welcome, since Mom usually ends up fixing two separate meals—one for the kids, and one for her and Dad.

7. Which best describes your own attitude toward the way your family eats?

A. You care a great deal about what your family eats and spend a lot of time shopping, cooking, and preparing well-balanced meals.

B. You've pretty much decided that even if your kids eat a lot of fast foods they'll still get adequate nutrition somehow. And you believe that an active lifestyle is just as important as eating well and healthfully.

C. You treasure mealtimes because they bring your family together for a certain period of time each day. You believe in serving wholesome, balanced meals your family will enjoy, and do your best to provide them on a regular basis, but they're predominantly a "backdrop" for family togetherness.

D. You believe that your kids should at least try everything that's served. More often than not, you give them what you know they'll eat, and you try to satisfy the individual food preferences of each person in your household.

Scoring:
Add up your A, B, C, and D responses. Write here the letter of the response you came up with most frequently: _____.

(In case of a tie, go through the questions again, quickly, to see whether there are any responses you wish to change. Since each of the family types described is so different from the others, a genuine tie is unlikely.)

INTERPRETING YOUR SCORE

If you scored mostly "A" responses:
Yours is what I call a "Type A" family.

A neighbor walking past your house at dinnertime and looking in the dining-room window would see a Norman Rockwell–type picture. Dad would be sitting at the head of the table, and Mom would be bustling out of the kitchen bearing a steaming dish. The kids would be waiting patiently for dinner to begin.

As a Type A family, you value togetherness over food. Missing a meal is practically inexcusable. Everything having to do with food is treated with respect and rather formally—planning, preparing, and serving. Someone—probably you—spends a large amount of time and effort on food-related tasks. Your mother probably did the same.

The kitchen is your exclusive domain. If Dad does any cooking at all, it's usually on the outdoor grill. The kids aren't welcome in the kitchen because they disrupt your routine, which you have down pat after years of practice.

You regard yourself as a good cook—in fact, that image is closely tied to your self-esteem—and you take pride in your skills. Maybe you're even a gourmet cook. You prize the recipes handed down to you by your mother (and grandmothers) and treasure your collection of cookbooks (which are kept out of reach of sticky fingers).

Snacks usually aren't permitted because they "spoil" appetites. You take it personally when the kids don't eat; it's as if they're rejecting your love.

One of your greatest pleasures is bringing in dessert at the end of the meal. You enjoy baking as well as cooking—you may even set aside a day of each week especially for that purpose—and the child who finishes his or her dinner without complaining is in for a real treat (dessert is not awarded to those who don't clean their plates).

Despite the cozy image, there may be trouble in this paradise. By insisting on togetherness over food, you may be placing *too much emphasis* on food. (Children in general don't appreciate gourmet cooking. The very young ones prefer simple foods; teens tend to be indifferent.)

Your earnest attempts to do well by your family may be perceived as controlling.

You may be pressuring your family to eat for the *wrong reason:* because you've spent the day slaving over a hot stove. And you may be encouraging your kids to overeat from an early age, a tendency that's hard to conquer later in life when the body is full of hungry fat cells.

Finally, you may be placing too much pressure on *yourself* to be the "perfect" mother, despite today's realities. If you're trying to juggle a job in addition to all your household duties, you're probably feeling the strain. On the other hand, you may be fortunate enough to have a housekeeper, or perhaps you're able to stay at home and not pursue a career. Even so, you may want to ask yourself if the amount of time you spend in the kitchen is really appropriate.

If you scored mostly "B" responses:
Yours is what I call a "Type B" family.

A neighbor looking into your house around dinnertime would probably see a totally different picture every night for a week. The dining-room table might be set for a meal—or it might be piled with laundry to be folded, or covered with newspapers or pieces of a jigsaw puzzle. Rather than being a center for family togetherness, the room itself is more likely a place people pass through on their way to somewhere else.

You're a person of many interests, and food preparation may be least among them. You may be a good cook, but you seldom have the opportunity to showcase your talents. Holidays are the exception, since they're the only times when your family can be counted on to sit down together.

In a way, your family's lifestyle is a relief to you. Since they care little about what they eat, you don't have to worry about pleasing them. You keep the freezer stocked with frozen dinners and the cabinets with instant foods. You use the microwave more than the stove because it enables you to make last-minute decisions about what to serve. It's not uncommon for the TV to be on during dinner, or for family members to read the newspaper or magazines or even schoolbooks.

You and your family enjoy your active lifestyle and feel no desire to change it, although sometimes you wish you could be together more often. That would require everyone to slow down, however, which isn't apt to happen.

But your boisterous, busy family may have a problem. Kids in Type B families often get too much of the *wrong kinds* of foods. There are reasons why fast food is called "junk food" (I'll talk more about fast food in chapter 12), and your kids' diets may be seriously lacking important nutrients. For better or for worse, a good nutritional variety takes a certain amount of kitchen preparation. Reliance on package foods and do-it-yourself microwave dinners has built-in limitations.

By not helping children form good eating and food preparation habits, you're allowing them to develop numerous bad ones. They're probably overdosing on salt, sugar, fats, and additives—all of which can have harmful effects over both the short- and the long-term.

If you scored mostly "C" responses:
Yours is what I call a "Type C" family.

Imagine that neighbor strolling past your house again. This time the scene indoors resembles a combination of a Norman Rockwell painting and the trading floor of the New York Stock Exchange. Everyone is gathered around the table, but no one is sitting still. Dishes are being passed, arms are being waved for attention, spoons are being dropped and retrieved, and people are popping up and down to get things from the kitchen.

You gave up your exclusive rights to the kitchen long ago (if you ever had them) because you want your family to be together as often as possible. In your meal planning, you allow for the extra time it will take for little, inexperienced hands to perform tasks you could do much more quickly on your own.

You value mealtimes as symbolic of your family's togetherness. If that togetherness is occasionally unpleasant, so what? You'd rather people talk to one another than sit there in silence, even if their talking gets a bit loud. You try to see that your family eats well and nutritiously, but you don't get upset if they fail to clean their plates. As long as they're together, you're content.

Type C kids often eat quickly and without pleasure. They may leave meals unfinished or resort to "sneaky snackery"—eating in their rooms between meals so they can legitimately claim that they're not hungry when mealtimes roll around. They learn to associate eating with conflict, and togetherness with tension and strain.

If you scored mostly "D" responses:
Yours is what I call a "Type D" family.

The Type D lifestyle—with parents and children dining separately— used to be considered the prerogative of the rich. The kids ate by themselves under their nanny's watchful eye, and Mother and Father took their meals later in the evening in the formal dining room, with servants in attendance. About once a month the kids were awarded the special treat of eating dinner with their parents.

At any rate, it's no longer true that this practice is confined to families who have money to spare (if indeed it ever was). In fact, it may be just the opposite. Today's typical Type D family is one in which both parents work (often because they need the added income), or where there's only one parent in residence and that parent has no choice but to work.

The kids don't eat with Nurse or Nanny; they eat alone. And sometimes meals aren't even prepared for them in advance; they fend for themselves. The old question, "It's 10:00 P.M.—do you know where your children are?" could be amended to, "It's 4:00 P.M.—do you know what your children are eating?"

If your family is Type D, perhaps it's because dinnertime is the only chance you and your spouse have to talk and you prefer to do it uninterrupted. Or perhaps you believe it's in your family's best interests for the kids to eat "kid food" and the adults to eat "adult food." Or perhaps you like to get the kids' dinners out of the way so you can enjoy your own meal later at a more leisurely pace.

Since you're not around to supervise their behavior during meals, your attitude toward snacking is liberal. You'd rather your kids eat something than nothing. You know that they're eating in front of the TV, and you wish they weren't, but you've given up trying to change them.

Today's Type D family may face more challenges than any of the other types. These challenges will be felt across all social strata as more mothers enter the workplace and the divorce rate remains high. Creative solutions are needed now more than ever.

Families with latchkey kids have special problems. (I hate the term *latchkey*, but it's entered our vocabulary and seems to be here to stay.) Their kids are at home unsupervised for hours each day. As a result, they're apt to eat anything they can find, and a dose of afternoon TV with its fast-food, snack-food, and candy commercials only makes matters worse. (Except for a great raisin commercial, try finding advertisements for foods kids *should* eat.) By the time dinner rolls around, they're not hungry because they've been nibbling for hours.

Without the presence of food "role models," children (latchkey or not) may develop poor eating habits or lose interest in food altogether. They'll eat aimlessly—sometimes because they're actually hungry, but more often because they're bored.

According to a recent National Children and Youth Fitness Study, modern children are "significantly fatter" than those of twenty years ago. There are various reasons for this—I'll address some of them in chapter 10—but two of the biggest culprits appear to be the lack of eating supervision at home and too much TV. According to a recent study conducted at the New England Medical Center and Harvard School of Public Health, kids who watch more TV are more likely to be overweight.

Feeling guilty about "abandoning" our kids is not the answer. Instead, we must find ways to influence them positively even when we're not around. Believe me, it *can* be done. An absent parent can still be a good parent, and a strong one.

I find it useful to assign categories because it helps me to define problems. Defining a problem is the first step toward discovering potential solutions. By calling yourself Type A, Type B, or whatever, you're not tattooing a letter on your forehead. What I *hope* you're doing instead is developing a clearer understanding of your family eating pattern—its good points and bad.

You won't have to change your family type to make Fat-Proofing work for you. It's designed to fit any lifestyle. Following are some tips to start you on your way. (Your family may have some characteristics of all four types, so be sure to at least read through all the tips, including those that at first seem not to apply to you.)

TIPS FOR THE TYPE A FAMILY

- If you get pleasure out of cooking, there's no reason why you shouldn't continue. But do examine your motives. Are you really doing it for your kids, or for yourself?

If you believe you're doing it for your kids, then you may not be considering their needs and preferences. Elaborate foods may be too rich for them. The sauces you spend hours preparing may be boosting their cholesterol levels. (Studies have shown that around one-third of all kids over 12 have too-high cholesterol levels.) And they may not like what you prepare—not because they don't like you, but because their tastes aren't that sophisticated yet.

If you're doing it for yourself, then why not expand your repertoire to include dishes better suited to their tastes? You can still take pride in a well-prepared meal. And many of the foods kids enjoy contain natural ingredients, so you can continue to prepare things from scratch.

- Do try to separate your self-esteem from your family's opinion of your cooking. Don't take it personally if they fail to praise your efforts or if they turn up their noses at your latest creation. Small children especially are suspicious of anything new.

- For the sake of your family's health, you *should* start eliminating desserts from their regular diet. In chapter 2, I outlined one way to do this. If you can't resist baking, again, there are plenty of healthful, nutritious recipes available.

- Start thinking about loosening your grip on the kitchen. Why? Because kids learn the most about nutrition from their parents. It's not enough for them to see the final products of your efforts. They also need to watch you cook, and to take an active role in meal preparation.

At first this may seem like opening a sanctuary to hordes of barbarians. For a while your kitchen may not be its old spotless self. But kids can be taught to clean up as well as to mess up!

Here are a few suggestions to get you going:

For very young children:

Little ones don't have the manual dexterity to perform kitchen chores, but they do have eyes and ears ready and eager to take in new information.

- Bring in a sturdy stepstool they can climb on to see above countertop level. They may be satisfied with nothing more than a clear view of your activities.

- If you've got the space, reserve one floor-level cabinet for unbreakables—plastic bowls, pots and pans, empty tins. Taking things out and putting things in (not to mention banging them together) can keep toddlers occupied for hours.

- Have fun with young children by exposing them to different smells, such as coffee, vanilla, and peanut butter. Take off those lids and enjoy your time together!

- If you've never before welcomed your little ones into the kitchen, you'll want to do some basic "kid-proofing" first. Put *all* knives well out of reach. Get in the habit of pointing pan handles toward the back of the stove.

For primary-school children:

- Upon returning from the grocery store, let your kids unpack the sacks. They'll enjoy digging in and making "discoveries," and they can also help you put items away. This will start familiarizing them with the ingredients you use.

▪ When baking, allow them to measure and pour dry ingredients.

▪ Assign simple chores—washing vegetables, snapping the ends off of green beans, putting napkins on the table, and so on.

COOKBOOKS FOR KIDS

There are many children's cookbooks available in bookstores or your local library. The first four listed below are special because of the lavish use of four-color photography.

▪ *Betty Crocker's Cookbook for Boys and Girls,* (Racine, WI: Golden Press/Western Publishing, 1975).

▪ *Microwave Cooking for Kids,* ed. by Better Homes and Gardens (Des Moines, IA: Meridith Corporation, 1984).

▪ *The New Junior Cookbook,* ed. by Better Homes and Gardens (Des Moines, IA: Meridith Corporation, 1984).

▪ *Step-by-Step Kid's Cookbook,* ed. by Better Homes and Gardens (Des Moines, IA: Meridith Corporation, 1984).

For younger cooks (ages 4–8):

▪ *Crunchy Bananas,* by Barbara Wilms (Helena, MT: Falcon Press, 1984).

▪ *My First Cookbook,* by Rena Coyle (New York: Workman Publishing, 1985).

For cooks 8 and up:

▪ *The Fun of Cooking,* by Jill Krementz (New York: Knopf, 1985).

▪ *Kids Cooking,* by Vicki Lansky (New York: Scholastic, 1987).

Another special cookbook is *Creative Food Experiences for Children,* by Mary Goodwin and Gerry Pollen. It contains 200 pages of activities, games, and recipes to introduce elementary-school-age children to the kitchen. For a copy send $5.95 to CSPI, 1501 16th St. NW, Washington, DC 20036 for a copy.

For older children:

- Stirring, mashing, peeling, grating, and scraping are all tasks that can be handled by older children.

- Let them prepare simple dishes by themselves at one end of the counter while you work at the other.

- Ask their advice in menu planning, and take the opportunity to discuss basic nutrition.

TIPS FOR THE TYPE B FAMILY

Take a lesson from the Type A mom; your life could use some planning! In fact, many of these tips have to do with planning ahead (something you may not be accustomed to):

- Try to do your grocery shopping once a week. If you're concerned about the kinds of foods your kids are eating, you can do something about it: buy *only* those foods you *want* them to eat. They won't be able to gorge on potato chips if they're not around.

- If frozen entrees are among your family's staples, you're in luck. A lot of companies that make them are finally responding to consumer demand for healthier prepared foods. Be sure to read the labels when you shop.

- Keep nutritious snacks in the refrigerator, prepared and ready to eat. Kids will happily munch on sweet carrot sticks—if they've been peeled and cut up for them ahead of time.

- No time for a leisurely breakfast? Set the table the night before and have everything ready, so that the whole thing takes ten minutes at the most to prepare.

- Make a new rule and stick to it: **No** TV during dinner. The kids may sit there in sullen silence for the first few days, but they'll get used to it in time. And they may discover that conversation isn't such a bad alternative.

If they simply *must* have some sort of entertainment, haul out the cassette player. Pop in some story tapes or, for older kids, tapes of old radio shows (the Green Hornet, for instance). They may sit there longer—and eat more slowly—just to hear how the tale ends.

Many bookstores are starting to carry large selections of books on cassette, and they're also available from your public library.

- If you don't have a microwave; consider getting one. Mine has been a lifesaver. And since it cuts cooking time down to almost nothing (compared to the stove or oven), you may be able to lessen your dependence on "instant" foods full of chemicals and preservatives (and calories).

Are your kids in the habit of gobbling their food? Try these suggestions for slowing them down:

- Have the whole family do a minute's worth of deep-breathing exercises before beginning to eat. (Put one child in charge of keeping count—"In . . . out . . . in . . . out.")

- Hold a contest to see who can turn a single serving into the most bites.

- Serve foods that can't be eaten in huge gulps (like peas, for example).

- Play word games at the table. Young children will enjoy "What am I?" Each person takes a turn describing a common object without using its name. ("I'm made of metal and have a big engine and fly to the moon. What am I?")

TIPS FOR THE TYPE C FAMILY

If your dinner table is the place where everyone in your family speaks his mind, you may need to channel conversations away from unpleasant or volatile topics. Mealtimes should be happy times!

Too many of my friends grew up in households where parents screamed at each other over the evening meal. To this day they can recall violent discussions about money, politics, jobs, drinking, and other topics that disturbed them deeply—partly because they didn't understand them, partly because they couldn't do anything about them, and partly because the arguments turned their parents into monsters.

Some couples promise each other that they'll never go to bed at night without settling arguments. For the sake of your children, you and your spouse should agree that the dinner table is a place for truce.

- If a whole-family brawl gets started (or even a spat between two family members), interrupt and schedule a conference for after dinner. Be calm but firm. If everyone chooses to fume quietly for the remainder of the meal, that's still preferable to a full-blown verbal battle.

- Save criticisms for later (if ever). This is no time to needle your kids because of how they dress, or to reprimand them for poor performance in school, or to nag them about their behavior. And never, repeat, **never** take this opportunity to get on their case for being overweight, if indeed they are.

It's confusing and humiliating for a child to have a forkful of food en route to his or her mouth and hear Mom or Dad say, "Haven't you had enough?" On one hand, they're there to eat; on the other, they're being told not to. If you need to limit a child's caloric intake, do so by preparing low-calorie foods and by limiting the size of servings.

- Kids who poke and kick one another under the table should be separated. Play "musical chairs" with your seating arrangement until you come up with one that works, but don't cast it in concrete. In fact, you may want to shift people around regularly. If Dad usually occupies the head-of-the-table position, put a child there on occasion as a special honor or reward.

Until your family becomes accustomed to these changes, they may not know what to talk about. Here are a few ideas:

- Ask your children to describe something they did during the day that they're especially proud of. Then praise them!

- Use the occasion to announce and discuss upcoming special events—a trip to the zoo, a family vacation, and so on.

- Schedule an "awards night"—perhaps for the Friday evening meal. Hand out "certificates of achievement" to children who have kept their rooms clean or performed assigned chores without complaining.

- Play soothing music during dinner. It's hard to argue while Bach's "Lute Suites" are airing sweetly in the background.

- Most important, *listen to your children* while they speak. Make it clear that you're interested in what they have to say. And ask other family members not to interrupt.

TIPS FOR THE TYPE D FAMILY

Fat-Proofing will probably be more difficult for you than for any other family type. But even though it's hard to instill good eating habits in your kids when you're not around, it's important to work at it.

- Children—especially young ones—should have adult supervision at mealtimes. Either you or your spouse should plan to at least sit with the kids while they eat. You may have to juggle schedules to accomplish this, but it's important.

- If you must leave the house before your kids eat breakfast, have it ready for them in advance. (In chapter 12 I'll give suggestions for breakfasts that don't require much preparation.)

- Pack nutritious school lunches the night before.

- If your kids arrive home before you do, you can still control what foods they snack on. Make sure that your refrigerator is stocked exclusively with nutritious snack foods (don't buy any other kind). Leave a note on the refrigerator telling them what they can and can't eat.

Even if your children are in daycare, this is no guarantee that they're getting snacks that are good for them. Ask the daycare provider what's being offered and when. If you don't like what you hear, do something about it. You may want to furnish snacks of your own choosing.

- Are you worried that your kids are watching too much TV in your absence? And that they're munching mindlessly when they do?

According to the experts, you've got plenty of reason to worry. A study done in the late 1970s noted that children prefer to eat the foods they see advertised on television (two-thirds of which are high in sugar content), and that the commercials themselves may have a "ripple effect" by stimulating demands for other edibles in the same category. When the children studied had viewed TV commercials for highly sugared foods, they opted for more of these; when they viewed pronutrition public service announcements, they opted for snack and breakfast foods considered higher in nutritional value.

Take action! If you must, buy a "channel blocker"—a device that allows you to lock out certain channels even when you're not at home. One brand name: the Censorview. (These are expensive, but many parents think they're worth it.)

TV manufacturers are looking ahead to what they think will be a growing market. General Electric has built channel blockers into several of its newer models, and RMS is selling a device that prevents access to video cassette recorders.

I've been known to leave for my office with the TV remote control in my handbag and the connector cables removed and hidden in the house. I hear plenty of grumbling, but no TV.

But don't just deprive your kids of TV without offering some constructive alternatives.

- Check into the availability of afterschool programs—sports, fun classes, and so on, that can keep your kids busy and *out of the house*. More and more of these are being made available because the need is so great. One excellent resource may be your nearby public school.

If your kids simply *must* come home, make plans to keep them occupied. Here are some strategies that have worked for me:

- Leave lists of things for them to do—some can be chores, and others can be fun.

- If they're old enough, and responsible enough, allow them to have friends in after school. Set up some games on the kitchen table.

- If your job permits, schedule a regular time or two when you'll phone them to see how they're doing.

- Plan "treasure hunts." Scatter a trail of notes throughout the house (or put paper arrows on the floor) that lead to a "prize"—a new book to read, a coloring book and crayons, a paint set, or a puzzle.

- It's not easy—and it can be scary—for children to walk into an empty, silent house. If you have a clock radio, set it to go on fifteen minutes or so before they're due to arrive. Or leave a recorded message on a cassette on the kitchen table from you to them. Some kids record their music practice on cassette to play back when Mom and Dad get home.

There are many other ways to make your presence felt. The critical thing is to let your kids know you care and are thinking about them even when you can't be with them.

A SPECIAL ASIDE
FOR SINGLE PARENTS

Single parents are under a great deal of stress and strain. Most are mothers who have suddenly found themselves the sole support of their kids, maybe without ever having worked outside the home.

Single mothers with children at home are the emerging lower class in our society. At least 30 percent are living at or below the poverty line. Often their children are left alone because the mothers can't afford daycare. Often their children eat poorly because there's no one around to look after them, and Mom has too many other things on her mind to worry about proper nutrition. Far too often it's a matter of having a very limited food budget.

Many publications produced by the U.S. government can help stretch a food dollar to cover the basic food groups. To find out more about government publications—many are free—request a copy of the Consumer Information Catalogue by writing to Consumer Information Catalogue, Pueblo, CO 81009.

Don't be ashamed to apply for food stamps. They can be a boon for a family temporarily down on their luck.

Finally, if you're a single parent, you don't have to go it alone. There are plenty of other parents out there with the same concerns you have. You can meet some of them through your local chapter of Parents Without Partners. For information, write Parents Without Partners International, 8807 Colesville Rd, Silver Spring, MD 20910, or call (301) 588-9354.

FOUR

WHEN TO START FAT-PROOFING YOUR KIDS

Choose one:
The best time to start Fat-Proofing your kids is:

A. during infancy

B. between ages 1 and 5

C. after age 5 but before adolescence

D. during adolescence

If you chose any of the above, you're . . . wrong.

The best time to start Fat-Proofing your kids is the day you learn you're pregnant—or even sooner. It's been said that the most critical years in a child's life are the two years *before* he or she is born. Mom's eating habits, physical condition, and overall health (and Dad's, too, since he contributes half of the genetic ingredients) are what baby is made of. Mom provides the building site, but both parents chip in on the materials.

If you don't yet have children but are planning to soon, *now* is the time to start Fat-Proofing: by eating healthful, nutritious foods, getting yourself into shape, and kicking bad habits (like smoking).

If you have a baby on the way, now is your golden opportunity to guarantee that he or she gets the best of everything. What goes into your mouth eventually makes it into his or her tiny body. Those fingers and toes you'll count at birth are forming right now, as is that miraculous brain. You're not only eating for two, you're wholly responsible for two. Your baby is counting on you.

More likely, though, you already have children. In this and the following chapters, we're going to look at how you can Fat-Proof your kids from infancy onward. I'll tell you the physiological variants to watch for and the milestones to note. I'll describe what goes on in each of the major age groups and discuss the key issues that arise. And I'll show you how Fat-Proofing can become an integral part of child rearing at any age or stage.

Along the way, I'll be citing norms and averages as reference points, *not* as hard-and-fast rules. The only rules you need to keep in mind are the Four Rules of Fat-Proofing—especially rule 1: *Don't assume that a heavier-than-average child is a fat child*. If you put a group of so-called average children in a room and studied each one, you'd find that some are taller, some are wider, some are leaner, some are chunkier, and all are different in countless ways. What's important to remember is that *your* child is unique, an individual. The whole focus of Fat-Proofing is to help your child be his or her best self.

FEEDING YOUR INFANT: THE FIRST YEAR OF LIFE

You've brought baby home from the hospital, tucked him or her snugly into the bassinette or cradle, and settled your exhausted body into an overstuffed chair for a few well-deserved moments of rest. And suddenly your head is buzzing with questions and doubts.

What's the best way to feed that tiny, fragile creature. Whom should you listen to—your mother, your neighbors, your friends, your doctor? If you're breast-feeding, how long should you continue? Should you feed on schedule or on demand? What if your baby won't eat? What if your baby won't *stop* eating?

And where does Fat-Proofing fit in? Is it just something else for you to worry about? What if your baby is a butterball? Does Fat-Proofing mean you should put your infant on a diet?

Absolutely not! *Relax!* And **don't** try to limit your baby's weight gain during these first several months.

He or she will grow faster this year than at any other time of life. By the end of the first 5 months, your child's birth weight will probably double. By the end of the first year it will probably triple. Meanwhile, his or her length may increase by as much as a foot. (Luckily, kids don't keep growing at this tremendous rate. If they did, they'd weigh 200 pounds by the time they were 10!)

For now, your primary goal should be that of keeping your baby healthy and well fed.

SHOULD I WORRY IF MY BABY IS FAT?

Not at all. In 1982, the American Academy of Pediatrics Committee on Nutrition concluded that most obese infants do *not* become obese adults, and most adult obesity is *not* due to obesity in infancy.

In fact, doctors are now encouraging women to have bigger babies. No longer are pregnant women put on strict diets if they gain more than 20 pounds (the horrible plight of women throughout the 1940s and 1950s). Instead, expectant mothers are encouraged to eat to their hearts' delight — as long as the food is safe and nutritious. That's because researchers have found a correlation between how much a woman gains during pregnancy and the birth weight of her baby. Women who put on only 15 pounds during pregnancy tend, on average, to deliver babies weighing 7 pounds; those who gain 24 pounds tend to deliver babies weighing 7 pounds 6 ounces; and those who gain 30 pounds produce, on average, babies with birth weights of 8 pounds 1 ounce. (Remember: these are only averages; your case may be different).

The ideal birth weight for a newborn is between 7 pounds 14 ounces and 9 pounds—what many of us refer to as "big" babies. It's ideal because it means the baby will have fewer diseases and be generally healthier than newborns of smaller size.

So, if you gave birth to a "big" baby, terrific! Your baby is off to a healthy start. And don't be worried that your baby will keep his or her baby fat for life. That fat, which babies put on during the last 3 months of pregnancy, is needed to insulate them against the colder world outside the womb. It's the period *after* that—from age 1 or 2 up to age 9—that seems most important as far as lifelong obesity is concerned.

In an ongoing study at the University of California, Berkeley, School of Public Health, 170 children were observed over a period of 9 years. Using a variety of measurements to determine body fat, including skin-fold thicknesses, the children were divided into three groups at birth: obese (the 15 percent with the most body fat); lean (the 15 percent with the least body fat); and nonobese (the 70 percent who fell in the middle). None of the 17 boys who were the fattest at 6 months was still fat at 9 years; of the girls, only 1 among 9 who were "obese" at 6 months was fat at 9 years.

In a study conducted by the French National Institute of Health, 151 children were weighed monthly from birth until age 16. Some clear patterns emerged. The babies put on weight during the first year, then slimmed down during the active growth years of 2 and 3. Then, at around age 6, their body fat began to increase again.

Significantly, *the earlier the fat came back, the more likely the child was to be overweight as a teenager.* The overweight teenagers in the study were those who had begun to increase their body fat before they were 5¹/₂ years old. The 16-year-olds of average weight had waited until age 6 or later.

AVERAGE LENGTHS AND WEIGHTS FOR BABIES (1 TO 12 MONTHS)

These averages are *for reference only.* Remember that they don't say anything specific about YOUR kids.

Girls

Age	Length (inches)	Weight (pounds; without clothing)
1 month	21.1	8.8
3 months	23.4	11.9
6 months	25.9	15.9
9 months	27.7	18.9
12 months	29.3	21.0

Boys

Age	Length (inches)	Weight (pounds; without clothing)
1 month	21.5	9.5
3 months	24.1	13.2
6 months	26.7	17.3
9 months	28.5	20.2
12 months	30.0	22.4

(Source: The National Academy of Sciences)

IS FAT HEREDITARY?

As I mentioned earlier, children of two fat parents have a 70 to 80 percent chance of becoming fat themselves. One study indicated some possible reasons why.

The babies were given two "tests." In the first, they were shown pairs of stripes. The babies of overweight parents looked back and forth between the stripes more often than did the babies of normal-weight parents, as if they couldn't decide which one to concentrate on. This "extraresponsiveness" to environmental distractions has also been found in adults who overeat.

In the second test, the babies were given a sweet solution to drink, followed by plain water. Both groups of babies eagerly drank the sweet solution. But they responded differently to the plain water; the babies of overweight parents tended to refuse it. In addition, the fattest babies preferred the sweetest solutions, while the thinner babies liked solutions that were less sweet.

In other words, it seems as though kids can have a "sweet tooth" long before they have teeth, period. And it may even be inherited.

New evidence is showing that obesity has a strong genetic component. A study in Denmark, as described in the *New England Journal of Medicine* (1986), looked at 540 adults who were adopted as children. Researchers found that their degree of fatness closely matched that of their biological parents but bore little correlation to their adopted parents. Even as evidence grows that fatness is inherited, it should not be used as an excuse for hopelessness. If being overweight is a family problem, all the more reason you should work at Fat-Proofing.

Are some children, then, "doomed" to become diet-addicted adults? Not necessarily. And here's where Fat-Proofing comes in. *Even though babies appear to have a built-in preference for sweets, a true "taste" for them must be acquired.* Whether your baby acquires such a taste is up to you. The example you set has just as much influence as any genetic predisposition, if such a predisposition exists.

In chapter 11 I'll talk in detail about the trouble with sugar; for now, here are some tips to keep in mind:

- Don't feed "sugar water." A thirsty baby will drink water plain.

- Don't sweeten bottled milk or formula.

- Resist the temptation to dip pacifiers in honey or jelly.

HOW MUCH SHOULD MY BABY EAT?

Never push your baby to eat more than he or she wants. At this stage, Fat-Proofing means two things: exercising good sense when it comes to feeding your baby, and *paying attention* to the messages your baby sends you. A baby who turns away from the breast or bottle and seems reluctant to take it again is *finished eating*. Don't push for more!

Even newborns are perfectly capable of making their wants and needs known. Most often, they communicate by crying—a sure-fire attention getter. Babies "say" lots of things by crying: "I'm wet; change me," "I'm bored; entertain me," "I'm grumpy; cheer me up," "I'm lonely," "I'm uncomfortable; turn me over," "I've got gas—burp me," and, "I don't feel well—help!" (And sometimes, when a baby is crying most energetically, all he or she is "saying" is, "I like the sound of my voice, and I've decided to see how loud it can go. Listen!")

You're communicating with your baby, too. Through your actions, your touch, your facial expressions, and your tone of voice, your baby is learning to recognize love, affection, annoyance, and impatience. You can tell that your baby is learning because he or she responds differently to your different messages. By the same token, *you* should respond differently to the different ones he or she sends you.

The key thing to remember is that *crying doesn't always indicate hunger*. So don't answer every whimper with the nipple. The mom who offers food every time her baby cries is establishing a pattern that can have serious aftereffects. The child learns that food is always the *first* response, the *first* solution—a cure-all for every dissatisfaction, a reward for every behavior. The mom who mistakes *all* cries for cries of hunger is usually the mom who will later bribe her child with sweets and use food to control.

Mothers who feed on demand seem to have the hardest time with this. But even mothers who feed on set schedules may have a problem. Their reaction is to feel guilty for *not* feeding their babies in between times.

Babies' needs can change rapidly. At certain stages in their growth, they may in fact be hungrier more often than at other stages. Still, don't assume that food is what they're asking for. If you've fed your baby fairly recently and have every reason to believe that he or she got enough to eat, try something else. Sing a song, wind up the mobile, cuddle in the rocking chair, change that diaper, do some simple body exercises (for suggestions, see chapter 10). Sometimes all a baby really needs is a little attention.

But please do not err on the side of underfeeding either, because of a fear of fat. It is a tragedy when parents mistakenly believe they can Fat-Proof their child by underfeeding. According to Bonnie Worthington-

Roberts, a professor of nutritional science at the University of Washington, "some parents actually underfed babies to the point of interfering with their growth."

AS A FAT-PROOFING MOTHER, SHOULD I BREAST-FEED OR BOTTLE-FEED?

For years, professionals and parents alike have been arguing about which is better—breast milk, bottled formula, or cow's milk. Before we go into the pros and cons of each, here's a comforting fact: recent studies have shown that a bottle-fed infant is *not* more likely to become obese than is a breast-fed baby. In other words, from a Fat-Proofing perspective at least, it doesn't matter which you choose.

However, it's generally agreed that breast milk is the ideal first food for babies. It's nutritionally sound, inexpensive, usually plentiful, and always served at exactly the right temperature. No formula has yet been able to match it point for point.

A study conducted from 1971 to 1981 revealed that breast-feeding in the hospital more than doubled during that ten-year period, rising from 24.7 percent to 57.6 percent. (In the mid-1950s, when bottle-feeding was the norm, that figure was only 18 percent.) And more mothers are now breast-feeding longer during the nutritionally critical first year of their babies' lives. Actresses breast-feed their babies on the set, as do television personalities; mothers are leaving the office on their lunch hours to go home and breast-feed their babies; a woman firefighter fought for her right to nurse her infant in the station house.

Interestingly, while bottle-feeding doesn't seem to produce any greater chance of future obesity than breast-feeding does, breast-feeding may help to protect a child against future obesity. In a study of 517 children, carried out by the Department of Pediatrics, Epidemiology and Health at Montreal's McGill University, evidence was found that this protection extends through adolescence. In addition, the degree of protection seems to increase the longer the child is breast-fed.

Breast-fed babies tend not to overeat because their mothers are less apt to overfeed them. Unlike a bottle-feeding mother who urges her baby to "finish the bottle," a nursing mother can't tell precisely how much milk her baby is taking and is more likely to let the baby decide when to quit. Breast-fed babies eat what they want and leave it at that. They may take 10 ounces at one feeding, 4 ounces at another. Miraculously, the mother's milk supply usually adjusts to accommodate the infant's eating patterns.

If you decide to breast-feed:

- **Do** increase your normal food intake by about 500 calories per day.

And don't worry that breast-feeding will cause weight gain. In fact, it can help you get in shape faster, since your baby more than drains those additional calories away. Plus, breast-feeding stimulates uterine contractions, which are good for the tummy muscles.

- Drink to meet your body's needs and satisfy your thirst. Recent research shows that lots of extra fluids don't have any effect on increasing milk production.

- Get enough rest.

- **Do** eat sensibly, just as you did during pregnancy.

This means eating a well-balanced diet. Breast milk will give your baby all the vitamins and minerals he or she needs *only if you eat a balanced diet.* The nutrients won't magically appear in your milk. You have to put them there by eating right!

LA LECHE LEAGUE

For more information on breast-feeding, contact your local La Leche League chapter. La Leche League was founded in 1956 by a group of mothers and has since grown to thousands of people nationwide with an active board of medical consultants.

Members will be glad to answer your questions, calm your doubts, and offer sound advice about breast-feeding (in addition to giving lots of support and encouragement). You can telephone a counselor anytime, day or night.

If you can't find the number in your telephone directory, write: La Leche League International, 9616 Minneapolis Ave., Franklin Park, IL 60131. Or call (312) 455-7730.

Other good sources of help and information include local childbirth-education associations, maternity hospitals, and, of course, other nursing mothers.

It used to be thought that breast-fed babies received too little iron after the 3-month store they are born with was depleted. But now it's recognized that the breast milk of a woman who eats a well-balanced diet contains plenty of iron for her baby. (Plus, it's absorbed more easily than is the iron contained in formula.)

Keep in mind that everything you ingest will eventually find its way to your milk—and to your baby. Some foods you eat will affect your baby. Surprisingly, cow's milk is one of these. Others can be chocolate, eggs, and broccoli. Avoid alcohol, caffeine, nicotine, food additives, and drugs— including over-the-counter drugs. Even aspirin, which may seem harmless, can reach dangerously high levels in your nursing baby through your breast milk. *Always* consult your doctor before taking *any* kind of drug while nursing.

Despite the many known advantages of breast-feeding, not all mothers can or want to do it. If either description applies to you, don't feel guilty! Millions of babies have been raised on the bottle and turned out perfectly fine; you may have been one yourself, since bottle-feeding was the rage when you were a baby.

FAT-PROOFING TIPS FOR THE FIRST FEW MONTHS

- **Don't** substitute pure cow's milk for formula.

Many modern formulas provide complete nutrition and are readily digestible. Cow's milk, on the other hand, was meant to feed calves, which double their birth weight in a third of the time human infants do (and start out a lot bigger). It's far richer in protein, calcium, and phosphorus than is human milk, and some of the substances in it are difficult for babies to digest.

The American Academy of Pediatrics now recommends that cow's milk be given to babies no earlier than their 6-month birthdays—and then only as a supplement to solid foods or to formula or breast milk.

Doctors also recommend that babies under 2 years of age receive only whole or 2-percent milk, not skim milk. With their small tummies and high caloric needs (they are, after all, growing at an incredible rate), they need to get their calories in as concentrated a form as possible. Skim milk takes out too many of those fat calories.

Besides providing too few calories (proportionally), skim milk also provides too *much* protein. That's because when the fat is taken out of the milk, a higher concentration of protein is left behind. This concentrated protein can be hard on a baby's kidneys.

Finally, skim milk lacks many essential fatty acids and vitamins C and E. So, the message seems clear: Give your baby whole or 2-percent milk at least until his or her second birthday.

- **Don't** water down your baby's formula.

The baby may "learn" from this that it takes *more* fluid to get the calories he or she needs to feel satisfied.

Water doesn't satisfy hunger; it just gives a temporarily "filled up" sensation before passing through. For a hungry baby who genuinely needs 8 ounces of formula, 4 ounces of formula mixed with 4 ounces of water won't do the trick. The baby will continue to demand food until he or she gets that second bottle of "half-and-half," and a pattern of overeating will have been established.

- Satisfy your baby's need to suck with things besides food.

An infant's need to suck is real and urgent. Studies have shown that frustrating it may lead to overeating and even compulsive overeating later in life.

But the need to suck doesn't always have to be met with feeding. If you've recently fed your baby and he or she is still rooting around for the bottle or nipple, try a pacifier, a bottle of plain water, a teething toy, or a nipple stuffed with cloth and the original aid, your finger (with nail well-clipped).

- If you're bottle-feeding, don't force your baby to down the last few ounces or drops. Let him or her decide when enough is enough.

- Don't answer all of your baby's distress signals with feeding. Try other noncaloric pacifiers—a backrub, a warm bath, a puppet.

- Don't worry if your baby refuses to eat at a feeding, or sleeps right through one. It's never too soon for babies to learn to eat only when they're hungry.

- Don't confine your baby to a playpen for long periods of time during his or her waking hours, since this diminishes physical activity. Instead, play with your child and provide space for rolling and (later) crawling and climbing.

- Spend feeding time cuddling your baby. The closeness that such physical contact establishes is essential to your child's overall development as a person. Take the time to look into your baby's beautiful eyes, stroke the fuzz of hair, trace the tiny ears, and otherwise *enjoy* this marvelous creature who so recently popped into the world.

WHEN TO START SOLIDS

Somehow we've gotten the idea that the earlier a baby starts on solids, the better. Why remains a mystery, although I suspect it has something to do with our pushing our children to achieve more and faster in all areas of their lives.

Myron Winick, M.D., has this to say in his sensible book, *Growing Up Healthy* (New York: William Morrow, 1982):

> It is difficult to ascertain just why the tendency to begin solid foods so early has developed. One reason often given is a belief that the infant is hungry, waking during the night crying for food, and that early introduction of solid foods will placate the child. There is no evidence to support this belief. If anything, the reverse is true. An infant who is on a variety of foods too early may develop gastrointestinal symptoms and appear "fussy" or "colicky," thus waking more frequently at night.

Think about it. Your baby is perfectly healthy, happy, and contented with breast milk (or formula) alone. Why rush into solids? Besides, feeding is a fairly tidy process when baby is plugged into a breast or a bottle. Do you *really* want to move that quickly into the food-on-the-floor, food-in-the-hair, food-on-the-ceiling, food-everywhere stage?

Some studies claim that giving a baby solids in the first few months of life does not appear to promote obesity. But solids contain far more calories per comparable serving than milk or formula, and baby doesn't need those extra calories.

And don't be fooled by that old wives' tale that you should start your baby on solids as soon as he or she is consuming a quart of formula a day. Many infants who are in the 90th percentile for height and weight start downing that much milk at 2 months! That doesn't mean they are ready— or need—to start solids. Certainly, by the time a baby is 1 year old, he or she should be getting most calories from solids rather than from formula or breast milk. But don't worry about it until then.

Plus—and this may be the best reason to hold off—solids can be hard on a baby's digestive tract. They contain starches that a baby's digestive system finds difficult to digest. Because the food is not fully digested, proteins and other relatively large substances sneak through the system—and often cause allergic responses (coughing, vomiting, or rashes). That risk doesn't seem worth taking.

No matter when *you* decide to start solids, pay attention to what *your baby* "tells" you. Babies who consistently push food out of their mouths with their tongues are making it known that their sucking instinct is still strong, and maybe they're not ready for gumming or chewing. Respect the fact that they're making a choice.

What are the signs of your baby's readiness? They're pretty clear. A baby who starts accepting food from a spoon and swallowing it—or who tries to grab food off your plate— is a baby who wants solids.

PREVENTING THE POWER STRUGGLE

Before starting solids, about all you have to worry about is making sure your baby gets enough to eat. From a Fat-Proofing perspective, it doesn't matter whether he or she is lean or roly-poly. And as long as you don't force-feed when your baby has finished eating, you aren't in too much danger of establishing poor eating habits.

Those easy days are over when you first strap your baby into a high chair; *that's when most feeding problems begin.* All at once, food is tied in with the parent's power to control when, what, and how much. And the child suddenly has the power to manipulate you, triggering waves of guilt and frustration.

This is the stage at which most moms start using food as a bribe, a reward, and/or a punishment. Food no longer serves only the baby's physiological needs; suddenly it splashes over into psychological needs as well— your baby's *and* yours.

I remember when Doug was a baby. Before he went on solids, he got fed when he was hungry, and I was relaxed and casual about feedings. All I cared about was that he was growing, just as he was supposed to. If he didn't finish a bottle, if he slept through a meal, no big deal.

That all changed with the first spoonful of cereal. He didn't want it. Why? I wondered. Had I done something wrong? I tried offering it again. He still didn't want it. Wait a minute—I had spent time choosing it, preparing it, putting it into the bowl, and now I was holding him in one arm, and grasping the spoon with the other hand, and he was *refusing* me!

I didn't realize it then, but I had committed a cardinal Fat-Proofing sin:

I had taken *personally* his rejection of a spoonful of cereal. From that point on, our lives were vastly more complicated. I was happy when he ate (and showed it), unhappy when he didn't (and showed that, too).

Fortunately for us all, Doug turned out okay in spite of my early mistakes. By the time Dana came around I was better informed (and more relaxed). What I learned should help you through your own.

- If children don't want to eat, *don't force the issue.* The sooner they learn to eat out of hunger rather than habit, the better.

- Don't insist on "three squares a day." A baby's stomach can't hold much at a time, and as your child grows, a series of smaller meals—or meals preceded and followed by healthful snacks— can be more wholesome. Jane Brody reports that studies of both

---

HOW MUCH TO FEED YOUR BABY

The following serving sizes are recommended for children 1 year old. Use them as *approximate* guidelines for feeding your baby.

Milk and cheese: 4 ½-cup (4-ounce) servings daily (1.5 ounces of cheese equals 1 cup of milk)

Vegetables and fruits: at least 4 ⅓-cup servings daily, including the following:

- vitamin C source (citrus fruits, berries, tomato, cabbage, cantaloupe): 1 ⅓-cup serving daily

- vitamin A source (green or yellow fruits and vegetables): 1 2-tablespoon serving daily

- other vegetables (potato, legumes): 1 2-tablespoon serving daily

- other fruits (apples, bananas): 1 ¼-cup serving daily

Protein foods (lean meat, fish, peanut butter, eggs): 3 2-tablespoon servings daily of lean meat, fish, and/or peanut butter **or** 2 2-tablespoon servings of the above plus 1 egg (kids don't need an egg a day, so you may want to alternate)

Cereals (whole grain and nonsugared), cooked pasta, and/or cooked rice: at least 2 ¼-cup servings daily

Bread (whole grain): at least ½ slice daily

laboratory animals and people have shown that eating several small meals a day produces less weight gain than large amounts of calories eaten all at once.

- Be pleasant during mealtimes, *no matter what*. Even the youngest children will catch on quickly if the table (or high chair) is a tense, unhappy place to be.

- Let children eat at their own pace and decide for themselves how much they want to eat at a single sitting.

Try to be flexible in *everything*—when your child eats, what your child eats, how your child eats, even whether your child eats. And respect strong food dislikes. Babies are curious, but their curiosity usually doesn't extend to new taste sensations. When your child spits something out, give it *one* more try and then wait a few weeks before offering it again.

- Introduce only *one* new food at a time. This will make it easy to see whether a particular food is causing an allergic reaction. (Babies grow out of many allergies, but they're likely to be supersensitive early in life.) Stick with single-ingredient foods.

Good first foods include instant rice cereal, mashed ripe bananas, applesauce, steamed pureed vegetables, and yogurt. (Some doctors feel that fruits should *not* be among baby's first foods because they can generate a taste for sweetness.)

- Take your time progressing from semisolids (thin cereals, strained fruits, and veggies) to lumpy foods to table foods. You may want to allow as long as 6 months for the entire process.

Begin with 1 teaspoon of baby cereal mixed with a few tablespoons of lukewarm breast milk or formula. Offer it to your baby twice a day, and gradually increase the amount until he or she is taking about 1/2 cup per day. Never add sugar as a taste bud incentive.

- Remember water is still an important and needed beverage for children. Create the water-to-satisfy-thirst habit early.

Offer solid foods after your baby has finished about half of a milk or formula feeding. In this 4 to 8 month period, be careful that the food doesn't reduce the amount of milk or formula your baby drinks.

If you are not sure how to go about making your own baby food, read *Feed Me I'm Yours* (Bantam). You'll be surprised how easy and convenient it is to do-it-yourself.

FIVE

FAT-PROOFING YOUR TODDLER

Although there's no apparent correlation between fat babies and later weight problems, there does seem to be one between fat *toddlers* and subsequent obesity.

Researchers at the University of California at Berkeley have found that girls are at particular risk between ages 1 to 2, while boys have two "danger zones": ages 2 to 3 and 4 to 6. Children who put on excessive weight during these times stand a good chance of later obesity.

Under the circumstances, it would be nice if toddlers were malleable, suggestible, cooperative creatures who ate when and what we wanted them to. If they were, Fat-Proofing them would be a snap.

Unfortunately, toddlerhood is the time when kids really start "feeling their oats." They develop their likes and dislikes, which are apt to change from day to day (or from meal to meal). They go on "food jags" (I'll talk more about these in a moment). They make messes at the table. They throw food. They're too curious and too energetic to sit still and eat.

You want them to finish lunch—and they want to lug the furniture around!

FEEDING YOUR TODDLER: OR, WHEN DID LIFE GET SO COMPLICATED?

Perhaps one of the most important things to realize about toddlers is that their appetites aren't what they used to be. They're more on the move, but they're not growing as quickly.

Remember that a child's birth weight triples during the first year of life. After that, things slow down considerably—at least on the surface. Much new development takes place "invisibly," inside the body. This is a period when the bones, teeth, muscles, and brain are going to town, the skeleton is forming and hardening, and the muscle mass is starting to fill out.

The *stomach*, however, is not growing quite as fast, and it can't hold all the food needed from one meal to the next. That's why toddlers want to snack around the clock.

Some snacking is not only permissible but desirable. Healthful, nutritious between-meal bites can actually help form sensible eating habits, and it can make it easier for a child to consume all of his or her daily nutrients. (See p. 92 for an assortment of sensible snacks for toddlers.) There's also some evidence that children who are frequent snackers have leaner builds—probably because they eat only when they're hungry rather than when they're *expected* to be hungry.

So remember, it's *what* your child eats, not necessarily *when* he or she eats, that makes the difference from a Fat-Proofing standpoint. Avoid giving your child fattening snacks—they can establish a pattern you'll regret in the months and years to come.

Toddlers require at least as many nutrients as they received during infancy (especially as they become more active, walking and running and climbing), but since they're often not as hungry, it may be harder to get them to eat what they need. Then again, there will be periods when they eat like horses one day and sparrows the next. Don't be alarmed if food intake varies. There are countless factors that can influence a child's appetite—health, activity level, distractions, moods, even the weather.

Rituals also emerge during this stage. Suddenly children want to eat foods in a certain order (meat, then fruit, then peas). Or they get terribly upset if different foods "touch" one another on the plate. (One mother I know handled this situation by serving everything in individual small bowls. Her toddler was delighted.) Rituals are a way for children to exert some control over their lives; go along with them as much as you can.

By the time most children reach age 2, they have established eating patterns that will remain with them for the rest of their lives. That's why it's so important to begin feeding your toddler the *right foods* for the *right reasons*—starting today.

HOW TO COPE
WITH TODDLER TYRANNY

If babies are self-centered and demanding, toddlers are tyrannical. Strong-willed and stubborn, they perceive the world as revolving around them and their wants. They're very much in the here-and-now, and when *here* is the high chair and *now* is the time they're supposed to eat, if they're not in the mood, forget it!

You certainly can't negotiate with them, and you may not even be able to bribe them. And while you may fool them some of the time with the old "here comes the airplane into the hangar" trick, they'll catch on soon.

Toddlers are adamant about their food preferences. They may not have the vocabulary (at first) to express them eloquently, but they're skilled at screwing up their faces and can spit a fair distance. Most toddlers—even those who formerly gobbled raw veggies by the handful—suddenly develop an intense aversion to vegetables, especially the green ones. This is a time when parents must call forth *all* of their patience and a large part of their creativity.

It's important to give your toddler permission to refuse certain foods—especially new ones. If you don't, you'll end up in a battle of wills that may bring you to the breaking point and set the stage for more serious eating problems later in life. Remember that saying "no" is one of the ways in which a child asserts independence and develops a sense of self.

Following are some techniques for introducing new foods that have worked for other parents. See which ones work for you.

- Present them one at a time in *very* small amounts, and serve them along with familiar and acceptable foods. If the kids turn up their noses, try again later, or incorporate the new foods into other dishes, such as soups, stews, or salads.

- Wait until your child is very hungry and then serve a new item as an "appetizer."

- Invite your child into the kitchen to "help" you prepare meals. This accomplishes at least three things: it removes some of the "mystery" from food preparation, it encourages an interest in different types of food, and it affords the child an opportunity to practice his or her developing motor skills.

- Pretend that certain foods are "for adults only." Forbidden fruits are somehow more attractive; children may actually ask for a taste or two.

- Always serve vegetables at the beginning of a meal, when your child is apt to be the hungriest.

- If your child has already refused a particular vegetable, try serving it in a different form.

Offer creamed corn instead of plain, or shredded carrots instead of diced. (Never, by the way, feed your toddler chopped or whole carrots; they could cause choking.) Or serve the refused vegetable a second time with a side "dip" of yogurt, creamed cottage cheese, or that perennial childhood favorite—peanut butter. Your child may have so much fun scooping out the dip that he or she will forget to hate the vegetable!

- If your child refuses meat, maybe what you're preparing is just too difficult for a toddler's teeth and jaws to handle. Try offering ground meat, or tender meat such as chicken. (Chicken is healthier, anyway. Ounce for ounce, it has as much protein as steak, with half the fat.)

- Be careful of the signals you send; your kids will be able to tell from them which foods *you* like and dislike. They pay close attention to your facial expressions; if you hate something you want them to eat, don't let it show!

There are some foods that toddlers simply *won't* eat. Be flexible! Substitute foods your child likes for foods on the "no way" list. Many contain essentially the same nutrients. For example, fruits have many of the same vitamins and nutrients as vegetables have, and a lot of kids prefer them.

Don't tease or cajole your child into eating more when he or she has had enough. You can, however, be sneaky in other ways. Many supermarkets today sell pasta made from spinach—or even colorful pasta "veggie spirals" made from spinach, carrots, and beets. Pureed vegetables can be added to sauces, soups, hot dishes, hamburgers, and pancakes without making their presence known. (Although there are toddlers who seem to have electron microscopes for eyes; I've known some who could detect a speck of green pepper or a shred of celery.)

THOSE AWFUL FOOD JAGS

Food jags are a lot like chicken pox. They seem to come out of nowhere, last for a specific period of time, and turn your entire household upside down.

Technically speaking, a food jag is nothing more—and nothing less—than a preference for a few foods over everything else on the face of the earth. I've heard of kids who subsisted on peanut butter for months, cheese for weeks, bananas for days. Formerly reasonable children have suddenly demanded liverwurst sandwiches for breakfast, oatmeal for dinner, and Spaghetti-Os around the clock. And if you think you're unique in this area, listen to these parents:

- "At eight months to a year, my baby would have been happy to eat nothing but puffed wheat. I would put a few puffs on other foods, which she would then eat readily."

- "Yogurt, yogurt, and yogurt—only peach. I did nothing for about two weeks and my son finally decided he wanted some of the baby's food. After three months, yogurt's still what he wants most. Okay, I don't have to cook so much."

- "My 2-year-old just wanted olives to eat for five days. He even woke up in the middle of the night once and was into them in the refrigerator."

Luckily, most food jags are short-lived. But they can still test the limits of your patience.

From a Fat-Proofing standpoint, a food jag is a *very* delicate situation. It can easily slide into a push/pull, "do what I say" power issue. And the more you insist, the more your child will resist.

A food jag is a way (albeit extreme) of expressing the desire for independence. It's also a way of getting attention, and the *kind* of attention you respond with is important.

Here are some tips to make your life easier during the food-jag times (which *will* happen, if they haven't already):

- Relax. Relax. Relax! Your child is *not* going to starve to death as long as he or she is eating *something*.

- Your child is probably eating a larger variety of foods than you think. List exactly what is eaten over a 2 to 3 day span and then look closely at the list to see what food groups are represented.

- Keep trying—offering new foods, new variations on old themes, etc.

- Make sure there are no "junk foods" around the house. At least the jag-times will be healthful!

- Go about business as usual. Serve the meals you'd normally serve at the times you'd normally serve them. If your child leaves the table and returns with a chunk of cheese, stay calm. In fact, if possible, pay no attention at all.

- If your child's food jag requires you to prepare foods separately, don't play the "guilt game" ("See the trouble I'm going to for you? Don't I have enough to do already?"). Just fix whatever the child is currently eating (hopefully, it will be fairly simple to produce) and put it in front of him or her in a matter-of-fact way. (Later in life, if your child is still finicky, he or she can do the fixing.)

- What counts are the *nutrients* your child receives, not the specific foods. Doctor peanut butter by stirring in some calcium-rich powdered milk or wheat germ. Slip milk into a favorite soup. Grate vegetables into spaghetti sauce.

- **Avoid fights.** Keep mealtimes pleasant at all costs. Don't compound the problem with emotional scenes or recriminations.

- Don't make an issue of a sudden dietary change; this may actually delay the return to normal eating patterns. Force-feeding and reprimands are out of line and have lasting harmful effects.

- Be inventive, creative, and "crazy" yourself. If your child develops a fondness for purple foods, then "dye" mashed potatoes or cooked cereal with blackberries, or "paint" bread. (I know, it *sounds* disgusting, but so what?)

- Hold on to your sense of humor—but don't laugh *at* your child. Think back to some of the nutty things you did when you were little (or even more recently). This should help you to retain your perspective.

- Finally: No matter how hard it may be to believe (especially if your child is entering Week Five of nothing but peanut-butter sandwiches), repeat these words. **This too shall pass.** Over time, most kids do manage to eat a balanced, if bizarre, diet.

What most parents fear during the food-jag years is that their kids won't get enough protein. We're taught that protein is vital to growth and development, and we want our kids to get plenty of it.

It's true: protein *is* important. It helps build everything from muscles to fingernails to the antibodies that enable the body to fight infection and disease.

But most Americans consume *twice as much protein as they need*—and children are no exception. Overconsuming protein might not be so bad if it weren't for the fact that many sources of protein (especially animal sources) are high in fat and calories. Getting your child hooked on a diet too high in protein now could spell trouble later.

According to the Food and Nutrition Board of the National Academy of Sciences—National Research Council, a child from 1 to 3 years of age needs .81 grams of protein per pound of body weight each day. In other words, if your toddler weighs 30 pounds, he or she needs $30 \times .81$, or 24.3 grams of protein daily.

Sound like a lot? Consider this: 1 cup of milk, a 1-ounce slice of cheddar cheese, and 2 tablespoons of peanut butter each contain about 8 grams of protein. If your child ate just that amount of food in a day, he or she would receive all the protein needed to keep his or her body running smoothly.

Other foods contain even more protein: 3 slices of bologna, 10.2 grams; 1/2 cup cottage cheese, 15 grams; 1/4 pound lean ground beef, 23.4 grams; 3 ounces of drained, packed-in-water tuna, 24.4 grams.

Protein is also found in vegetables—especially legumes (dried peas and beans), such as soybeans, chickpeas, lentils, pinto beans, and black-eyed peas. But, although vegetables may contain a high amount of protein (1 cup of lima beans, for example, contains 12 grams), they don't always have all the essential amino acids that make up a complete protein molecule and are needed for protein to do its work in the body.

That's where "protein complementation" comes in—a fancy phrase for something that's really quite simple. It means combining two or more vegetable proteins, each of which offsets the other's amino-acid deficiencies, to create a complete protein that the body can use. Some common protein-completing food combinations are peanuts and wheat (also known as a peanut-butter sandwich), or milk and cooked oatmeal (what child would eat oatmeal *without* milk?).

Since protein comes in so many forms, it's hard to imagine a child being a "protein-picky" eater. But what if you want your child to eat a particular protein-rich food, and he or she refuses? Try changing its form. Puree tuna in a blender to make an appetizing spread for crackers. Serve tiny

---

PROTEIN COMPLEMENTS

To create a high-quality protein meal, simply combine foods from any two of the following groups.

Group One: Grains
baked goods or cereals containing whole wheat, cracked wheat,
    rye, cornmeal, and/or oats
whole-grain pasta
buckwheat
brown rice
wheat germ
barley
millet

Group Two: Seeds and Nuts
sesame, pumpkin, and/or sunflower seeds
Brazil nuts, black walnuts, hazelnuts, and/or cashews (also wal-
    nuts, almonds, pistachios, and/or pecans, although these don't
    contain quite as much protein)
tahini
alfalfa sprouts

Group Three: Beans and Legumes
anything·made from soybeans
any common beans, including kidney, black, navy, and/or mung;
    peas, including dried green or yellow or chickpeas (garbanzos)
lentils
bean sprouts
peanuts and/or peanut butter

Proteins from animal products can stand alone—in other words, they're sufficient *without* having to be combined with any other protein. Sources of animal protein include milk and/or dry milk powder, cheese (except cream cheese), yogurt, lean meat, poultry, and fish.

---

meatballs on doll dishes. Make milky puddings or blend cottage cheese into bite-size pancakes.

Your child's protein consumption should probably be the *least* of your worries. Chances are that even a food-jag food is chock-full of it.

HOW CAN I TELL IF MY TODDLER IS FAT?

First, understand that most 1- and 2-year-olds *appear* chubby because of their relatively short legs and large heads (the skull and brain reach 70 percent of their full growth by age 2). And, in fact, toddlers *do* have more body fat than they did as babies.

At birth, an infant's body is about 11 percent body fat. By age 1, that percentage has more than doubled to 24 percent. Then it gradually decreases to 22 percent at age 2 and about 18 percent at age 3.

All that body fat in a toddler is both *normal* and *good*. The store of extra calories comes in handy if he or she becomes too ill to eat. The fat also protects the toddler's internal organs and acts as an insulator to maintain normal body temperature.

AVERAGE HEIGHTS AND WEIGHTS FOR TODDLERS (12 MONTHS TO 3 YEARS)

For reference only:

Girls

Age	Height (inches)	Weight (pounds; without clothing)
12 months	29.8	21.0
18 months	31.9	23.8
2 years	34.2	26.0
2½ years	36.0	28.5
3 years	37.0	31.0

Boys

Age	Height (inches)	Weight (pounds; without clothing)
12 months	30.0	22.5
18 months	32.4	25.3
2 years	34.2	27.2
2½ years	36.3	30.3
3 years	37.4	32.2

(Sources: The National Academy of Sciences and The National Center for Health Statistics)

What about your toddler's protruding tummy? This, too, is quite natural and normal. It has to do with the fact that his or her abdominal muscles—the ones *you* use to hold *your* stomach in—are not yet fully developed. As the child grows older, the muscles will strengthen and the tummy will gradually pull in toward the spine.

Starting at around age 2, the toddler's body fat should begin to decrease as muscle mass increases. Arms and legs will also begin to lengthen at a relatively quicker rate than the trunk of the body, until by age 5 your pudgy toddler will have turned into a slender, long-legged child.

In other words, if your 1- or 2-year-old seems chubby to you, *don't worry*. Just make sure that he or she is eating a healthful, nutritious diet and wait for nature to take its course.

What if your child doesn't show signs of thinning out by age 3 or 4? Then it's time to take a closer look at his or her diet. Is it too rich in high-fat and high-sugar foods—the kinds that may be contributing too many calories and too few nutrients? Could you be offering your child better food choices? That's what Fat-Proofing is all about. Remember that the food habits your child learns *now* will carry forth into his or her later life.

WHAT THOSE PERCENTILES MEAN

You're in the pediatrician's office for your child's annual checkup. At some point the doctor says, "Well, little Jenny (or Johnny) is in the 60th percentile for height and the 50th percentile for weight." You're about to ask for an explanation when the doctor sails off onto some other topic.

Let's clear up the "percentiles mystery" once and for all—and maybe dispel a few myths while we're at it.

Percentile figures are derived from studies of children. These studies don't take into account *all* children, but they do try to use representative samplings. The results of those samplings are what your child is compared to.

If Jenny is in the 60th percentile for height, all this means is that 60 percent of children her age are shorter than she is, and 40 percent are taller. If she's in the 50th percentile for weight, then half the children her age weigh less than she does and half weigh more.

A lot of people view height-and-weight percentiles as "test scores." They seem to like it when their child zooms past the 50 percent mark—the "average." The fact is that most children fall somewhere between the 25th and 75th percentiles.

Should a child's height and weight percentiles be more-or-less equal?

That is, if Johnny is in the 65th percentile for height, should he also be in the 65th percentile for weight? Ideally, maybe; realistically, it doesn't much matter, unless the differences are extreme. For example, if Johnny is in the 15th percentile for height and the 80th percentile for weight, then he probably weighs more than he should. Even if he's in the 50th percentile for weight, that 15th percentile for height indicates that he's shorter than most children his age and therefore should weigh less than the average.

From a Fat-Proofing perspective, a knowledge of percentiles can help to pinpoint a tendency toward overweight. The next time you visit the pediatrician, ask to review your child's growth records to date. If the weight percentile *always* exceeds the height percentile, then you can safely assume that your child is forming a pattern. One or two instances of great disparity between the percentiles may simply indicate growth spurts. (See the appendix for complete percentiles charts, *for reference only*.)

What if your child far exceeds both percentiles? Remember Fat-Proofing rule 1: *Don't assume that a heavier-than-average child is a fat child*. If Jenny's in the 90th percentile for height and weight, then all that probably means is that she's a big girl. Take a look at yourself and your spouse, at your parents and your spouse's parents, at other relatives. Being taller and heavier than average may just run in your family.

WHAT—AND HOW MUCH— SHOULD MY TODDLER EAT?

Although it may seem as if your child is growing like a weed, the truth is that he or she isn't growing anywhere near as fast as during the first year of life, when birth weight tripled and height almost doubled.

That's why toddlers' calorie needs temporarily *decrease*—and why some are such finicky eaters. They simply aren't as hungry as they were as babies.

Specifically, toddlers need 35 to 40 calories per pound of body weight each day. (That's down from 45 to 50 calories per pound during their first year.) In other words, if your toddler weighs 30 pounds, he or she needs from 1,050 to 1,200 calories each day.

Where those calories come from is important to the toddler's health, both now and for the future. Here's the ideal breakdown:

- 55 percent should come from carbohydrates
- 20 percent should come from fats
- 15 percent should come from protein

Does this mean that you have to sit with a calculator and a food chart on hand at every meal, figuring out whether your child is getting enough calories from each food group? Of course not—you'd go crazy! Instead, make an effort to include a lot of high-carbohydrate foods in every meal. Kids usually have no trouble getting enough fats and protein.

HOW MUCH TO FEED YOUR TODDLER

The following serving sizes are recommended for children ages 2 to 3. Use them as *approximate* guidelines for feeding your toddler.

Milk and cheese: 4 ¹/₂-cup (4 ounce) servings daily (1.5 ounces of cheese equals 1 cup of milk)

Vegetables and fruits: 4 servings daily, including:

- vitamin C source (citrus fruits, berries, tomato, cabbage, cantaloupe): 1 ¹/₂-cup serving daily

- vitamin A source (green or yellow fruits and vegetables): 1 3-tablespoon serving daily

- other vegetables (potato, legumes): 1 3-tablespoon serving daily

- other fruits (apples, bananas): 1 ¹/₃-cup serving daily

Protein foods (lean meat, fish, peanut butter, eggs): 3 3-tablespoon servings daily of lean meat, fish, and/or peanut butter, **or** 1 egg plus 2 3-tablespoon servings of lean meat, fish, and/or peanut butter (kids don't need an egg a day, so you may want to alternate)

Cereals (whole grain and nonsugared), cooked pasta, and/or cooked rice: at least 2 ¹/₃-cup servings daily

Bread (whole grain): at least 1 slice daily

What are good high-carbohydrate foods? Fruits, whole grains, and vegetables. Most of these foods also contain a sizable chunk of nutrients. Plus, they're an excellent source of dietary fiber—the "roughage" that helps keep the digestive system running smoothly and regularly.

HELP! MY CHILD **WON'T** DRINK MILK!

Most pediatricians agree that 16 to 24 ounces of milk a day is plenty for a toddler. And toddlers who eat yogurt, cheese, and other dairy products can get by with a lot less. Too much milk can lessen the child's appetite for other necessary foods. Overconsumption of milk, for example, is a leading cause of iron deficiency in toddlers.

But what if your child refuses to drink milk, period? Will his or her teeth fall out from the lack of calcium?

Many parents worry about this, because many children go through a stage when they dislike (or even despise) milk. The good news is, it's no big deal. Ignore it and the child may quietly return to milk on his or her own.

Meanwhile, here are some creative ways to slip the child's daily requirement of 800 mg. of calcium into the food you serve:

- Add powdered milk to your casseroles or baked dishes—about 2 tablespoons per cup of casserole or flour.

- Chocolate milk, served a few times a week, is another alternative. Cartons of chocolate milk are very sweet. Mix it half and half with skim milk and you and your child will both feel good when a glass of milk is finished.

- Serve lots of cheesy dishes—macaroni and cheese (an almost universal favorite with kids), cheese tacos, or grilled cheese sandwiches.

- Serve ice milk, yogurt, or puddings. Few children can resist these.

- Use high-calcium vegetables, such as beans and green leafy vegetables, in soups and salads.

If your child continues to refuse milk *and all other dairy products*, you may want to talk to your doctor about calcium supplements. **Never** give a calcium supplement to a toddler without professional advice, as some supplements interfere with iron absorption.

WATCHING OUT FOR FOOD ALLERGIES

A child who's going to develop food allergies will likely show signs during the toddler years, if not earlier. These signs, which include coughing, vomiting, wheezing, rashes, or hives, can start as early as age 1, with the incidence peaking at around age 3 and then falling off sharply. The foods that seem to cause the most trouble are citrus fruits, tomatoes, eggs, strawberries, and fish; for infants, add cow's milk to this list.

Is there any way to prevent food allergies? Studies have shown that breast-fed babies develop fewer of them, both during infancy and later in life. Other than that, however, there seems not to be anything we can do. Introducing new foods one at a time, and spacing out their introduction, is a good way to find out which, if any, foods our children are allergic to.

Some children outgrow their symptomatic sensitivities to foods, but many don't. The longer a sensitivity persists, the less likely it is to disappear.

If you suspect that your child is having an adverse reaction to a particular food, check with your doctor. He or she may then refer you to an allergist—your best source of information on rearranging your child's diet.

It may be that your child doesn't have an allergy at all, but instead has an *aversion* to a certain food. In kids, an aversion can be a temporary dislike that fades with the coming of food "fads" (more about those in chapter 7). In adults, however, a food aversion can be a serious psychological condition, with deep-seated connections to unpleasant memories or associations formed during the early years. (Yet another good reason not to "force" foods that your toddler genuinely dislikes.)

Both food allergies and food aversions are the focus of much attention these days. A whole new science, called "clinical ecology," is springing up around various theories—most of them controversial—about the relationship between food and behavior. You may already have seen articles in the popular press that link food to behavior disorders, hyperactivity, depression, and fatigue.

Most experts are hesitant to jump on this bandwagon. (Some dismiss clinical ecology as quackery, plain and simple.) Until the hard evidence comes in, I'd recommend exercising common sense and taking your doctor's advice.

And don't make the word *allergic* a part of the vocabulary you use around your child. One mother made the mistake of wondering aloud whether her preschooler was allergic to milk. He adamantly refused to drink it, and whenever she pushed it on him he would take a tiny sip and cough vigorously. The next thing she knew, he was claiming to be "allergic" to bedtime—something else he didn't like!

FAT-PROOFING TIPS FOR THE TODDLER YEARS

If you managed to bring your child through infancy without using food as a tool, congratulations. But you may find your resolve weakening as your toddler becomes increasingly vocal and opinionated.

It's *too* easy to pacify a shrieking 2-year-old with a sugar cookie, or to hand a demanding 3-year-old a bag of potato chips. It's tempting to take pity on a child who spends an entire meal staring morosely at his or her (untouched) plate. Thus, the first—and most important—Fat-Proofing tip for this phase is:

- Stick to your principles!

Toddlers learn quickly to start whining for sweets as soon as Mom answers the telephone. They figure out in a hurry that the dinner table is a useful place to throw a tantrum. Don't let food become either payment or punishment.

With that attitude firmly in mind, you should find these tips both practical and workable:

- Set a good example. If your child sees you eating and enjoying a variety of foods, he or she may learn to do the same by copying you. (This is one of those rare cases when kids' talent for mimicry works for rather than against you.)

- Allow your toddler plenty of time to eat. An excited child has trouble eating, so keep mealtimes relaxed and calm.

- Serve juice in a cup rather than in a bottle. Juice is sweet. In a cup it will satisfy thirst rather than become a "pacifier."

On the other hand, don't let your child sit there forever while cobwebs form on his or her corn. After a reasonable period of time (no longer than half an hour), clear the table in a matter-of-fact way. If your child is truly hungry later, offer him or her something to eat *without* a lecture on "you should have eaten when you had the chance."

- Give healthful, nutritious snacks at appropriate times during the day. When your child asks for something to eat at other times, ask if he or she is feeling hungry. If asked routinely, this may reinforce the message that food is a solution to hunger, not boredom.

- Offer small servings in child-sized bowls, plates, or cups. These are less intimidating than heaps of food on full-size plates. Let your child tell you if he or she wants more.

- Serve your toddler what the rest of the family is eating—including introductory portions of any new foods.

Don't, however, challenge your child with too many gourmet specials. Children's palates are unsophisticated. If you really want them to try something "exotic," go ahead and prepare it—but have a peanut-butter sandwich ready and waiting as backup.

- Encourage self-feeding—another step toward independence.

Can't face the prospect of hosing down the kitchen or dining room after every meal? Then restrict self-feeding to one meal a day, to less-messy foods, or to favorite foods, at least until your child gets the hang of it.

Your toddler needs opportunities to practice self-feeding, which develops skills vital to gaining control over fine and large muscle movement. But these same skills can be developed elsewhere than at the table. For example, you may want to allow more water play in the bathtub or kitchen (which is preferable to splashing in the soup). Or schedule lunches for outside on the picnic table where the mess won't matter as much.

Food that makes it into the mouth is always more important than food that falls on the floor. Ignore spills and drops; praise successful efforts. Never criticize "bad manners" or punish or shame your child for accidents; he or she isn't trying to be "naughty." And offer help willingly if the self-feeder tires or gets discouraged. It's okay if your toddler sometimes reverts to being a baby. (In many ways, that's what he or she still is.)

- If your child sometimes refuses to eat, let it pass. He or she may simply be tired, excited, or not hungry. No child has ever starved to death after skipping a single meal.

- Serve foods that are colorful and have interesting shapes. Visual stimulation is important.

- Permit some "food play" and experimentation. But remove a child who starts to throw food from the high chair or table.

Kids naturally want to feel their food, squish it in their fingers, smear it on their faces, and paint the table with it. Some degree of messiness is normal and reflects a child's natural curiosity. (For your own peace of mind, spread a dropcloth under your toddler's chair.)

- When discipline is necessary, speak in positives, not negatives. For example: "Keep your peas on your plate, please," is preferable to, "Stop throwing your peas on the floor!"

INFORMATION ON TODDLER NUTRITION

For more information on feeding and nutrition for toddlers, see the "Nourishing and Nurturing Two-Year-Olds" fact sheets prepared by Cornell University. Designed for teachers, they can help parents, too. To order, write: Distribution Center, 7 Research Park, Cornell University, Ithaca, NY 14850. Enclose a check or money order for $1.75, made payable to Cornell University. Or check your local library's pamphlets drawer under "Children: Care & Health."

CONVERTING THE DAYCARE PROVIDER

You've been luckier than many mothers today in finding a daycare provider you like and trust. There's just one problem: She feeds her own toddlers sweets and junk food, and you don't want those things in your child's diet. Yet, you don't want to switch sitters. What are your options?

A. Keep the sitter and have your child eat healthy foods.

This sounds like the perfect solution, but it can happen only under certain circumstances:

- You can send along the foods your child should eat. But your sitter will have to feel comfortable with—and be willing to enforce your child's eating of—these foods. (If they take extra time or effort to prepare, forget this approach; it probably won't work.)

- You can request—and hope—that your sitter will change her food-buying habits. (This can be like asking someone to change religious or political preferences.) You can tell her your feelings and ask if she might read some of the material you could give her (like this book, for example, or *Feed Me, I'm Yours*, or *The Taming of the C.A.N.D.Y. Monster*). She may be open to reading first, changing habits second.

B. Keep the sitter and let your child eat whatever she serves.

How many meals does your child eat at her house? That might color your decision. As much as I believe in Fat-Proofing and in promoting nutritious foods, I *don't* believe that less-nutritious foods harm kids forever—*as long as they're not all they get to eat.* You can probably balance your sitter's lunches and snacks with your breakfasts and dinners.

C. Switch sitters.

While this is not what you want to hear, it's your only choice if the first doesn't work and the second isn't acceptable to you. Yes, you'll have to spend time looking for another—and be inconvenienced for a while—but there *is* more than one daycare provider in the world.

SENSIBLE SNACKS WITH TODDLER APPEAL

Nutritious snacking should be part of every toddler's day. Remember that their stomachs are still small and can't hold enough to last them between meals. Plus, they're less likely to become cranky or overtired if they come to the table without feeling starved. (But don't serve snacks any closer to meals than an hour and a half, or your kids may not be hungry when it's time for the family to sit down together.)

Like babies, toddlers should be supervised while they snack to make sure their food gets chewed and swallowed properly. Choking is a major health concern for kids this age. **Don't** give your toddler popcorn or similar-size foods that could get stuck in his or her throat. The same **don't** goes for hot dogs, the most frequent lethal choking food. If you *must* serve them—and with their high fat content you're better off not—at least slice them lengthwise, turn, and slice again. The same goes for grapes! And don't spread peanut butter too thick on bread; young children have been known to gag on that, too.

Be careful with foods that come on sticks. The sticks can splinter and cause injury to mouth and eyes.

- Keep on hand such good-for-them choices as diced cheese, un-salted crackers, and fresh fruits.

- A half-slice of whole-wheat bread may be enough to tide a child over between lunch and dinner.

Add interest with your own homemade grape jelly. Thaw 1 12-ounce can of frozen grape concentrate. Stir in 1 package of unflavored gelatin. Pour the mixture into a saucepan and heat to boiling. Remove from heat, cool slightly, and pour into a wide-mouth jar. Store in the refrigerator. (From *The Taming of the C.A.N.D.Y. Monster,* Bantam, 1982.)

- Fill a plastic cup with dry, unsweetened cereal; mix several types together for fun.

- Don't mistake thirst for hunger. A glass of water or fruit juice may be enough to satisfy a child until mealtime.

- Try rice cakes. Happily, more and more supermarkets are start-ing to carry these easy-to-handle, low-calorie snacks. (Basically, they're nothing but whole-grain rice puffed and stuck together in fat, rounded cakes.) They're yummy, too, especially to the child who's never developed strong tastes for sugar and salt.

- Stir drained, canned fruit (the kind that's packed in its own juice, not syrup) together with plain yogurt for a creamy snack. Or give a single-serving-size carton of fruited yogurt (the less sweetened, the better).

- Give a plastic cup full of cold cooked macaroni (elbows are best). Complement with grated cheese.

Following are some sure-thing snack-food recipes.

QUICK WHOLE-WHEAT BANANA BRAN BREAD

$^1/_4$ cup oil
$^1/_3$ cup honey
1 egg
1 cup bran
2 tablespoons frozen concentrated orange juice, undiluted
1 $^1/_2$ cups mashed bananas
1 $^1/_2$ cups whole-wheat flour

2 teaspoons baking powder
$1/2$ teaspoon baking soda
1 teaspoon vanilla extract

Optional:
$1/2$ cup chopped nut meats

Preheat oven to 350°.

Combine oil and honey; add egg, then bran; mix thoroughly. In a separate bowl, combine orange juice and bananas. In another bowl, combine flour, baking powder, and baking soda. Gradually add banana mixture and dry ingredients to the bran mixture, alternating between them. Mix thoroughly. Add vanilla.

Bake in greased 5″ x 9″ loaf pan for 1 hour.

FRUIT STRIPS

Make these at home instead of buying the commercial "roll-ups" or bars, which contain almost nothing but calories.

a quantity of any very ripe fruit, including apples, pears, berries, etc.
water

Preheat oven to 125°.

In a blender, puree fruit with a little water. Line the bottom of a flat pan (or cookie sheet) with plastic wrap. Pour the fruit mixture into the pan and spread thin. Place in oven with door slightly ajar for 8 to 12 hours. Dry the mixture until you can easily peel it away from the plastic. Cut into strips and serve.

SUPER WHEAT-GERM COOKIES

$1 1/2$ cups old-fashioned oats
$3/4$ cup wheat germ
$3/4$ cup sugar
1 teaspoon ground cinnamon
$1/4$ teaspoon ground cloves

$^1/_2$ cup cooking oil
2 eggs
$^1/_2$ cup raisins, chopped nuts, snipped prunes, mixed dried
    fruit, or flaked coconut

Preheat oven to 350°.

In a large bowl, combine oats, wheat germ, sugar, cinnamon, and cloves. Mix in oil, eggs, and fruit. Spoon teaspoonsful onto lightly greased and floured baking sheets. Garnish with coconut or nut halves. Bake 10 to 12 minutes or until lightly browned. Makes 3 dozen.

ORANGE FROTH

3 cups water
1 6-ounce can frozen unsweetened orange juice concentrate
1 cup powdered dry milk

Optional:
nutmeg, coconut powder, or banana

Whip all ingredients together in a blender and serve.

SIX

FAT-PROOFING YOUR PRESCHOOLER

Preschoolers have a lot in common with toddlers (although they'd never admit it), so much of what I've already said about toddlers applies to this age group, too.

One big exception: This is a time when, if excess weight takes hold, it's apt to stick. (Luckily, the 6-year-old growth spurt is just around the corner.)

The most apparent differences between preschoolers and toddlers have to do with motor-skills development and language. By now, kids are getting pretty good at using forks and spoons. Most of the food they start on the way to their mouths actually ends up there. The bad news is that they like to talk while they eat, and you just have to bear with them while they spill and drop. Remember, they're not out to get you!

Food jags pop up again, along with meal rituals and appetite fluctuations. Kids this age are expert dawdlers and stallers. They're also adept at coming up with crazy excuses for all sorts of things. Don't worry, and *don't nag*. There are plusses at this stage, too! (For one, you can start having real conversations with your children.)

FEEDING YOUR PRESCHOOLER: GROWING BUT NOT GROWN

Your child's rate of growth will slow even more during the preschool years of 4 to 6. That doesn't mean you won't be driven crazy by jeans and shoes that seem to be outgrown before their second washing. Your child *will* be growing during these years, but not anywhere near as fast as those first 12 months or even as fast as the toddler years. (On average, children gain about 5 pounds and 3 1/2 inches between ages 2 and 3, compared to 4 1/2 pounds and 2 1/2 inches between ages 4 and 5.)

Most kids thin down during the preschool years—often to the point where they look downright skinny. Their toddler tummies begin to flatten out as their abdominal muscles get stronger, and their arms and legs continue to lengthen. Yet, although the toddler fat has disappeared, muscle is slow in taking its place. Until more muscle develops, lithe and leggy is the look for most preschoolers.

WHAT IF MY PRESCHOOLER IS PUDGY?

First, remember that kids' bodies, like their minds, develop at different rates. So, although *most* kids start to slim down between their third and fourth birthdays, *some* kids put it off until later. Just be aware that sometime during these preschool years, you should begin to notice a gradual reduction in weight gain. That doesn't mean your child will lose weight; rather, he or she simply won't gain it as quickly as before.

You can keep track of your child's development by weighing and measuring him or her twice a year. (You or your pediatrician should do this anyway to make sure the child is growing at a healthy rate.) If your child's weight is 15 percent more than what is considered average for his or her height, he or she may—repeat, *may*—be overweight.

The problem with using only height and weight to judge pudginess is that athletic, muscular children may appear overweight when they're not. A better indication of fatness can be obtained by measuring the thickness of skin on the back of the upper arm—called a "triceps fat-fold measurement." For boys 4 1/2 to 8 1/2 years old, the average triceps skin thickness is 8 mm.; for girls, it's 10 mm.

A special caliper instrument is needed for the triceps measurement. (Don't worry, it's painless.) So, if you're concerned that your preschooler is overweight, talk to your pediatrician and ask him or her to do a triceps measurement for you.

Never put your preschooler on a calorie-restricted diet without consulting your pediatrician first. That doesn't mean you can't put your child on a healthful diet by cutting back on sweets and fatty foods. But always let your child eat as many healthful foods as he or she wants. Generally, it's only with junk foods that kids go overboard and eat more than their bodies need. (See chapter 7 for more about why kids shouldn't diet.)

AVERAGE HEIGHTS AND WEIGHTS FOR PRESCHOOLERS (4 TO 6 YEARS)

For reference only:

Girls

Age	Height (inches)	Weight (pounds; without clothing)
4 years	40.0	35.2
5 years	42.7	38.9
6 years	45.1	43.0

Boys

Age	Height (inches)	Weight (pounds; without clothing)
4 years	40.5	36.8
5 years	43.3	41.2
6 years	45.7	45.6

(Source: The National Academy of Sciences)

WHAT—AND HOW MUCH— SHOULD MY PRESCHOOLER EAT?

During the preschool years your child will need approximately 1,300 to 2,300 calories each day. Obviously, taller and more active kids will need closer to 2,300 calories, while the caloric need of children who are shorter (or who spend more time watching television than riding bicycles) will fall nearer the low end of that range.

Just as during the toddler years, these calories should ideally be broken down as follows: 55 percent from carbohydrates, 30 percent from fat, and about 15 percent from protein. Again, you don't have to spend hours with a calculator figuring out the percentiles. Just lean heavy on carbohydrates (fruits, vegetables, and whole grains) when you're planning family menus.

HOW MUCH TO FEED YOUR PRESCHOOLER

The following serving sizes are recommended for children ages 4 to 6. Use them as approximate guidelines for feeding your preschooler.

Milk, cheese, yogurt and/or other dairy products: 4 1/4-cup (2-ounce) servings daily

Vegetables and fruits: At least 4 1/2-cup servings daily, including the following:

- vitamin C source (citrus fruits, berries, tomato, cabbage, cantaloupe): 1 1/2-cup serving daily

- vitamin A source (green or yellow fruits and vegetables): 1 1/4-cup serving daily

- other vegetables (potato, legumes): 1 1/4-cup serving daily

- other fruits (apples, bananas): 1 1/2-cup serving daily

Protein foods (lean meat, fish, peanut butter, eggs, meat substitutes): 3 5-tablespoon servings daily of lean meat, fish, peanut butter, and/or meat substitutes, **or** 2 5-tablespoon servings of the above plus 1 egg (remember that kids don't need an egg a day)

Cereals (whole grain and nonsugared), cooked pasta, and/or cooked rice: at least 2 1/2-cup servings daily

Bread (whole grain): at least 1 1/2 slices daily

Another good rule of thumb is to allow *1 tablespoon per dish* (meat, fruit, vegetables) *for every year of the child's age.* A 4-year-old should get 4 tablespoons of meatloaf, 4 tablespoons of peas, and 4 tablespoons of applesauce; a 6-year-old should get 6 tablespoons of each. (A rule of thumb is not the same as a hard-and-fast rule. There will be times when your child will want more, and times when he or she will want less.)

HOW CAN I MAKE SURE MY CHILD IS GETTING ENOUGH NUTRIENTS?

Pound for pound, children need a lot more vitamins and minerals than adults do. That's because kids need nutrients not just to maintain the status quo in their bodies (as adults do), but also to make new cells for growing.

A preschooler, for example, needs two times the amount of thiamine, riboflavin, niacin, and vitamins A and C, and three times the amounts of vitamins B-6 and B-12 as a 25-year-old man.

Children, by the way, are *least* likely to consume iron and vitamin C in sufficient amounts, and are *most* likely to overdo it with riboflavin. (For examples of foods rich in these nutrients, see "Where to Find Vitamins and Minerals . . . Naturally," p. 103.)

The best way to make sure your child is getting all the vitamins and minerals he or she needs is with a varied diet that is heavy on the healthful foods and light on "empty calorie" foods, such as soda pop, candy, and sugared breakfast cereals (which includes the vast majority of ready-to-eat cereals). These foods are "empty" because they have few, if any, nutrients to offer.

You're probably wondering why breakfast cereals are described as empty. After all, aren't most children's breakfast cereals "fortified" with vitamins and minerals?

Yes, cereal manufacturers do add vitamins and minerals to their products. That's because most of the cereals' nutrients—and fiber—are lost during the manufacturing process. The manufacturers then return some, *but not all,* of those lost nutrients (and none of the fiber) when they "enrich" or "fortify" a cereal. And they also add something else—lots of sugar, sodium, and preservatives, and often artificial colors and flavors. (In fact, much of the important nutrition in breakfast cereals comes from the added milk.)

Some scientists question whether these added vitamins and minerals fortifying processed cereals can be absorbed and used properly in the body. A study conducted by the Consumers Union concluded that "there is no consistent connection between added vitamins and minerals and nutritional quality of breakfast cereals."

Ready-to-eat cereals, especially those containing lots of sugar, sodium, and additives, are not a healthful breakfast choice. If your child *must* have them, at least make sure they are eaten with milk and sliced fruit.

The same holds true for drinks. Water that is colored and flavored and sweetened and has vitamin C is *not* the same as orange juice even if the vitamin C content is the same. There is more to orange juice than vitamin C.

WHAT ABOUT SUPPLEMENTS?

Some moms start feeding vitamin/mineral supplements to their kids on the day they bring them home from the hospital. Others wait until the preschool years, when it's safe to give children those colorful little tablets they're seeing advertised on TV. (This is also the time when kids start asking for those cute Fred Flintstone or Bugs Bunny vitamins, precisely *because* they've seen them advertised on TV. More about television—and how you can fight against it—later.)

I have mixed feelings about supplements. Personally I don't recommend or give my children vitamins. I really don't believe they're necessary. On the other hand, I've offered them on occasion, as a sort of "insurance" for those days (or weeks) when one of them is on a food jag or just being picky about what goes into his or her mouth.

The truth is that the basic vitamins and minerals kids need are available in sufficient quantities in ordinary, everyday foods, and it's best if they get them that way.

If you have doubts about your kids' daily vitamin/mineral intake, go ahead and supplement—keeping these tips in mind:

- Vitamin/mineral supplements are just that—*supplements*. They're no substitute for healthy eating habits. If your child refuses to eat breakfast, don't think that a tablet will make up for lost nutrients. In fact, most of the good stuff will pass right on through if the child's stomach isn't full. Vitamins and minerals work *with* food, not solo.

- Read labels on vitamin supplements. Your kids don't need artificial coloring, flavoring, or sweeteners.

- If you're worried about "natural" versus "synthetic" vitamins, don't be. The chemical formulas in both are the same, and the body uses both kinds in precisely the same ways.

- Pay attention to USRDAs—for U.S. Recommended Daily Allowances. These tell you how much of each nutrient is needed by a child of a specific age or sex. Be advised, however, that many kids' vitamins are formulated to meet the needs of teenage

WHERE TO FIND VITAMINS
AND MINERALS . . . NATURALLY

WHAT IT IS	WHAT IT'S GOOD FOR	WHERE TO FIND IT
vitamin A	normal growth, good vision, healthy skin, teeth, and nails, resistance to infection	milk, fortified margarine, eggs, leafy green and yellow veggies, liver
vitamin B-1 (thiamine)	heart, nervous system, muscle coordination, helps body use carbohydrates	enriched and whole-grain cereals, whole-grain breads, fish, poultry, lean meats, liver, milk
vitamin B-2 (riboflavin)	healthy skin, body tissue	enriched breads and cereals, leafy green veggies, lean meats, liver, dried yeast, milk, eggs
vitamin B-6 (pyridoxine)	healthy teeth and gums, red blood cells, nervous system, the formation of certain proteins, helps body use fats	whole-grain cereals, wheat germ, veggies, dried beans, bananas, lean meats
vitamin B-12	growth, nervous system, preventing anemia	lean meats, liver, kidney, milk, salt-water fish, oysters
vitamin C	teeth, gums, bones, body cells, blood vessels	citrus juices, berries, tomatoes, cabbage, green veggies, potatoes
vitamin D	teeth, bones, helps body use calcium and phosphorus	milk, cod liver oil, salmon, tuna, egg yolk—and sunlight!
vitamin E	red blood cells, helps the body use vitamin A	vegetable oils, wheat germ, whole-grain cereals, lettuce

WHAT IT IS	WHAT IT'S GOOD FOR	WHERE TO FIND IT
folic acid	preventing anemia, helps the intestinal tract function	leafy green veggies, cantaloupe, apricots, beans, whole wheat
vitamin B-3 (niacin)	nervous system, helps the body convert food to energy	enriched cereals and bread, eggs, lean meats, liver, brewer's yeast
vitamin H (biotin)	adrenal glands, nervous system, skin, helps the body use carbohydrates, proteins, and fats	egg yolk, green veggies, milk, liver, kidney
vitamin B-5 (pantothenic acid)	helps the body use carbohydrates, proteins, and fats	almost all foods
calcium	healthy bones and teeth, cardiovascular health, blood clotting, enzyme and hormone activity	milk and milk products, cheese, sardines, salmon, dark green veggies, sunflower seeds
phosphorus	involved in nearly every chemical reaction in the body	whole grains, cheese, milk
iron	healthy blood	organ meats, beans, leafy green veggies, shellfish

boys. They may be too much of a good thing for your pre-schooler, so you may want to supplement every other day instead of daily.

RDA lists can be confusing, since they employ many different types of measurements—milligrams, micrograms, REs, TEs, IUs, and the like. Fortunately, you don't need to worry about "translating" them, or about converting one type of measurement to another. All you have to do when reading a supplement label is to make sure that the RDA meets the needs of the *average* child of your child's age and sex.

- **Don't** promote supplements as a "treat"—"Finish your breakfast, and I'll give you your vitamin." One child I know has to be tied down to eat meals—and every morning after breakfast he runs to the bathroom and begs Mom for his vitamin.

- **Never** give a child a megadose of **anything**. A megadose can actually be poisonous to the system.

Water-soluble vitamins (all eight Bs plus C) are used up or washed out of the body on a daily basis, so they don't pose a problem. It's the fat-solubles—A, D, E, and K—that you need to watch out for. These are stored in the body fat, meaning that your child doesn't excrete them or sweat them out. So it's possible for them to build up to toxic levels.

- Although vitamin C is water-soluble and won't accumulate in the body over time, some researchers have drawn a link between too much of it and possible damage to the teeth. It makes good sense to avoid chewable tablets containing extra vitamin C.

FAT-PROOFING TIPS FOR THE PRESCHOOL YEARS

Preschoolers are extremely, often irritatingly, curious. Take advantage of this natural inquisitiveness to press your Fat-Proofing message.

- Since kids this age want to know *everything*—often more than *you* know—this is a perfect time to explain how food acts in their bodies.

Where does it go and what does it do once it gets in and goes down? (And, of course, how does it make the stuff that comes out? This is the beginning of the potty-jokes era, and no matter how delicate your sensibilities are, you're going to have to put up with them.)

- Respond to their interest with simple, straightforward answers. Get help with the questions that stump you.

A mother I know has developed a wonderful routine with her two preschoolers. Whenever they have a question she can't answer, she writes it down in a notebook; then, after accumulating five or so, she packs up the kids and they head off to the local library. The children's librarian has been terrific (most of them are), pointing the way toward information on topics ranging from "What do butterflies eat?" to "Where does the poop go?"

- Bring home books to read. You don't have to stick to "dry," educational-type materials; there are plenty of others that incorporate food into entertaining stories. Some examples:

  - *Bread and Jam for Francis,* by Russell Hoban (New York: Harper Junior Books Group, 1964).
  - *Green Eggs and Ham,* by Dr. Seuss (New York: Beginner Books, a division of Random House, 1960).
  - *The Berenstain Bears & Too Much Junk Food,* by Stan and Jan Berenstain (New York: Random House, 1985).

For a clever "twist" on the fussy-eater theme, try *Gregory, the Terrible Eater,* by Mitchell Sharmat (New York: Four Winds Press, 1980). Gregory is a goat who has his parents worried because he won't eat proper "goat food"—tin cans, bottle caps, wax paper, and shoelaces. Instead, he insists on fruits, vegetables, eggs, fish, bread, and butter. The story of how Gregory learns to eat a balanced diet (good stuff *plus* junk food—from the junkyard!) is sure to amuse.

- When the sheer quantity of questions has you at the end of your rope, turn the tables by querying your kids. "Can you guess why water is good for you?" "Do you know why protein makes you grow?" "What foods are important for strong bones?" "What vegetable helps you to see better at night?" "How does your tummy tell you when it's hungry?" "Do you know where milk (or butter, or bacon, or eggs) comes from?" They like to show off their knowledge—and they like to make things up.

- Now is the time to assign new and more demanding kitchen duties to your youngsters. They can help set and clear the table; they can be responsible for feeding pets; they can mash and stir and wash veggies in the sink (while standing on the ever-present stepstool).

- Never force your kids to eat foods they genuinely hate. Instead, try to find out what they like. One approach: Spend a half-hour or so with your child going through *Good Housekeeping* or *Ladies Home Journal* or *Family Circle*—or some other magazine with lots

of pictures of foods. Have him or her point to favorites. Then try
to fit at least one into every meal.

- Be willing to serve foods in slightly unusual ways, if that's what it
takes to get your kids to eat them. (Some children who won't
drink milk out of a cup will happily spoon it from a bowl.) Carve
animals out of whole-grain breads and vegetables. Let the kids
serve their own mashed potatoes with an ice-cream scoop.

Look back at p. 54 for cookbook ideas. Cooking with kids creates new
food awareness.

FIGHTING BACK
AGAINST TELEVISION

Television has been termed the Great American Babysitter, and
that's what it is in a lot of households today. But whether your kids
watch TV, and how much, when, and what they watch, are not the issues
here. What's important from a Fat-Proofing perspective is that fact that
TV—especially advertising—teaches kids the wrong things about nutrition.

Jane Brody has gone so far as to call TV a "nutritional subversive." Of
the literally thousands of food commercials a child sees within a given year,
the vast majority (80 percent, according to one study) are for sugary products or junk foods. Candies, cookies, burgers and fries, cakes, chocolate-
dipped granola bars, ice cream, frosted cereals, ad infinitum, are paraded
on screen and praised. The moms, dads, kids, grandparents, teachers,
friends, and neighbors shown eating them are invariably happy (and, even
more deceptive, most of them look physically fit).

Why do companies spend millions of dollars on commercials aimed at
kids who (usually) don't have money of their own? Because they know the
power of persuasion. The advertisers persuade the child, and the child in
turn persuades the parent—by whining, begging, and pleading. There is a
direct correlation between the number of commercials kids see and the
number of times they ask for an advertised product.

The problem as far as preschoolers go (and some older kids, too) is
that they often *can't tell the difference* between fact and fantasy, between
commercials and regular programs, between a sales pitch and something
meant purely as entertainment (or even as education). This is made worse

by the recent proliferation of cartoon shows based on commercial products (toys, games, and the like). Kids believe what they see on TV. They can't tell when they're being conned, and they're still too innocent to suspect that what they are seeing and hearing may not be the truth.

As a parent, you may or may not choose to remove TV from your kids' lives; that's your decision. But *if* they watch it, you *must* take responsibility for helping them to become discriminating viewers and put in perspective what they see. Even very young children can be made aware that eating a bowl of cereal won't enable one to leap over skyscrapers or beat up bullies. Some suggestions for fighting back:

- First, and most important, *watch TV with your kids*. If you don't, you won't know what they're seeing, so you won't have much to say about it one way or the other.

- Make your feelings and opinions about commercials very evident. You may not be able to hold lengthy conversations with your toddler, but you can certainly say *"Yuck!"* when a commercial for some particularly noxious food item appears. And you can talk to your preschooler about what advertising is.

Keep your explanation simple. Try: "That person is trying to talk us into buying something. That person gets paid for saying those words. That person doesn't know us, and doesn't know what we like or what's good for us."

- Question your kids about what they're seeing. For example: "What is that mommy giving her children? Do you think eating candy is good for them?" Then discuss why it isn't. (If you need ammunition—you'll have to "translate" it for your kids—see "The Trouble with Sugar," in chapter 11.)

- Tell your kids why you have no intention of running out to buy an advertised product: "I don't want you to get cavities in your teeth"; "I want you to grow up strong and healthy." Even, "I love you too much to feed you that stuff."

- Switch the dial to the Public Broadcasting Service. Big Bird and Mr. Rogers won't try to sell your kids anything.

Where most parents have real trouble is in the supermarket. There, all the products kids have seen on TV are in front of them, life-size, and usually at eye level. If you take your kids shopping, you'll have to be firm from the beginning.

- Make it clear that you're not going to fill your cart with junk. At first your kids may scream and argue (and even throw tantrums in the cookie aisle), but in time they'll get the message.

- Announce *before* you leave home that only certain kinds of treats will be allowed—sugarless gum, fresh fruits, rice cakes, and the like.

- Don't buckle under pressure, no matter how unrelenting it is!

GIVING GRANDPARENTS THE WORD

You've made the decision to Fat-Proof your kids. Unfortunately, the rest of the world doesn't know about it. And there are people out there who may be reluctant to convert to your new way of thinking.

People like Grandma with her floury hands and kitchen full of goodies. Or Grandpa with his pockets full of treats and his willingness to run out for ice-cream cones.

It doesn't have to be you against them. If it is, your kids may end up in the middle.

Your parents and/or in-laws may well view Fat-Proofing as just another newfangled notion you've gotten into your head. Before you start trying to change them, take a moment to think back to the way things were when they were growing up—and when they were raising you and your spouse.

In *The Grandmother Conspiracy Exposed* (Santa Barbara: Capra Press, 1974), author Lewis A. Coffin, M.D., treats this issue with a great deal of sympathy:

> I drew on my many years of talking with mothers about the diets of their children, and one fact that kept coming up was that almost everything I was trying to accomplish was in direct opposition to the Grandmother's theory of feeding. This is true of many grandmothers, but certainly not all of them.
>
> Years ago the grandmothers of today were young mothers. They absorbed some of the dietary traditions of their parents, their friends and even their doctors. In those days the thing to do was to produce a fat baby, since everybody felt that a fat baby was a healthy baby. Natu-

rally, these diet patterns are deeply rooted in the memories of these currently older ladies, and they feel that what was good for their children must also be good for their grandchildren. Add to this that as soon as a person becomes a grandparent, he or she undergoes a radical personality change—stern fathers becoming cooing grandfathers, harpie-type mothers melt and crawl on the floor, sing lullabies and cram cookies and cookies and cookies down their sweet little grandchildren's throats, take them to the ice cream store, bake cakes and pies for them, and stand back admiringly as the little loved ones swell, tweak their obese little cheeks approvingly, and raise a terrible hue and cry if anyone tries to interfere. . . .

Grandmothers, of course, are not being malicious. They are showing love for the children by wanting them to experience as much pleasure and good health as possible by *their* standards. To restrict all the goodies and treats, particularly those they have toiled lovingly to produce themselves, is unthinkable.

Have you *ever* been able to change your parents' minds about anything? (In-laws are another matter entirely.) If not, what makes you think you can start now? Does that mean that you must suffer in silence?

The answer to that last question is: it depends. On the sort of relationship you have with your kids' grandparents, on how openly you can talk with them, and on how willing they are to listen.

Not knowing the details of your personal situation, I can only give you some suggestions:

- Have a heart-to-heart with the offending grandparent(s). Tell them what you're trying to do, and why, and enlist their help and support.

- Invite them to dinner and serve your favorite Fat-Proofing dishes. Let them know that you're in this as a family, and since they're family, too, you'd appreciate their going along (or at least giving that appearance when their grandchildren visit).

- When swapping recipes, include some from your Fat-Proofing file.

What if they resist your pleas and insist on sticking to their own routines? My advice then is to throw in the towel. How much time do your kids spend with their grandparents anyway? All of your good work is not going to be destroyed by occasional encounters with apple pie or fresh-baked cookies or chocolate cake. Give in, give up, be quiet. Sooner or later your Fat-Proofed kids may take things into their own hands by saying "no" to sweets.

GOOD-FOR-THEM SNACKS FOR PRESCHOOLERS

Like toddlers, preschoolers should be given healthful, nutritious snacks throughout the day.
Keep supplies of the following on hand:

- unbuttered, unsalted, popped popcorn

Once you train your kids' palates away from a taste for salt (see chapter 11), they'll learn to appreciate the natural flavors of foods like popcorn.

- unsweetened applesauce for spreading on whole-wheat bread

Make your own; it's easy. Wash, core, and slice apples; **don't** peel them. Add water (just enough to cover), cover tightly to keep the vitamins in, and boil until tender. Blend them, peels and all, in a blender or food processor. Cool and store in a jar in the refrigerator.

- whole-grain or rice crackers
- fresh fruits (serve a berry mix for a special, colorful treat. No sugar necessary!)

Add the following to your recipe file—and use them to inspire your own ideas.

PEANUT BUTTER–BANANA POPS

1 cup milk
1 ripe banana, cut into chunks
1/2 cup creamy peanut butter
1/2 teaspoon vanilla extract

Optional:
chopped nuts

Combine milk and banana in blender and puree until smooth. Add peanut butter and vanilla and blend well. Pour into freezer molds, seal, and freeze until very firm. Unmold and serve immediately. Roll in chopped nuts, if desired.

PINEAPPLE POP

  1 pineapple wedge (⅛ of a pineapple)
  2 teaspoons toasted wheat germ

Insert Popsicle stick into end of pineapple wedge. Roll in wheat germ. Stand in jar and freeze.

FRUIT YOGURT POPS

  8 ounces plain yogurt
  2 to 3 bananas
  1 6-ounce can frozen orange juice concentrate

Mix all ingredients in blender. Pour into freezer molds and freeze.

ANTS ON A LOG

  celery sticks
  cream cheese (or Neufchâtel, for fewer calories)
  raisins

Kids will enjoy spreading the cheese into the "valleys" of the celery sticks and positioning the "ants."

VEGGIE DIP

  1 cup low-fat, small-curd, uncreamed cottage cheese
  1 cup plain low-fat yogurt
  2 tablespoons chopped fresh parsley
  4 teaspoons onion powder
  4 teaspoons Worcestershire sauce
  1 teaspoon lemon juice

Blend cottage cheese and yogurt together. Add parsley, onion powder, Worcestershire sauce, and lemon juice. Serve in small cups with carrot strips, green-pepper strips, thin celery stalks, zucchini slices, cauliflower bits, broccoli pieces, etc., for dipping.

GRAPE-APPLE PUDDING

1 cup grape juice
1 cup hot water
5 tablespoons minute tapioca
pinch of salt
6 tart apples, cored and quartered
1/2 cup chopped nuts
3/4 cup sugar

Mix grape juice and hot water and bring to a boil. Add tapioca and salt and cook until clear (about 12 minutes). Add apples, chopped nuts, and sugar. Cook until apples are just tender, or bake in a greased baking dish at 400° for 40 minutes. Serve warm or cold.

BANANA SMOOTHIE

1 1/2 cups milk
1 large banana
1 tablespoon honey
1/4 teaspoon vanilla extract

Whir all ingredients together in a blender and serve.

SEVEN

FAT-PROOFING FOR THE PRIMARY SCHOOL YEARS

Studies have shown that ages 6 to 9 are the critical years for preventing weight problems. Children who are overweight by this time (or become so during it) usually end up fighting fat for the rest of their lives.

The day your kids first climb onto the school bus signals the end of an era. No longer can you know where they are and what they're doing every second; no longer can you run over to kiss their boo-boos or praise an accomplishment. And the time when you can monitor every bite of food that goes into their mouths is gone for good.

This doesn't mean that Fat-Proofing has to stop. It just gets harder from here on.

Suddenly peer pressure becomes a factor. A whole second-grade class may decide that carrots are "yucky." You may pack lunches that would win prizes at a nutritionists' convention, but there's no guarantee they'll get eaten. Food jags are replaced by eating fads.

Bolstered by peer pressure, the power of TV becomes stronger than ever. Before, dealing with commercials was a family matter, a dialogue between you and your child. Now a third party—someone named "everyone else," whom no parent has ever met—gets involved. "Everyone else gets to go to McDonald's!" "Everyone else's mom buys Pringle's!" "Everyone else drinks Kool-Aid!" "Everyone else brings Oreos for lunch!"

Again, your kids' developing language and logic skills can work *for* you rather than against you. All it takes is the right approach.

- A school-age child is capable of sitting through—and comprehending—an explanation of why some foods are better for the body than others, how certain foods affect different parts of the body, and so on.

- Kids *should* be hearing this stuff in school, but even if they are you can supplement their education at home. Don't forget your on-site "laboratory"—the kitchen. School-age children can get involved in nearly every facet of meal preparation.

- Emphasize that your child is more special to you, and more important, than the mythical "everyone else."

FEEDING YOUR CHILD: NUTRITION ON THE RUN

Even for kids who are in daycare from infancy, going off to school means major changes in their lives. At last they're entering the outside world. It's almost as big a step as entering the world outside your body, when they're born; it's a shock to their systems, and to yours.

Suddenly they're on a whole new schedule. While before they ate lunch at noon, the size of the school they're in (and the space limits of the cafeteria) may dictate that they eat at 11:00 (or even as early as 10:30). When one mother I know began sending her child to a private school, she was told to pack a mid-morning snack; lunch was at 12:30.

A fourth "meal" is added to the daily routine: the afterschool snack. No longer is it possible for kids to eat whenever they feel hungry. In most schools, lunch is *it*, and it's a long time between then and the final bell. Especially if kids are involved in afterschool activities, they arrive home wanting—and needing—an immediate energy boost.

Depending on what and how much that snack consists of, kids may not be ready for dinner at the usual time. Some families start eating later once their kids are in school. Others take that opportunity to begin eating lighter evening meals.

Entering the outside world also means making new friends. Kids start running in packs, and they may spend their afternoons going from house to house around the neighborhood. Another mom's notion of an afterschool snack is apt to be quite different from yours.

Scouts, sports, extracurricular activities, and homework consume chunks of their time. Kids start having legitimate reasons for missing meals or eating on the run. And it gets more difficult for you to plan the sit-down-together dinners you're used to.

One thing hasn't changed, however: Your child still needs to eat a *balanced* diet on a daily basis. And it's best to pack most of those nutrients into breakfast, dinner, and at-home snacks, since those are the only meals that remain under your immediate supervision. I'll talk later about school lunches; for now, let's look at what a child needs to stay healthy and keep growing at a normal rate.

WHAT—AND HOW MUCH—SHOULD MY CHILD EAT?

During the school years, your child will need from 1,650 to 3,300 calories each day. Bigger and more-muscular children will obviously require more calories (within that range) than smaller, less-muscular kids. How active your child is will also play a role in the number of calories he or she needs; more-active kids need more calories.

The proportional protein needs of kids actually *decrease* during the school years. A child 7 to 10 years old needs .55 grams of protein per pound of body weight, while a toddler (ages 1 to 3) needs .81 grams and a preschooler (ages 4 to 6) .68 grams per pound of body weight. Most kids consume twice as much protein as they need.

They also consume more than twice as much fat as is good for them—about 40 percent, according to a recent survey. (For more on the dangers of fat in your child's diet, see chapter 11.) This may help to explain why one out of four school-age kids is overweight.

Interestingly, girls seem to eat better than boys during childhood. According to a study conducted by the Johns Hopkins University School of Medicine, girls consume less fat and less cholesterol than boys.

What should your child eat during the school years? By now the answer is probably starting to sound very familiar: Your child should eat a variety of foods, with an emphasis on the high-carbohydrate ones like vegetables, fruits, and whole grains. Keep the junk snack foods—soda, potato chips, candies, cakes, and sugared cereals—out of the house. Replace them with healthful foods such as natural fruit juices and fresh and dried fruits. You may not be able to control what your child eats away from home, but you *can* control what's eaten where you live.

Remember, too, that school-age children in particular need a good, healthful breakfast. According to a University of Iowa Medical College study, kids who skip breakfast are more likely to lose the ability to concentrate by late morning. And skipped breakfasts can leave your child more susceptible to infection and fatigue. (Recent attempts to duplicate this study's findings have not been successful, but it's hard not to agree with the "Mother's wisdom" it backs up.)

Getting your child to eat breakfast is still a good Fat-Proofing technique. A recent Clemson University study reported that kids who skip breakfast snack more often and tend to be overweight. They also tend to have higher blood pressure, eat more salt, and exercise less than kids who eat breakfast.

ABOUT SCHOOL LUNCHES

Fat-Proofing the school-age child involves extending your reach beyond the family table. You can make sure your kids eat a healthful breakfast, and you can usually see that they down a good dinner. But the *only* way to have any direct influence over what your kids eat for lunch during school is to pack it yourself the night (or morning) before. (If they're "traders," you can only hope that they're not bargaining their whole-wheat sandwiches for Twinkies!)

Each lunch you prepare should include (1) a protein-rich food (probably a sandwich); (2) a fruit or vegetable; (3) a no-sugar (or low-sugar) "treat" of some kind; and (4) a beverage (unless the kids get milk at school). Check out my *Taming of the C.A.N.D.Y. Monster* Cookbook, too. Some additional food for thought:

- Take a few extra moments to make the meal look appealing. Use cookie cutters to shape sandwiches, crinkle-cut carrots, and add a colorful paper napkin.

- Rather than go the sandwich route, pack apple quarters, orange slices, pieces of cheese, bread and butter, and peanuts.

- Pack extras like berries, cut-up fruit, and veggie slices in a small paper cup with a toothpick. Enclose in a sandwich bag and twist-tie shut. Pack a banana or apple by cutting it in half, spearing it with a Popsicle stick, and wrapping tightly.

- Cut a "cap" off the top of an apple and core the apple. Stuff the hole with chunky peanut butter mixed with raisins or chopped dates. Replace the cap—and send a child off happy.

- Spread tuna salad or egg salad into celery-stick "valleys."

Lunchtime is no time to introduce your child to something new. Pack things he or she likes and is familiar with, and they'll be less likely to end up in the wastebasket.

Sandwiches, those old standbys, are versatile enough to allow for almost any kind of experimentation. For example:

- Smash a slice of whole-wheat bread with a rolling pin. Spread with peanut butter, add peanuts and wheat germ, and roll the whole thing up like a jelly roll. Cut into half-inch slices.

- Stir together peanut butter and any of the following: honey, sliced bananas, grated carrots and raisins, applesauce, toasted wheat germ and honey, cut-up dates, etc.

- Mix tuna fish with any of the following: sliced cucumbers, sunflower seeds, sprouts, grated carrots, chopped celery, etc.

- Blend cream cheese with any of the following: raisins, crushed pineapple, chopped nuts, luncheon meats, sliced egg, etc.

Always start with a good bread. Thankfully, some bakeries are now offering breads that are worthy of the name. Have the bakery slice them for you or buy them whole and slice them yourself.

Of course, we're talking about *whole-grain* breads here. If you think your family isn't yet ready for a 100 percent whole-grain bread, get them used to the idea gradually. Start, for example, with a bread that contains a partial amount of whole wheat; then, once your family has grown accustomed to the richer flavor and texture, bring on the "real" thing—one that is made from 100 percent whole wheat.

Why is whole wheat so important? Because it contains wheat germ and bran, the parts of the wheat berry that are eliminated in the making of white bread. Wheat germ and bran give whole-wheat bread its healthful fiber and most of its B vitamins, vitamin E, protein, and trace minerals (minerals needed by the body in very small amounts). Enriching white bread puts back *some* of these nutrients, but not all of them. And it doesn't return the lost fiber.

Read labels carefully when choosing breads. Make sure that all the flour in the bread, or at least the first flour listed, is described as "whole wheat," not just "wheat." A "100 percent wheat" bread is *not* a "100 percent whole-wheat" bread. And just because a bread looks "dark" does not make it a whole-wheat bread. Many bread manufacturers add caramel coloring to their "100 percent wheat" breads. Those are just white breads in disguise.

Don't bore your kids to death by *always* packing apples or oranges. Get a couple of plastic containers with lids that will stay on, and you can provide all kinds of exciting alternatives: mandarin oranges, pineapple chunks, a small fruit salad, or applesauce. And don't think that the "treat" has to be cookies or candy. A bag of popcorn, a small container of yogurt, and graham crackers are all possibilities.

What if they don't eat what you pack? What if you prepare the world's most nutritious lunches, and your child happily swaps them for bologna sandwiches and Ho-Hos?

You can try ordering your kids *not* to trade. Good luck! Or you can give them certain things to trade, along with strict instructions to eat everything else themselves. (Or you can hope that the other kids won't want the nutritious sandwiches and fruit salads and carrot curls you pack.)

What if your child participates in the school lunch program? Unfortunately, many of those programs are not all they should be. The foods are unappetizing, and the vending machines, laden with unhealthful alternatives, are too accessible. (Some county boards of education have banned all vending machines.) These are things a concerned parent (or, better, many concerned parents working together) can often do something about.

How can you find out what's going on at your child's school? Ask your children what they're eating. Many school systems send home weekly menus; read these carefully. Arrange to have lunch at school with your child one day and pay attention to the foods being served (and the ones kids are choosing).

If you believe a change is in order, contact the school principal or PTA at your child's school and ask if anyone has conducted a study of the school's lunch program. If not, volunteer to head such a study.

It isn't easy to change a school's attitudes about food and nutrition, but it can be done. Parents and school officials in East Aurora, New York, threw junk foods out of their schools a few years ago and replaced them with wholesome, healthful meals. In the process, kids, teachers, and parents learned lifetime lessons about good nutrition—and the school system saved a lot of money besides.

Here is a guide for parents who are interested in improving school lunch programs:

- A pamphlet called *Nutritional Parenting: How to Get Your Child Off Junk Foods and Into Healthy Eating Habits* offers a fairly detailed report on what parents in one school system did to ensure healthy school meals. It also provides a list of "dos" for fledgling parent activists. Send $2.95 postpaid to: Keats Publishing, Inc.,

27 Pine Street (Box 876), New Canaan, CT 06840. (This pamphlet is part of the publisher's "Good Health Guides" series; you may want to request a list of other publications in that series.)

SOME EARLY WARNING SIGNS OF A KID IN TROUBLE WITH FOOD

Many parents express feelings of losing control over their kids as soon as they start school full-time. They *are* becoming more independent, and that's as it should be. But because this is a critical period in a child's development—one in which putting on excess pounds can have lasting effects—it's important to stay on top of your child's eating patterns.

Be alert to behavioral changes that may indicate a trend toward eating problems. Following are some warning signs to watch for—and some suggestions for handling those that become apparent.

1. *Eating in secret*—or "sneaky snackery."

In cleaning your child's room, you come across candy wrappers under the bed, cookie boxes in the closet, cake crumbs on the desk.

You didn't buy them. Where did they come from?

Maybe the guilty party is the neighbor down the street—the one your child always seems eager to visit. Or maybe it's time to find out what your child is doing with his or her allowance. (See p. 123 for more on the allowance issue.)

- Ask, *don't accuse.* Confrontation may meet with resistance or even outright lies.

What's important is to find out *why* your child feels the need to hide the evidence from you. Is it because you often react with anger when he or she does something you don't approve of? Is it because your antisugar campaign has gone to extremes?

Kids like sweets because sweets taste good. That's a fact that no amount of Fat-Proofing can change. If a child is indulging in sneaky snackery, it may be because he or she feels ashamed of eating sweets in front of you, or afraid of incurring your disapproval. Try to bring things out into the open—*gently*.

- Fill a large bowl on the kitchen counter with all sorts of snacks—including pieces of hard candy, mini-packages of M&M's and Reese's Pieces, bite-size candy bars. Also include boxes of raisins, individually wrapped whole-wheat cookies, and other healthful alternatives. Then make it known that the kids can eat what they want, when they want. Establish only one rule: they can't take food into their rooms.

If candy is readily available, it loses some of its desirability; if it's not forbidden, eating it becomes less of a game and a challenge. What will probably happen is that the kids may indulge on occasion without going overboard. (They may stuff themselves at first, just because of the novelty, but this shouldn't last for long.)

- Kids often eat out of boredom, so start a Boredom Box. Fill it with an assortment of surprises wrapped in gift paper: crayons, small toys, cards, colored pencils. Keep it in a corner and allow kids to draw from it when they come to you claiming "I'm hungry."

- See if the kids will consider doing their homework at the dining-room table—or some other place in the house other than behind closed doors.

- Bring the kids into the kitchen and fix healthful snacks together.

- Set times when sweets may be consumed. For example: after dinner, but *not* before. As long as they're eating nutritious meals on a fairly regular basis, an occasional brownie won't matter.

2. *Eating fewer meals with the family.*

Kids who don't eat at home may be eating somewhere else—at a friend's, for example. Some kids start skipping family meals because the dinner table has become the scene of fights and arguments. In their understandable desire to avoid unpleasantness, they stay away.

- Try to make mealtimes pleasant and positive. Declare a moratorium on arguments.

- Find out where they are when they're not at the table. Again, *ask*, don't accuse. If there's a genuine scheduling conflict—an afterschool activity, for example—try to reschedule the family dinner to include them.

- Declare a no-eating-in-bedrooms policy.

- Get them more involved in preparing meals. They're apt to stick around to find out how their achievements are met by the rest of the family. Be generous with praise for any and all efforts.

- Ask your kids for mealtime suggestions and do the preparing yourself (or let them do it under your supervision). Then at least you'll have some control over the ingredients.

- Insist that they eat at the table, along with everyone else. They can fix what they choose, but they have to join the family to eat it.

3. *Taking dinner into their rooms.*

"I'm doing my homework," "I don't feel well," "I just want to be alone," "I'm too busy to come to the table"—to a child, all seem like pretty good reasons to eat in his or her room. There they're free to eat at their own speed (or not at all), and to snack on foods they've hidden away.

A mom I know had this problem, and she solved it with this approach: "Okay, Timmy, you can eat in your room tonight. But only if you promise to sleep on the dining-room table when it's time for bed."

4. *An obsession with food.*

This can take one of two forms: extreme finickiness (eating only one or two foods), or a fixation on food, period—any and all kinds.

- If it appears to be no more than finickiness, ignore it and it will probably go away. Be thankful you're not dealing with a toddler and a full-fledged food jag. (Besides, if you're keeping a Fat-Proofed kitchen, your child should have primarily healthful foods to choose from.)

Take a look at what else is going on in the child's life. Have there been big changes at school, or in the child's daily routine? Consider your cooking habits. Have you made any major alterations in what you prepare and when? Finickiness can be symptomatic of a need to control. (Then again, it can simply come out of the blue with *no* apparent reason.)

- If it appears to be a fixation, pay attention to what your child is eating. Ask him or her to cooperate in keeping a food diary for a week or so. That should reveal any serious imbalances in his or her diet and, perhaps, the source of the problem.

A child who is frustrated or depressed may turn to food as a "cure." (We adults do it, so why shouldn't our kids?) A bored child may eat almost mindlessly. Come up with some activities the child can do instead of eating, especially after school and during the mid-evening hours.

5. *Spending their allowance money on food.*

Often we declare that kids' allowances are theirs to spend as they please (as long as they do the chores necessary to earn it). If your kids' spending money is being spent on the wrong things, here's what to do:

- Give each child a small notebook and ask them to keep a written record of how they spend their allowances—down to the penny, if possible. Explain that this is a good way to learn where their money goes. (And it's a good way for *you* to track their spending habits.)

- Open a savings account and have your kids put half of their allowances there each week. Perhaps they can be saving for something special—partial payment on a new bike or a pair of roller skates. If they know they're working toward a goal, they may save even more. And it makes them feel important to have passbooks of their own.

- Set an upper limit on what they may spend on sweets per week. Then let them spend it on whatever they choose. A candy bar every now and then won't do them lasting harm.

- Keep a supply of sweet-tasting "extras" at home, such as frozen fruit-juice pops and sugarless gum. Don't limit your kids' intake of these. They may not *want* to spend their hard-earned quarters on satisfying their "sweet tooth" if they can do it for free.

- If you know that your kids are stuffing themselves with candy at the movies, make sure they eat a snack *before* leaving the house. Then give them "popcorn money" to take along.

- Find out where your kids are spending their off-hours. If they're hanging around the corner store, it's time for you to suggest alternatives. What about a swimming class at the local Y, or a volleyball team at your community center?

YOUR CHILD'S CHANGING BODY

The years from 7 to puberty are in many respects the "plateau" years. Although your child is still growing, it's at a much slower rate than during infancy. And the next great growth period—puberty—is yet to come.

Legs are the fastest-growing part of the body during these preteen years and contribute the most to added height. In general, kids with long, lanky arms and legs will enter puberty later than those with short, stocky ones.

Muscle growth begins to slow down around age 7 and continues at a gradual pace until puberty. Also, girls begin to increase their subcutaneous fat (the layer of fat just under the skin) starting at around age 7; for boys, in contrast, this layer of fat generally starts decreasing at this age.

Up until about age 10½, girls and boys are around the same height and weight. Girls experience a big growth spurt between the ages of 10½ and 13; boys experience it a bit later—between the ages of 12½ and 15. For this reason, between the ages of 10 and 13, girls tend to be taller and heavier than boys. This is natural, and isn't necessarily a sign that a girl is overweight.

WHAT IF MY CHILD IS OVERWEIGHT?

You can generally tell if your child is overweight simply by looking at him or her. The best place to look is at the upper arms and thighs. Are they thick and chubby with rolls of fat? Do clothes fit too snugly in these areas? If so, your child is probably overweight.

If you think your child has a weight problem, *now* is the time to do something about it. Not by nagging or bribing or making the child feel ashamed or "different," but by calmly developing a plan of action.

Your first step should be a visit to your child's doctor to get a better assessment of just how overweight your child is. *Your child must agree to this appointment.* Don't drag your child there if he or she doesn't want to go. If he or she is under pressure, your child will probably resist whatever assessment is made—and any weight-reduction program that follows.

"If you want your child to lose weight, there are two things you should never do. Never tell him he's fat and never put him on a diet," says Gerard Musante, head of a weight-loss clinic in Durham, NC.

At the doctor's office, your child's height and weight growth charts should be examined. If your child's weight is 15 percent more than what is considered average for his or her height, he or she is most likely overweight.

Because naturally muscular children may wrongly be considered overweight using this system, your doctor may choose to do a simple triceps fat-fold measurement. This test uses a caliper to measure the fold of skin on the back of the upper arm (both fat and muscle). If your child's fat-fold measurement is above average for his or her age, a weight problem is probably indicated.

AVERAGE HEIGHTS AND WEIGHTS
FOR PRIMARY SCHOOL CHILDREN
(7 TO 12 YEARS)

For reference only:

Girls

Age	Height (inches)	Weight (pounds; ordinary indoor clothing, no shoes)
7	47.5	48.1
8	49.8	54.8
9	52.0	62.7
10	54.4	71.8
11	57.0	81.5
12	59.6	91.6

Boys

Age	Height (inches)	Weight (pounds; ordinary indoor clothing, no shoes)
7	47.9	50.4
8	50.0	55.8
9	52.1	62.0
10	54.1	69.3
11	56.4	77.8
12	58.9	87.7

(Source: The National Academy of Sciences)

Here are the triceps fat-fold averages to use for comparison:

Boys

Age	Average Triceps Fat-Fold Measurement
6½ to 8½	8 mm
8½ to 9½	9 mm
9½ to 11½	10 mm

Girls

Age	Average Triceps Fat-Fold Measurement
6½ to 9½	7 mm
9½ to 11½	8 mm

After a weight problem has been verified, your child should keep a "food calendar" for at least a week. The calendar can be a real eye-opener—and motivator—for your child. This is especially true if the child is asked to write down when and *why* he or she ate each food as well as what was eaten. The child may recognize that he or she is eating out of boredom or simple habit as much as out of genuine hunger.

The food calendar will also help you recognize how you and other members of your family may be contributing to the child's weight problem. (Who is buying or preparing the high-calorie, high-fat foods that appear on your child's calendar?)

The next step in your plan will depend on what you learn from the physical examination and the food calendar. You may need to do nothing but allow your child to keep on growing. Or you may need to reexamine your home menus—the meals you serve your family. Is everyone starting the day with a good, nutritious, nonfattening breakfast? Are meals balanced among the food groups and attractively presented—and, most important, is everyone eating them?

Maybe the need for more exercise is indicated. Often the main cause of obesity isn't overeating (or even eating the wrong foods), but simple inactivity. Is your child spending too much time in front of the TV? Is your whole family spending too much time there? (For ideas on how to get your kids moving, see chapter 10).

Arrange to watch your child at play with his or her friends. Overweight children tend to burn fewer calories than their slender age-mates. In a team game, for example, slender kids are usually moving, fidgeting, and horsing around, even when they're supposed to be standing still, while overweight kids are taking their time, letting other kids run for the ball or reach for it.

If your child does in fact have a weight problem, you can use the basics of Fat-Proofing to get him or her back on the track of healthful eating and regular physical activity. It won't be easy—bad habits are hard to break—but it can be done.

- Support your child's fight against fat, don't just give verbal support. Eat what your child eats. Exercise with him or her.

- Keep mealtimes free of arguments, scoldings, and criticisms.

- Serve smaller portions and try to eliminate second helpings.

- If junk foods have sneaked into your refrigerator and cabinets, get rid of them!

- Don't expect miracles. Getting in shape takes time, effort, perseverance, patience—and love.

- Overweight children often turn inward and become reclusive. If this is the case with yours, encourage him or her to get out and get involved. Scouts, community activities, noncompetitive sports, and even the local drama club are all possibilities. Use your imagination; your child is counting on you.

HOW TO TALK TO AN OVERWEIGHT CHILD

Rule 4 of the Fat-Proofing program tells you, "Send your child the message, *'You're Okay.'*" That's "okay" *no matter what.* You must make it clear that you love the clean-plate child and the child who throws peas on the floor, the child who eats everything you serve without complaint and the child who claims to hate your cooking. And you must make it *very* clear that you love the child who has a weight problem.

Remember that fat children often don't love themselves. They don't like the way they look, and while it may seem as if they enjoy their food, they may not like the way they eat. They know that eating is somehow connected to weighing too much, having too few friends, feeling clumsy and tired and isolated. Their self-esteem falls, and they may be deeply ashamed of themselves and their eating habits.

I've emphasized over and over throughout this book that you should *never* criticize a child's eating habits, appearance, or weight. But that doesn't mean you can't discuss these matters with your child. What's important is *when* and *how* you do it.

- Don't choose a time when you're feeling grumpy or frustrated. It's too easy to "lash out" at a child and make him or her the victim of your bad mood.

- It's best if the child comes to you with a desire to talk about his or her problem.

"Mom, my favorite dress doesn't fit anymore," or, "Mom, I feel tired all the time," are good openers for a loving, supportive conversation. Don't respond, "That's because you're fat!" Don't make statements, period. Lead the child to reveal more of his or her feelings by asking gentle and sensitive questions.

Some examples: "Why do *you* think your dress doesn't fit?" "Can you think of a reason why you feel tired?"

- If you have to go to your child and bring up the topic, do so with all the kindness and patience you can muster. Your child may already have been the butt of jokes and name-calling at school. He or she needs to know that home, at least, is a refuge.

In his book *Helping Your Child Grow Slim* (New York: Simon and Schuster, 1982), Dr. Warren P. Silberstein describes a way of approaching a child with a weight problem. His advice is so sound (and supportive) that I want to pass it along.

> [You] mustn't attack the child head on, you mustn't emphasize his excessive weight—but rather, you must minimize it and then minimize the treatment.
>
> You say to the child, "You are a little bit overweight. A little bit." And you show him the growth chart. [*Note: You may want to use the one found on page 126.*] He can't understand the chart.
>
> But rather than looking at the child and pointing to his body and saying how fat a body he has, you have him look with you at the chart, and you say: "Well, you see here how we've plotted your height and weight, and how you compare with other children of your age, and you are a little overweight. And I think if you could be more the same weight as other children of your age and size, you would probably be happier. And if it weren't too hard to do, you would be glad to do it.
>
> "Now, the trick is," you go on to say, "you don't have to lose any weight. You just have to be careful not to gain weight as quickly as you've been doing."
>
> You go further: "You see, last year you weighed seven pounds less then you do now. And if you had not gained any weight instead of gaining seven pounds, you would be right about where you belong. Now, do you think it would be too difficult for you not to keep gaining as much weight?"
>
> And most children can handle that idea. Most are likely to say, "Yes, I think I can do it."

What you're doing with this approach is enlisting your child's support. Once you've got that, and once it's evident that you're *not* at war with your child or attacking him or her, you stand a far better chance of succeeding.

SHOULD KIDS DIET?

Let's say you're 5 pounds overweight. You look in the mirror, or you find that the zipper won't budge on last year's pair of pants, and you know what you have to do: diet and exercise until you reach your "ideal" weight.

Let's say your child is 5 pounds overweight. Now, you might be tempted to apply the same solution to his or her situation: diet and exercise until those 5 pounds are shed. That seems to make sense, right?

Wrong. It fails to take into account Fat-Proofing rule 2: *Realize that your child's body is different from your own.*

It's not different just because it's smaller; it's different because it's still growing. You've reached your maximum height; your child hasn't. Your bones are as long as they're going to get; your child's aren't. Your ideal weight is set, more or less, for the rest of your life; your child's is increasing every year, and sometimes, during a growth spurt, every month (it may seem like every minute!).

For most overweight children, dieting is not the answer. In fact, it can cause more problems than it cures. Deprive a child's growing body of essential nutrients and the effects can be long-term and devastating. Even restricting food intake can be harmful. An overweight child put suddenly on a rigid diet may end up undernourished or malnourished.

You know how *you* feel when you're dieting, and you know why you feel that way. As an adult, you can reason away your hunger pangs. For a child, though, a diet may seem like a punishment. Suddenly Mommy (or Daddy) is holding back food that used to be given freely. And there's something terribly wrong with a child's having to go hungry for extended periods of time.

A hungry child is a cranky, grumpy, fussy child. A malnourished child may also be sluggish, tired, listless, and uninterested in things going on around him or her. Malnourished children have short attention spans. They do poorly in school. And their bodies become less able to fight off illness and infection.

In *Helping Your Child Grow Slim*, Dr. Silberstein claims that children can be helped to grow into their right weight over a period of years. "In most instances," he writes, "unless a child is extraordinarily obese, he or she shouldn't lose any weight at all!" Instead, he advocates what he terms "zero weight gain." The only exception he makes is for adolescents nearing the end of their growth period.

The main focus of any attempt to control a child's weight should always be the formation of good eating habits. Most dieting adults lose and gain weight again and again because they immediately revert to their old ways once they lose their targeted number of pounds. The diets that work are those that stress maintenance, not quick results. That's been proved over and over.

With this in mind:

- Unless you're under doctor's orders, don't restrict your child's calorie consumption. *Do* avoid serving calorie-rich, nutrition-poor foods.

- **Never** put a child on a fad diet. (This might be worth turning into Fat-Proofing rule 5!)

If you've gone through periods of diet addiction yourself, then you already have a good idea of the wide variety of diets out there. Maybe you've spent weeks eating nothing but grapefruit or drinking canned diet drinks. (A friend of mine remembers what the inside of her family's refrigerator looked like when she was a child. The top shelves were loaded with "regular" foods for her and her father and brothers to eat; the bottom shelf was packed with her mom's Metrecal.)

Concern about parents' fears of fat has prompted the American Academy of Pediatrics to publicly warn against putting children on diets. An article in *Pediatrics* cited a lack of compelling evidence to suggest that stringent low-fat, low-cholesterol diets were necessary for children.

I can't emphasize strongly enough that *fad diets are not for children*. (Technically speaking, they're not for adults, either. But adults are supposed to be able to make their own choices, while children have many of their choices made for them by their parents.)

A fad diet can be a real hardship for a child, physically and psychologically. A lot of them are based on cutting back on (or cutting out) a particular substance, usually carbohydrates or fats. These diets may result in short-term weight loss, but once normal eating is resumed the weight is almost always regained. Meanwhile, the child's growing body is deprived of things it needs.

Fad diets can be dangerous in other ways. Low-carbohydrate diets (also known as high-protein diets) tend to be very high in cholesterol and fats, which can lead to cardiovascular disease. Some deliberately induce "ketosis"—a condition that results when the body begins burning its own fat stores too rapidly. Ketosis can cause appetite loss, nausea, low blood pressure, fatigue, and dizziness.

Low-protein diets force the body to consume its own lean muscle tissue. And liquid protein diets may be the most perilous of all. Some dieters have developed irreversible heart problems; others have died.

- **Never** feed a child diet pills.

Amphetamines, diuretics, laxatives, and caffeine don't belong in your child's body—and they're the main ingredients of most diet pills. Plus, there's no scientific proof that they work.

- Avoid gimmicks in general.

- Forbid fasting.

Some children—especially teens—will resort to fasting in an attempt to lose weight quickly. Fasting amounts to self-starvation, and it's been linked to numerous health problems, including dehydration, nausea, dizziness, muscle wasting, and massive protein loss.

If your child is severely overweight and dieting seems the only possible solution, get advice from your doctor or a nutritionist. This is one area in which getting creative yourself is not recommended.

WHERE TO GET HELP FOR AN OVERWEIGHT CHILD

If you feel you need help, *don't be afraid to seek it.* There are plenty of professionals whose job it is to know the best and latest methods for working with overweight kids. You don't have to go it alone.

- Find out if your child's school offers a program for overweight children. Start by checking with the guidance counselor.

Many such programs offer sound nutrition advice, regularly scheduled physical activity, and peer support. A school program may be all you need to support your own Fat-Proofing efforts.

If your child is truly obese—something you'll find out from a physical examination—you'll need to take stronger measures. Here are a few suggested routes:

- Ask your doctor to recommend a bariatrician.

A bariatrician is a doctor who specializes in treating obesity. He or she may recommend a supervised diet and exercise plan.

- Consider a weight-loss clinic.

Weight-loss clinics for kids are cropping up across the country. The good ones offer several advantages, including up-to-the-minute advice and techniques and plenty of peer support. When overweight kids meet others like themselves and they're all working toward the same goal, there's strength (and motivation) in numbers.

Start by asking your pediatrician for a reference, or check with your local children's hospital or university medical school. Once you've got two or three possibilities, examine each closely. Many such programs have prepared information packets that are free for the asking; read these through and jot down your questions and concerns. Then make an appointment to speak with the program director or other full-time staffperson—and be sure to bring along the notes you've made.

Here are some questions you'll want to have answered when evaluating a weight-loss program for your child:

1. Who's on staff?

In addition to trained counselors, the program should offer the services of a nutritionist and a psychologist. Plus, there should be *ongoing* medical supervision.

2. Does the program emphasize self-esteem and self-confidence?

Overweight kids need help feeling good about themselves. Is there a rewards system? (See chapter 9 for more on building self-esteem in the obese child.)

3. Does the program stress the importance of physical fitness?

Look for a focus on *lifetime* aroebic exercises such as running, swimming, or bicycling.

4. Is the program centered around a nutritionally balanced eating plan?

No fad diets, diet pills, or drugs! The plan should be sensible and fairly easy to follow. It shouldn't cause chaos in your kitchen, nor should it be based on "special" foods that will make your child feel even more isolated and "different" from everyone else.

5. Does the program emphasize *gradual* weight loss and maintenance afterward?

Be alert to promises of quick and easy results. Weight loss and weight control are hard work, even for kids. This doesn't mean that the program has to be sour and dour, however; on the contrary, it should be upbeat and enthusiastic. Your child will have to make a commitment to it, and no child will want to do something that doesn't have *some* element of fun.

Ask about follow-up, too. What happens *after* your child reaches his or her target weight? Is continuing support available? Are there monthly or semiannual checkups.

6. What are the program's success rates?

How many kids have gone through it? How many have succeeded in reaching their target weight? How many have *kept off* the weight lost—and for how long? Have follow-up studies been conducted? Ask to see copies.

Rank the programs according to what you learn about them. If your first choice and your child don't "fit," then move on to your second choice. Don't insist that your child stay in a program he or she genuinely dislikes. Overweight kids already have enough problems with food and self-image; they shouldn't be forced to follow programs or attend meetings that make them even more miserable.

Some weight-loss programs require family involvement, whether in the form of group counseling or changes in household meal preparation and eating habits. Upholding your end of the bargain will indicate to your child that you're in this together.

- Consider sending your child to a weight-loss or "slim-down" camp.

Each summer, thousands of boys, girls, women, and men lose tens of thousands of pounds at weight-loss camps around the country. Many regain some or all of it during the winter months, but some keep those pounds off for years—because they've learned (and stuck to) good eating habits.

WEIGHT WATCHERS CAMPS

Weight Watchers camps are franchises of the enduring and reputable Weight Watchers International organization. They're a good place to start your search for the right camp for your child. For information write: Weight Watchers Camps, 183 Madison Ave., New York, NY 10016. Or call (800) 223-5600 (in New York state, (212) 889-9500 or from Canada (800) 251-4141).

There are many such camps to choose from these days; weight loss is big business. Evaluate any camp you look into with the same criteria listed above for rating weight-loss programs.

WHAT TO DO AFTER
YOUR CHILD SLIMS DOWN

Even after your child has lost weight, he or she may continue to "feel" fat and show it in the way he or she walks, dresses, moves, and behaves.

- One way to reinforce the "new image" is by helping it along with some new clothes and/or a new haircut.

Your child will feel better and may reap the added bonus of recognition from his or her peers. They may not notice the weight loss, but they will see—and, hopefully, compliment—the new outfit or hairdo.

- Communicate to your child in word and deed that you're behind him or her all the way. Your support and confidence are crucial at this stage.

Don't make the mistake one well-meaning mom did. When she brought her daughter back from a day's shopping and the two of them were putting their purchases away, the daughter started cleaning out her closet and piling her old clothes on the bed. Mom asked, "What are you doing?" and Daughter said, "Getting rid of this stuff." To which Mom replied, without thinking, "Don't you think you'd better save some of it, just in case?" Daughter was crushed and Mom was mortified.

- An occasional "binge" is to be expected. Don't make a big deal about it, but *do* have a talk with your child about the consequences.

A week's worth of stuffing oneself may take months to work off; a single afternoon of potato chips at a friend's house won't exact as high a price. Make sure your child understands the difference. (No recriminations allowed in either case.)

A FEW FINAL FAT-PROOFING
WORDS ABOUT SCHOOL-AGE
KIDS

The elementary-school years are critical to Fat-Proofing. In a very real sense, they're your "last chance" before adolescence sets in. If a child hasn't learned the rudiments of healthful eating by the time he or she becomes a teen, it may be too late.

The child who grows up in a household where nutrition is the norm, where mealtimes are pleasant, where the parents make the effort to Fat-Proof from an early age and *stick with it*—that child stands an excellent chance of never becoming a diet-addicted adult.

AFTERSCHOOL SNACKS FOR THE FAT-PROOFED HOUSEHOLD

If your kids are like mine, they'll walk in the door after school and head straight for the kitchen. Nutritious snacking is still an important part of their diet (and besides, dinner is so far away!), so it's up to you to keep the kitchen well stocked with the kinds of foods you want them to eat.

- Since schoolage kids like to be self-sufficient, post a "what's in-side" list on the refrigerator door and let them help themselves.

- If they've learned their way around the kitchen and know how to use appliances responsibly, give them free rein with the toaster oven (or microwave) and the blender. Let them try their own creations—banana-carob "malts" (made with low-fat milk), fro-zen fruit slushes, melted cheese on crackers.

- Keep pocket bread on hand, along with plenty of filling possi-bilities. Sprouts, shredded cheese, chopped tomatoes, and tuna with a half-mayonnaise, half-yogurt dressing make a yummy "portable" sandwich.

- Shop in health-food sections for carob-coated peanuts, trail mix, granola, and muesli (a combination of grains, ground nuts, and shredded dried fruits that's tasty with milk or plain yogurt). Store in airtight containers on a "snacks shelf."

You can make your own trail mix from almost any combination of ingre-dients. Start with seeds (pumpkin, sesame, sunflower) and add nuts (pea-nuts, almonds, unroasted cashews). Flavor with raisins or currants, chopped dates, or any other chopped dried fruit (apples, pears, bananas, pineapple, peaches, apricots). For a special treat, toss with chocolate or carob chips and/or shredded unsweetened coconut.

Add the following recipes to your growing file.

HOMEMADE GELL-O

1 package unflavored gelatin
2 cups cold fruit juice (orange, apple, grape, cherry—anything
    but pineapple, which will keep the gel from setting)

In a saucepan, stir the gelatin into half of the juice. Heat on the stove over a low flame until the gelatin is completely dissolved. Remove from heat, stir in the rest of the juice, pour into a mold (or individual cups), and set in the refrigerator.

APPLE CRISP

4 to 6 apples, peeled, cored, and sliced
1 tablespoon lemon juice
1 cup oatmeal, uncooked
$1/3$ cup whole-wheat flour
$1/3$ cup packed brown sugar
1 teaspoon ground cinnamon
$1/4$ cup toasted wheat germ
$1/3$ cup melted margarine

Preheat oven to 375°.
Place the apple slices in a greased 9″ baking pan and sprinkle with lemon juice. Combine the dry ingredients and mix in the melted margarine until the mixture is crumbly. Sprinkle over apples. Bake 20 to 30 minutes, or until apples are tender. Tasty warm or cold.

EGGNOG FOR TWO

Delicious in winter or summer.

1 egg
2 cups skim milk
2 teaspoons vanilla extract
dash of nutmeg

In a large bowl, beat egg for 1 minute. Add milk and stir; add vanilla and stir; beat mixture until frothy. Top with nutmeg.

EIGHT

Teens:
Too Late
To Fat-Proof?

If there are teenagers in your house, does that mean it's too late to start the Fat-Proofing? No—but it can be more difficult than starting when they're young.

You already know that it's hard to tell teens what to do. They like to show their independence and self-reliance, and a lot of that involves doing the opposite of what their parents want. Push them in one direction and they're sure to pull in the other.

Fat-Proofing teens takes imagination, patience—and a large measure of tact. But if there's ever a time when the old saying "better late than never" applies, this is it. One out of five teenagers in the United States today is at least 20 percent overweight—and about 80 percent of these will grow up to be overweight adults.

FEEDING YOUR TEENAGER: FUELING THE SECOND GREAT GROWTH SPURT

Kids grow faster during adolescence than at any other time since infancy. They add from 15 to 25 percent of their adult height, and they nearly double their weight.

And that's about all we can say about boys and girls in the same breath. From this point on, we must consider each sex separately, because the changes that take place in the two are so very different.

- In boys, the growth spurt usually begins at around age 13; in girls, at around age 11. In boys, it peaks at around age 14; in girls, at around age 12.

During the peak year of the growth spurt, your son or daughter may add anywhere from 2 to 5 inches to his or her height.

- Both get broader, but not in the same places. Boys develop wider shoulders; girls, wider hips.

In girls, the pelvic bone actually enlarges, and fat begins to deposit around the hips and the upper thighs. This is the body's way of preparing for childbearing.

- Boys gain an average of 57 pounds during adolescence; girls, an average of 45 pounds.

The two sexes deposit this additional weight in different ways. In boys, most of it goes into muscles and other lean tissue. In girls, nearly half is deposited as fat.

These differences are due to the sex hormones the adolescent's body is producing at such an alarming rate. Testosterone, the male hormone, goes to work building muscles and burning fat. Estrogen, the female hormone, does just the opposite, promoting—and maintaining—body fat.

The results are seen in the mature adult body. The average, healthy, reasonably fit man carries about 14 to 16 percent of his weight as fat, while for the average, healthy, reasonably fit woman this amounts to between 23 and 26 percent. The male usually weighs more because he's taller *and* because muscle is denser and heavier than fat.

What this means is that females are *naturally* rounder, softer, and "fatter" than males. *You should explain this important difference to your teenage daughter.* Girls have a hard time understanding why they're growing "plumper" while their brothers (and boyfriends) are becoming more streamlined. They're especially appearance-conscious and susceptible to the lures of fad or crash diets. (They're also, as we'll see, more prone than boys to dangerous eating disorders.)

What should you feed your developing teen? The same daily *balanced* diet you feed to the rest of your family. Include foods from the groups I've discussed all along as essential to Fat-Proofing:

- milk, cheese, yogurt, and/or other dairy products

- vegetables and fruits, including daily servings of vitamin C sources (citrus fruits, berries, tomato, cabbage, cantaloupe), vitamin A sources (green or yellow fruits and vegetables), potatoes and legumes, and other fruits

- protein foods including lean meats, fish, peanut butter, eggs, and/or meat substitutes

- whole-grain and nonsugared cereals, pasta, and/or rice

- whole-grain breads

There are three reasons why I don't indicate serving sizes and frequencies. First, it isn't really necessary. (Their appetites will probably be greater than yours, which is to be expected since they're so busy growing. If you've never seen your teenage son down a whole quart of milk in a gulp, just wait.) Second, they're not children anymore; they've been feeding themselves for years, and you shouldn't be doling out portions to them. Simply make available reasonable quantities of healthful and interesting foods. Third, teens have differing nutritional requirements, depending on their sex, their size, how active (or inactive) they are, and where they are in their growth spurt.

On average, adolescent girls need from 2,100 to 2,400 calories per day. Since their growth spurt comes earlier than boys', they should decrease their calorie intake as they approach physical maturity. Adolescent boys, *on average*, need to increase their calorie intake from 2,500 per day at ages 10 to 12, to 2,700 calories per day at ages 12 to 14, and to 3,000 calories per day at ages 14 to 18. Unless your teen is extremely overweight, you should not restrict his or her calorie consumption. Teens still need plenty of calories to grow on, and cutting back can interfere with and even stunt their growth.

Studies have shown that teens get about 80 percent of the calories they consume each day from regular meals, and the other 20 percent from snacks. The Fat-Proofing household is one in which healthful snacks are always available. Stock up on whole-grain baked goods, fresh fruits, fresh veggies, and cheeses. Buy a hot-air popcorn popper, if you don't already have one; most teens I know can *always* eat popcorn, and it's best if it isn't prepared in oil. Encourage yours to eat it unsalted, too.

Normal, healthy teens don't need to follow special diets. But some nutrients are of particular importance during the adolescent years, simply because the foods teens prefer tend to be short on them. So you'll want to be sure to feature these at your family table:

- foods high in folic acid (leafy green veggies)

- foods high in vitamins C and A (citrus fruits, leafy green veggies, cantaloupe, potatoes, carrots, sweet potatoes)

- for girls especially, iron-rich foods (meats, egg yolks, leafy green veggies)

- calcium-rich foods (milk, cheese, yogurt, leafy green veggies)

Don't push protein. You may think that your teen needs an extra "boost" during this stage, but it isn't necessary. In fact, a very high protein diet may be harmful, since too much protein over the RDA may increase calcium loss from the bones.

If you're uncertain as to whether your teen is eating a balanced diet, now may be the time to bring vitamin/mineral supplements into the house, if only for your own peace of mind.

WHO'S IN CHARGE HERE?

Now that we've talked about *what* to feed your teenager, let's explore *how*.

If you don't know this already, you'll learn it soon: You *can't* control your teens' eating habits. You can't watchdog every hastily grabbed lunch, every afterschool gathering at the local pizza parlor or malt shop, every party or school function. And *you shouldn't try*. Growing up involves learning how to care for oneself, and that includes taking responsibility for a healthy lifestyle. You can lead your teens in the direction of good eating habits, but you can't force them to follow.

Some tips for helping these habits along:

- Encourage your teen to help with shopping and food preparation.

Many teenage boys are now taking home-economics courses in school and learning their way around a stove. Most teens are responsible (and coordinated) enough to take on the task of preparing a meal from beginning to end. And most feel proud of themselves when they do.

One family I know has three teenagers, and each week they take turns planning and fixing the evening meals. Monday is Mom's night; Tuesday, Wednesday, and Thursday belong to the kids; Dad takes over on Fridays; weekends are up for grabs. Nobody carries the entire burden of feeding five people every evening, and the kids actually enjoy their turns as chief chefs.

Most teens will eat what's put in front of them if they're hungry, so this may be your only opportunity during the day to see that they eat right.

Even if they're busy with schoolwork, extracurricular activities, and friends, they can still make time to join the family at dinner. Make it a rule and stick to it.

- Do respect your teens' food preferences. By now, jags and fads should be mere memories. But your kids are old enough to know what they like (and don't like), and you should no longer insist that they try a bite of everything.

On the other hand, teens' palates are more sophisticated than those of younger kids, so they'll probably like a wider variety of foods. And they may be willing to experiment with new tastes, if only because they're new.

- Don't even *attempt* to use food as a way of controlling your teens' behavior.

If you do, your kids may naturally rebel in that direction by eating less (or eating more of the wrong kinds of foods).

In contrast to the advice I've given up to now, I don't recommend banning junk foods from a house where teenagers are present. Especially if they are lean, the extra calories will certainly not hurt. Let the kids have them—as long as they buy them *with their own money,* and as long as they continue to eat at least one meal a day with the family. It's been my experience that kids would rather buy the latest hit record than spend their hard-earned allowance on consumables.

- Don't bring food into discussions that are really about other things.

Your teenager's room looks as if it's been bulldozed. What do you say? "It's time to clean your room," **not** "Your room is a disaster, and I'm tired of watching you stuff your face with potato chips."

Your teenager's hair looks as if it's been bulldozed. What do you say? Maybe nothing (it depends). But certainly **not** "Can't you do something with your hair? And why are you always eating?"

IF YOUR TEEN IS DETERMINED TO DIET

Teens diet for all sorts of reasons—because they're overweight, because they're afraid of being overweight, because their friends are dieting, and sometimes "just because." Sadly, some teens diet because it's a family tradition—Mom and Dad are diet-addicted, and teens learn what they see.

If it hasn't happened already, there's a good chance that someday in the not-too-distant future your teen will push away his or her plate and announce, "I can't eat that—I'm on a diet." How should you respond? **Not** with, "Don't be silly; you don't need to diet; eat!"

First of all, your daughter or son will bridle at being called "silly." Second, he or she won't care about *your* opinion of what he or she needs. Third, he or she will rebel against the order to "eat"!

What's the alternative? Keep calm and try to find out what kind of diet your teen is following. Maybe there's a fad going around school. Maybe your teen has succumbed to the claims of the latest Hollywood star promoting her own book.

Have your child give you a complete description of the diet in question. If all it involves is skipping a meal once a week, don't worry. The same goes for a "no meat," "no butter," or "no bread" diet—*as long as nutritional needs are being met with other foods.* It's *not* okay to cut out an entire food group.

If the diet comes out of a book, ask to see it—and then read it. Pay attention to the author's credentials. Is he or she reputable—and does he or she have a solid background in nutrition? Look carefully at the first chapter or two, which should tell you about the origins of the diet and whether it's been tested—and, importantly, on how many people it's been tested, and under what circumstances.

If you're lucky, your teen may have chosen a diet that's based on sound nutritional principles. If not, let a doctor or nutritionist be the one to break the news. As an "outside" authority figure, he or she will likely have more influence than you over your teen in this matter.

> For an excellent source of information on which diets are safe and which aren't, see *Rating the Diets* by Theodore Berland. The March 1986 issue of Consumer Guide's *Health and Exercise* magazine, *Rating the Diets* looks closely at many popular weight-loss plans. Your local library should probably have a copy in its reference section; if not, write Consumer Guide, 3841 W. Oakton St., Skokie, IL 60076. If available, they will send it to you for $3.75 ppd.

ON COUNTING CALORIES

If your teens insist on counting calories, make sure that they know about *output* as well as input. Take this opportunity to stress the need for exercise—the only known way to efficiently burn calories.

Teens should get at least 30 minutes per day (or an hour every other day) of vigorous exercise. The fact that teenage obesity has increased by 40 percent over the past twenty years indicates that too few have made regular exercise a part of their lives.

If they're not at the tennis courts, the track, or the pool, where are they? Studies have revealed the answer: they're parked in front of the TV.

Television may be a leading contributor to the rising numbers of too-fat teens. A July 1, 1985, article in *The Wall Street Journal* reported some shocking facts:

- Today's adolescent spends 25 hours per week *or more* watching television.

- Kids who watch a lot of TV are more likely to be overweight than kids who don't.

For many, 25 hours of TV means 25 hours of snacking.

What do they see on the flickering screen? Commercials that urge them to eat—and programs that urge them to be thin. These conflicting messages pave the way for trouble.

During a time when their bodies are growing, their level of activity is slowing down. Part of the problem may be due to changes in the labor market. It used to be that kids had afterschool jobs; in 1974, 50 percent of teenagers did. That figure has since dropped to 30 percent. Instead of going off to work, teens are coming home to empty houses, full refrigerators, and uninterrupted time alone.

If you're a parent who works outside the home, you still don't have to commit your teen to endless hours in the Twilight Zone. Some alternatives:

- Encourage your teen to get involved in afterschool activities— team sports, clubs, whatever, as long as he or she stays out of the house for a period of time.

- If those hold no appeal, bring up the possibility of volunteer work. Maybe there's an elderly neighbor who needs help with lawn mowing or snow shoveling. Perhaps a local hospital could use another aide.

- Assign chores that cut into TV time. Preparing dinner, weeding the garden, teaching the dog new tricks—anything your teen agrees to do.

- Insist that homework be done immediately after school, and ask to see the evidence.

■ Send your teen on errands that must be done on foot. Walking is terrific exercise. Between ages 5 and 11, even obese kids normally walk the equivalent of at least 6 miles per day. During adolescence, boys sustain that pace, but girls fall back to only 3 miles.

If your teen hasn't yet made a commitment to some form of exercise or sport, make it a priority. Here's where counting calories may help.

CALORIE EXPENDITURES PER HOUR FOR DIFFERENT ACTIVITIES*

Activity	Calories Expended Per Hour of Continuous Exercise
Bicycle riding	200–600
Walking moderately fast	200–300
Football	560
Soccer	560
Frisbee	200
Basketball	500
Tennis	500–700
Volleyball	300
Swimming	300–600
Dancing	400–500
Jogging	400–500
Skiing (cross-country)	650–1,000
(downhill)	350–500

*Based on an individual weighing approximately 130 to 150 lbs. Add on more calories if the person is heavier.

(Source: Nutrition and Health, ed. M. Winick, vol. 2, no. 4, 1980.)

WHAT IF MY TEEN IS OVERWEIGHT?

If you have a teenager with a serious weight problem, the first thing you should do is to recognize the pain of it.

For an adolescent, extra pounds and bulges can be emotionally tragic. They can also be very difficult to shed. That's because the onset of puberty gives the green light to a whole new crop of fat cells. Weight added during

AVERAGE HEIGHTS AND WEIGHTS FOR TEENAGERS (11 TO 18 YEARS)

Note: Because adolescents grow at such varying rates, this chart reflects a *range* of heights and weights for each age.

For reference only:

Girls

Age	Height (inches)	Weight (pounds: ordinary indoor clothing, no shoes)
11	56	78
	57	82
	58	86
12	58	86
	59	90
	60	95
13	59	92
	60	97
	61	101
14	62	109
	63	112
	64	117
15	63	116
	64	119
	65	122
16	63	117
	64	120
	65	123
17	64	122
	65	125
	66	129
18	64	123
	65	126
	66	130

Boys		
Age	Height (inches)	Weight (pounds; ordinary indoor clothing, no shoes)
11	55	73
	56	77
	57	81
12	58	85
	59	89
	60	92
13	58	85
	59	89
	60	93
14	61	99
	62	103
	64	108
15	64	115
	65	120
	66	125
16	65	122
	66	128
	67	134
17	66	132
	67	136
	68	141
18	67	139
	68	143
	69	149

(Source: Baldwin-Wood)

this stage of life doesn't just "fill up" existing fat cells left over from infancy; instead, it's stored in the new fat cells. And remember that fat cells are forever.

There are two options for an obese teen. The first is to *stop gaining weight* and "grow into" the weight he or she is carrying around. Whether this is possible depends on how far along he or she is on the growth spurt.

The second is to *lose weight* on a medically approved and supervised diet. As I have made clear, I do not recommend that parents put their children on diets. Even if you are a trained nutritionist, you should consider enlisting outside professional help. Otherwise you will enter the realm of food-as-control. And it can be especially counterproductive when dealing with a rebellious adolescent who is sure to resent your efforts.

WHERE TO GET HELP FOR AN OVERWEIGHT TEEN

There are many resources available to obese teens and their parents.

- Start by scheduling a complete physical examination for your teen. Your doctor may recommend a diet or refer you to a specialist.

- Find an adult third party—someone your teen respects—who will encourage him or her to lose weight. Some possibilities: a church adviser, a school nurse, your child's PE teacher.

- Contact your local hospital or medical center. Many now offer safe and nutritionally sound weight-loss programs geared to teens.

- Avoid *all* programs that promise miracles.

- Consider hypnosis. Some physicians are now using it to treat everything from phobias to speech disorders. Studies have shown that when combined with behavior therapy it can be effective in treating obesity.

Techniques vary, but usually they consist of putting the patient into a hypnotic trance and implanting specific suggestions. For example, the patient might be instructed not to eat at certain times. Another technique involves "imaging"—seeing oneself as lean and fit—and working gradually toward attaining that image.

Be sure to find a competent, ethical professional. Start by calling your nearby medical center and ask whether anyone in the psychology, psychiatry, or nutrition department uses hypnosis for weight control.

DANGER SIGNS:
TEENS AND EATING DISORDERS

I'm glad I'm not a teenager today. I don't know if I could handle the mixed messages adolescent girls are getting: be smart, be successful, be pretty, be natural, be assertive, be feminine, be athletic, be soft, be career-oriented, get ready to be Supermom.

And, of course, Be Thin. Which may be the most prevalent, the most demanding, and, it seems, the most dangerous message of all.

The problem is, there seems to be a single standard of "in" looks. Why can't it be okay for bodies to come in a variety of shapes and sizes? We no longer insist that skirts conform to a single length. In fact, kids today seem to have more of a sense of individual "style" than any preceding generation (certainly more than mine did when we were that age). Take a look around a local hang-out. You'll see a dozen different hairdos, all kinds of jewelry, mix-and-match clothes that seem like conglomerations of the past and the future. Anything goes as far as color is concerned. Still, those clothes had better hang on bony bodies or they're "out" no matter how "in" they are.

I watched a program on television not too long ago about looks and how they affect our lives. I saw a perfectly lovely young girl, 10 or 12 years old, confess her biggest worry: she was "fat" (she wasn't!) and convinced that if she didn't lose weight she wouldn't attract boyfriends.

Whoever first said "you can never be too rich or too thin" may have meant it as a cocktail party bon mot, but it's teenage girls who are taking it to heart. And some of them are dying because of it.

Adolescents go overboard on almost everything they do. When they fall in love, it's forever. When they're embarrassed, they want to crawl in a hole and stay there. When they're happy, they're irrepressible. When they convince themselves they're fat—or when they believe that people around them think they are—they become obsessive about losing weight.

Millions of young women today (and men, although far fewer) are suffering the effects of the severe eating disorders known as *anorexia nervosa* and *bulimia*. Anorexia involves literally starving oneself; bulimia involves binging (eating to excess) and purging (vomiting).

If you suspect from what follows that your teenager has either of these conditions, it is vital that you consult your family doctor and request referral to a specialist experienced in treating eating disorders.

- Estimates vary as to how many adolescent girls are affected by anorexia and bulimia. One source claims that 1 out of every 100 to 250 adolescent females is anorexic, while 1 to 4 percent of females age 14 to 25 are bulimic. Another maintains that anorexia is found in 1 out of every 20 teenage girls, bulimia in 1 out of 3 women age 18 to 30.

Either estimate is horrifying. We seem to have an epidemic on our hands.

- Boys and young men are in general less susceptible; more than 90 percent of all anorexics and bulimics are female.

- While these disorders normally occur in the teen years, they can begin as early as age 7 or relatively late in life.

- Until recently, it was believed that anorexia and bulimia were diseases of the middle and upper classes. It was also thought that they most frequently struck adolescents with above-normal intelligence. Now, however, research has shown that they occur in all socioeconomic, racial, age, and intellectual groups.

Anorexia is considered the more lethal of the two, with an estimated mortality rate of 5 to 15 percent. Perhaps its most famous victim was the singer Karen Carpenter. People were shocked when they heard the news: Karen Carpenter had long been a star, a people-pleaser, a high achiever, a "good girl"—characteristics common to anorexics.

Food is the fuel our bodies need to function. Damage to vital organs and heart failure are among the most serious side-effects of self-inflicted starvation. The good news is that most of the problems resulting from anorexia or bulimia can be reversed—if treated early enough.

HOW CAN YOU TELL IF YOUR TEEN IS ANOREXIC OR BULIMIC?

Alan E. Bayer, a professor of sociology, and Daniel H. Baker, a medical psychologist, have developed a list of signs and symptoms that may indicate the presence of anorexia or bulimia. They caution that *both diseases require medical diagnosis and testing*. If you're worried about your teen, consult your doctor before jumping to conclusions.

(The following is adapted from Alan E. Bayer and Daniel H. Baker, "Adolescent Eating Disorders: Anorexia and Bulimia," *Family Life Educator,* winter 1984.)

PHYSICAL SIGNS

1. *Extreme weight change.* Anorexics may lose up to 25 percent of their body weight over a period of several months; a bulimic's weight may zoom up and down.

2. *Hypothermia.* Because extreme weight loss inhibits the body's ability to retain heat, the anorexic or bulimic may often feel chilled.

3. *Insomnia.*

4. *Constipation.* Insufficient food and liquid intake wreaks havoc on the internal organs, including the intestinal tract. Bulimics may aggravate this by abusing laxatives, diuretics, and/or emetics.

5. *Skin rash, dry skin.* May indicate dehydration.

6. *Hair loss, poor nail quality.* Signs of protein deficiencies.

7. *Dental problems.* Signs of nutritional deficiencies. These may be especially noticeable in a bulimic; vomiting brings up stomach acids.

8. *No menstrual periods.* Both diseases lower female hormone levels, which may interrupt the menstrual cycle.

BEHAVIORAL SIGNS

1. *Unusual eating habits.* These may include food rituals, unexplainable new preferences, hoarding food, stealing food, taking a very long time to eat, and so on. Watch for excuses for avoiding family meals.

2. *Hyperactivity and/or an overemphasis on exercise.* If your formerly sedentary teen suddenly shows an interest in fitness, terrific—unless it's extreme.

3. *Lots of trips to the bathroom scale.* Anorexics especially may weigh themselves several times a day.

4. *The use of laxatives, diuretics, emetics, or diet pills.*

5. *Academic achievement.* This is a problem? In combination with the other symptoms, it may be. Anorexics and bulimics are into total control: over their bodies and their minds.

EMOTIONAL AND PERCEPTUAL SIGNS

1. *A distorted image of the body; denial.* Anorexics are convinced they're fat even when they may be skeletal. Bulimics may express a fear of becoming fat. Both are apt to deny that they have a problem, if questioned or confronted.

2. *Unclear thinking.* Starving people can't think straight.

3. *Dichotomous thinking.* Anorexics and bulimics tend to see the world in black-and-white terms. They may have trouble making decisions and choices.

4. *Taking everything personally.*

5. *Low or no self-esteem.*

6. *Low or no sense of self-control.*

7. *Perfectionism.*

8. *Concealing emotions—especially anger.* Fearing rejection, many anorexics and bulimics will "stuff" their anger.

9. *Classifying foods as "good" or "bad."* Over time, more and more foods may be relegated to the "bad" list.

Writing in *Infants to Teens* (November 1984), Berget B. Jelinch, RN, LMFT, stresses that control plays a major role in eating disorders. "Children don't have control over too many things in their lives," she notes, "but they *can* control what goes in and out of their bodies."

Professionals recommend relaxing some of the control you may hold over your kids. Let them make choices. Encourage them to show their emotions, including the negative ones. Don't tell them how they feel; listen while *they* tell *you*. Give them room to move, to grow, to stretch their wings.

I'm convinced that we could reverse this terrible trend toward eating disorders by easing up on the pressure to be thin. As long as "thin is in," women especially are going to suffer. In a recent survey of 33,000 women, 75 percent reported that they felt "too fat" while 42 percent claimed that losing weight would make them happier than success at work, a date with a man, or hearing from an old friend.

There may be a new eating disorder on the horizon, one that won't be as confined to girls and women as anorexia and bulimia seem to be. A study reported in the *New England Journal of Medicine* reveals some troublesome findings. Fourteen children ages 9 to 14, mostly males, had limited their food intake so severely that their growth and sexual development were stunted. They were afraid of getting fat.

These were boys who, according to the study, had normal body images, did not abuse laxatives, and were not compulsive exercisers. What, then, was the common denominator? *Most came from families in which a high value was placed on thinness and in which there was conflict over meals.*

Add to this the fact that children and teens are constantly bombarded with messages from the media that are really adult-oriented. Models—even the youngest—are made up and dressed up to look and act older and more mature than they are. Kids don't stop to think about this; they just want to emulate their idols. They take such messages personally.

One message they *never* hear is that growing takes calories. Instead, they see already-skinny teens drinking diet soda on the beach. No wonder so many kids today conclude that calories are poison; no wonder our job as parents—to build those healthy bodies—is getting harder every day.

WHERE TO GET HELP FOR A TEEN WITH AN EATING DISORDER

- If your teenager exhibits some or all of the signs described above, *contact your doctor immediately*.

While neither anorexia nor bulimia is a brand-new disease, both are newly prevalent. Find out if your doctor is up-to-date on them. Has he or she seen and treated cases before? If not, request a referral to someone who has.

Most treatment today is delivered on an out-patient basis, although in-patient programs are commonly available in major cities across the country. Since eating disorders are often rooted in psychological problems, treatment usually involves counseling and may include family therapy.

Family therapy is recommended because food attitudes and body attitudes are usually developed at home. Researchers have discovered a number of cultural and familial patterns that are common to anorexics and bulimics. Usually food has been an "issue" in the family for years, or food has been equated with love. Doctors frequently find that the relationship between mother and daughter in particular needs work and healing.

- Contact one of the following national organizations, any of which can provide information and/or a list of treatment professionals who deal with anorexia and bulimia.

  - The American Anorexia/Bulimia Association, Inc., 133 Cedar Lane, Teaneck, NJ 07666. AA/BA has regional offices in several states (maybe yours). Send $2 for an information packet. (201) 836-1800
  - The National Anorexic Aid Society, Inc. (NAAS), 5796 Karl Rd., Columbus, OH 43229. Send $2 for an information packet. Or you may request information and referrals by calling (614) 436-1112.
  - The National Association of Anorexia Nervosa and Associated Disorders (ANAD), Box 7, Highland Park, IL 60035. ANAD is a self-help organization with chapters or groups in most states. Send $1 for an information packet or call (312) 831-3438.

- Check with your local mental-health association for other organizations or agencies in your geographical area.

- Educate yourself by reading about eating disorders. Look in your local library for books on the topic. There are several good ones available.

- Consider starting a support group. In New York, the mother of an anorexic child started a self-help group for parents and relatives called SPAN (for Supportive Parents of Anorexics and Bulimics). Often parents need help almost as much as their children. They feel guilty, confused, frustrated, and afraid.

If you have a child with an eating disorder, be sure to get help for yourself, too.

NINE

BUILDING YOUR KIDS' SELF-ESTEEM

Central to successful Fat-Proofing—or, for that matter, to successful living—is a sense of *self-esteem*. A child who lacks it is often unhappy and troubled. He or she may also be a prime candidate for obesity.

A child who feels worthless may overeat to cover up that feeling. A child unable to cope with the world may overeat to escape it. A child unsure of his or her own abilities and powers may overeat to prove that there's *something* he or she has control over.

Babies new to the world need self-esteem. Preschoolers need it. Grade-schoolers need it. Teenagers need it. Their self-esteem determines how they behave, how well they learn, how they get along with others, how they face problems and challenges, and the kinds of people they are both inside and outside.

Self-esteem is like our emotional "central nervous system." We don't function smoothly unless it's in tip-top shape. Jean Illsley Clark, author of *Self-Esteem: A Family Affair* (Winston Seabury/Harper & Row, 1978), calls self-esteem the very core of our beings. She writes:

> Positive self-esteem is important because when people experience it, they feel good and look good, they are effective and productive, and they respond to other people and themselves in healthy, positive, growing ways. People who have positive self-esteem know that they are lovable and capable, and they care about themselves and other

people. They do not have to build themselves up by tearing other people down or by patronizing less competent people.

Where do our children get their self-esteem? In the beginning, at least, from *us*, their parents. Later in life it's strengthened by teachers and peers and friends and neighbors, but only if *we* first plant the seeds in the rich soil of a healthy, supportive, nurturing home environment. Even after our kids grow up and become self-sufficient, our opinions of them remain critical to their sense of self. (How many of us—regardless of age—are *still* trying to please our parents, *still* trying to figure out how to win their praise, *still* wishing that we could be "better" children and more "worthy" of their love?)

How can you create an environment in which your kids' self-esteem will take root and thrive? According to the authors of the pamphlet "Our Children's Self-Esteem" (Network Publications, 1983), there are four "ingredients" essential to this process:

- We must accept our children totally (or almost totally) for exactly what they are.

- We must clearly define limits, and enforce them consistently and fairly.

- We must respect their individual actions within those limits, and give them latitude to take those actions.

The fourth ingredient may surprise you:

- We must have high self-esteem *ourselves*.

The responsibility for helping your kids to develop self-esteem is just as important as your other parental responsibilities. Nothing can take its place. The most nutritious foods, a closet full of clothes, piano lessons from age 4, a room full of toys, the best schools, and so on—the list can be endless—won't begin to fill the "hole" inside a child who does not like or value himself or herself.

There is no such thing as too much self-esteem. It's not the same as egotistical fat-headedness; as Jean Illsley Clark points out, "Positive self-esteem is not to be confused with self-centeredness . . . being a braggart, or acting superior, all of which are attempts to hide negative feelings of self." The child who boasts constantly and struts around being bossy is a scared, uncertain little kid inside.

Clark outlines the kinds of messages we shouldn't—and should—send our children:

"You are important as long as you act tough, accomplished, or 'smart'" is a negative, unhealthy central message around which to organize one's life. "You are a worthwhile person" is a positive, healthy message. "You are capable!" is an important message to offer children at every age. Telling the baby he is clever for learning to call you by crying when he needs dry pants, complimenting a seven-year-old for figuring out what to take with her to play with in the car, commending the sixteen-year-old for passing his driver's test are "You are capable" messages. The offerings change as the child grows, but the message remains the same—"You can do well."

SELF-ESTEEM-BUILDING TIPS

In 1984 I asked the readers of my *Practical Parenting Newsletter* to respond to the question, "How do you build your child's self-esteem?" Use their suggestions as jumping-off points for coming up with your own.

How will you know if they work? Children aren't modest; if something you say makes them happy, you'll know! Maybe they'll tell you; maybe they'll laugh; more likely they'll just beam.

- "We have started traditions to help our children realize their important place in the family. We enjoy celebrating birthdays especially. This spring when our little girl turns 3, we will show pictures and slides of her birth and of her first and second birthdays. We did this last year and she was so happy she cried tears of joy." (*Cheryl Sedlmeyer, Fort Wayne, IN*)

- "On each child's birthday I present him/her with a book of pictures from the preceding year, showing his/her growth and development with a little rhyme under each picture. My kids love their birthday books and want to hear me read them over and over." (*Janet Gift, Davis, CA*)

- "I never ask 'What's that?' about his artwork. Instead I ask him to tell me a story about it." (*Eileen Schanelklitsch, Havertown, PA*)

- "I consciously and consistently think to comment on what our children have accomplished or done right *daily*: 'You did your zipper all by yourself without getting frustrated.!' 'I liked the way you shared with Jason when he was over today.' Any little compliment helps." (*Jodi Junge Bryn, Athyn, PA*)

■ "We sing a lot about her, using her name in the songs." (*Joy Goldwasser, Denver, CO*)

■ "Compliments go a long way, especially when they overhear you telling your spouse or another adult about something they did or said." (*Cynthia Wagner, Montebello, CA*)

■ "I always tell Jamie (3) what a lucky day it was for Mommy and Daddy when he was born." (*Linda Newberry, Jermyn, PA*)

■ "Every night at bedtime I tell my son how much Daddy and I love him. I also tell him that he is a good person and we will always like and love him. Sometimes he does things we don't like, but we always like *him*." (*Mona Hanlin, Hartland, WI*)

■ "I tell my sons regularly how much I like being with them, because I do! They are great people and they make me laugh." (*Nancy Wrather, Los Angeles, CA*)

■ "We use definite statements about actions: 'You jumped high.' 'You brushed your teeth before you were told.' This is recommended in *Between Parent and Child* by Dr. Haim Ginott." (*K. Darnell, Hueytown, AL*)

When Barbara Woodhouse says, "There is no such thing as a bad dog," we believe her. Why do some parents have such a hard time accepting that there is no such thing as a bad child? A child can deal with changing his or her actions; changing his or her *self* is another proposition entirely, and an impossible task.

If you *must* criticize, soften it by giving your child a compliment before and after. And let your kids know that it's okay to make mistakes, too, and that mistakes—even Mom's and Dad's—show people ways to learn and improve.

Just as words can build and strengthen a child's sense of self-esteem, they can also bruise or shatter it. As one mom wrote, "My mother was fond of labels: 'You're stupid,' 'you clumsy idiot,' etc." Often the words that slip off our tongues so easily go straight to our children's hearts.

Another way to help kids learn self-esteem is by *letting them make choices*. You can start doing this at a very early stage in their development— as soon as they start understanding the language. The trick lies in *structuring* their choices. One mom I know used to tell her toddler, "It's bedtime now.

Do you want to walk up the stairs by yourself, or do you want me to carry you up?" Bedtime was a fact and not open to negotiation, but the child could decide how he wanted to get there!

In my book *Practical Parenting Tips for the School Age Years* I devoted an entire section to developing self-esteem, with special emphasis on showing respect to children. Here are some of the suggestions offered there:

- Don't reserve "please," "thank you," and "I'm sorry" for adults.

- Don't belittle your children, and correct or punish them in private, when you can, to help them save face.

- If you expect your children to knock at your closed door and wait for an invitation to enter, extend the same courtesy to them.

- Ask your children's permission before borrowing their things, as they must before borrowing yours.

- Take the time to introduce your children to others, as you do for adults.

- Let even very young children participate in family councils. Listen to them, and try to adopt their suggestions somehow.

And some I'm saving for the next revision:

- Don't interrupt your children when they're speaking. Even if a story threatens to go on forever, it won't.

- Allow your children to finish things they've begun, even if it means waiting for them. Why should your schedule always take precedence?

- Give them their privacy. Don't open their mail, don't read their diaries, and, unless you suspect a serious problem (such as drug use), don't go through their stuff.

If you want to give your young kids "warm fuzzies" to enhance their self-esteem, read *The Original Warm Fuzzy Tale*, by Claude Stein ($7.95, Jalmar Press, 1977). Jalmar also publishes several other books for children in the area of self-esteem. Write for their catalog at: 45 Hitching Post Drive, Bldg. #2, Rolling Hills Estates, CA 90274.

THE BODY IMAGE BATTLE

One day when Dana was 8, she came home from school and announced that she wouldn't be eating dinner. Why? Because she was afraid of getting "fat"!

I was furious—not with Dana, but with a society in which little girls become aware of (and unhappy with) their looks at an increasingly early age. Preteen "makeup" kits and seductive "kiddy" clothing are symptomatic of what I view as a growing sickness. Girls believe that to succeed they must be pretty, and to be pretty they must be thin (and even "sexy"). Who are their models? Models, actually—the ones they see on magazine covers, on billboards, in the ever-present TV commercials.

Numerous studies have shown that far more women than men are dissatisfied with their bodies, particularly their weight. They diet more, weigh themselves more, and describe themselves as fat more often. And many trace the beginnings of these feelings to their childhood. "I've always had a weight problem," "I've been fat ever since I was a little girl," "I was a fat baby, and I guess I just never grew out of it."

No wonder so many women hate their bodies; they've been practicing for years. And no wonder most of the people who suffer from anorexia nervosa and other severe eating disorders are women (90 percent, according to one study).

Society doesn't deserve all the blame. Parents play a significant role, too. Mothers who harp "Don't eat that; you'll get fat" are setting the stage for big problems down the road. Fathers who tease mothers about "letting themselves go" are making it known that thin is appealing and anything else is second best.

Many children become obese not because they eat too much but because they exercise too little, and once again most of the victims are girls. Boys are expected to be active; girls are expected to be polite, and stay clean, and not make noise. As I noted earlier, girls outnumber boys in the fat-kids league after about age 11, and lack of activity is a major cause. (In chapter 10, I'll talk about how to get kids of *both* sexes moving.)

Although it's tough to counter the enormous pressures of society, there are things you can do at home:

- If you have both boys and girls, don't assume that only the boys will be athletes.

And when your daughter does become involved in competitive sports, don't preface every track meet or softball game with, "Be careful!"

- Pay attention to how you speak to your children. Do you find yourself saying, "You're such a pretty girl," versus "You're such a good boy"? Try to keep your praises—and scoldings—non-gender-specific.

One of my friends remembers what happened whenever she and her brother—both pianists—gave recitals as children. People would come up to them afterward and say to her, "Miriam, what a beautiful dress! How lovely you look!" Then they'd turn to her brother and say, "Terry, how well you played!"

- Don't assign tasks according to gender. Girls can take out the garbage; boys can set the table. Girls can mow the lawn, boys can sweep the floors. And both girls *and* boys can—and should—help with meal preparation and cleanup.

- **Never** warn your child away from certain foods by saying they're "fattening." And **never** call an overweight child "fat."

Girls in particular need to be taught self-esteem for who they are and what they do, not how they look. They need to be praised for their character and achievements, not just their appearance. Maybe you can't change society, but you can monitor—and modify—your own casual habits. It takes practice, but it can be done.

Fathers must help, too. Most dads I know treat their sons and daughters very differently. They slap their sons on the back, challenge them to arm-wrestling contests, and toss footballs back and forth with them, while behaving as if their daughters are made of glass. An athletic son is "a chip off the old block"; an athletic daughter is a "tomboy."

Old habits and attitudes are hard to break, and both parents must work together. The sooner you start, the more likely it will be that *all* of your children grow up liking themselves.

BUILDING SELF-ESTEEM IN THE OVERWEIGHT CHILD

In chapter 1 I described some of the problems fat children face. In addition to the physical hazards—including a propensity for life-threatening diseases—there are numerous psychological and emotional ones. Not the least among these is the fact that their parents are often ashamed of them.

Fat kids often see themselves as failures. If their parents don't like them, who will? Are their parents echoing this judgment against them? Fat kids often regard themselves as unable to control their lives. Are their parents reinforcing this sense of powerlessness and fear?

Even the most loving and well-meaning parents can unwittingly do great harm to their overweight children. Instead of building their self-esteem, they break it down. The child's life becomes a litany of criticisms: "I think you've had enough to eat," "You're getting fat," "It's time to buy you new clothes again; you're bursting out of those," "Don't be a pig," "Pull in your stomach," "You're a bottomless pit," "Just look at you—you look *awful*." And on and on, day in and day out.

Nobody needs self-esteem as badly as a heavy child does. The best way to get in touch with this need is to think back to the days when you were overweight, if you ever were (maybe you still are!). How did *you* feel? What was it like when *your* parents criticized you?

Very young children don't even know what being fat means. They haven't yet gotten the message from society that thin is in and bones are beautiful. But they can sense when their parents disapprove of them, and it's shattering.

School-age children are particularly vulnerable to the cruelty of their classmates. We know how fat children counter teasing from others; they learn to make fun of themselves. And this drives their self-esteem lower and further compounds the problem. To effectively bring about any major change in ourselves, we must start with a powerful sense of self-esteem— the conviction that we're strong enough to succeed. The overweight child stands little chance of developing this inner motivator.

Teenagers are in such turmoil already that obesity may propel them into extremely self-destructive behaviors, including severe eating disorders. The hormonal roller-coaster they're riding, combined with brand-new social pressures, can be too much to bear. Suddenly it's more important than ever to "look good"—to be popular, to attract members of the opposite sex, to wear the "right" clothes. Because overweight teenagers don't fit in, their self-esteem plummets further.

Helping a fat child build self-esteem takes extra effort and an especially delicate touch. Here are some tips to get you started:

- **Never** make fun of your child for being overweight. This only increases his or her shame and guilt.

- Resist the temptation to offer nagging "helpful hints." ("Why not have half a piece of pie instead of a whole one?" "Don't you think that dress would look better without a belt?") This can only increase the child's resistance.

- Don't draw unfavorable comparisons between your fat child and other children in your family. ("Your brother is three inches taller than you and weighs less!" "How come your sister can eat as much as you do and still stay slim?")

- Don't give the child special treatment. Unless your doctor instructs you otherwise, for example, don't prepare meals for him or her that are different from those the rest of the family eats.

If you're preparing healthful, balanced meals for your family, then they're equally suitable for your overweight child. The child doesn't need to eat "other" foods. Instead, he or she needs to eat *less* of what everyone else is having—and exercise *more*.

- Plan physical activities that the whole family can participate in without leaving the fat child out or behind. Start with walks rather than bike rides if the child is very out of shape. The point is to *include* the child in the family.

- Help your child set weight-management goals that are realistic and easy to achieve. Even a small success can give him or her the confidence to attempt the next goal.

- Watch what you say to others in front of the child or in the child's hearing. Make sure that if you're talking about the child you're saying something positive.

- Let your child know that you love him or her, whether heavy or thin, and that your love is not conditional on weight loss.

Most of all, remember Fat-Proofing rule 4: "Send your child the message, *'You're Okay.'*" This goes for the fat child, too. Accept the child for what he or she is. Show your love. Make it clear that your approval of him or her has nothing to do with weight or size or appearance.

As parents, we have tremendous influence over our children. Some think of it as the power to shape them; I prefer to think of it as the power to enable them to be whatever they can be. So much of their potential hinges on their self-esteem—how *they* see themselves, what *they* think they're capable of. And so much of their self-esteem hinges on how we treat them, what we say to them, and even how we look at them. If we love them, openly and honestly, it's that much easier for them to love themselves.

TEN

HOW TO GET YOUR KIDS MOVING

F itness is not only healthy—it's also fashionable. Jogging, bicycling, lifting weights, huffing and puffing on Nautilus machines, swimming, jumping up and down in aerobics classes—whatever; *everybody* seems to be exercising these days.

Everybody, that is, except our children.

In 1984, the Office for Disease Prevention and Health Promotion released the final report on a three-year National Children and Youth Fitness Study. Based on a survey of nearly 9,000 children, it yielded shocking results. Apparently our kids are in worse shape than ever before in our history. Boys and girls of the 1980s are significantly fatter than boys and girls of the '60s were. They don't measure up on tests of endurance and strength.

Other studies have revealed equally disturbing facts. In Texas, nearly half of the kids tested scored "poor to weak" in the 600-yard run. In Florida, kids scored lower on fitness tests than their older brothers and sisters did nine years ago. In California, more than a third of the children participating in pilot aerobics programs couldn't do ten minutes of exercise. Nationwide, some 4 percent of all elementary-school children have high blood pressure, 10 to 20 percent have elevated blood fats, and 25 percent are overweight and can't pass a fitness test. Over 60 percent have at least one risk factor for heart disease, while 36 percent have two or more.

It's not only their bodies that are affected. When children in one Canadian school were given time each day for vigorous exercise, their language and math test scores rose right along with their fitness levels. When kids in Michigan underwent a three-year fitness program, their self-esteem improved measurably. They felt better about themselves and about life in general.

We grownups have been pursuing our "perfect bodies" and leaving our kids behind. While we're watching our weight, they're watching TV. While we're running around the block, they're walking to the refrigerator. While we're bending and stretching, they're sitting or sleeping.

Plus, in schools with dwindling budgets, physical education programs are often among the first to be cut or cut back. A paltry 36 percent of the kids included in the National Children and Youth Fitness Study were found to have daily gym classes. And the kinds of exercise they're getting don't promote physical fitness. Team and competitive sports and informal games don't do it. Running, swimming, bicycling, and walking are what count; these are the kinds of exercise that contribute to cardiorespiratory (heart-lung) health and start kids on a lifelong fitness program.

About ten years ago, we bought a good sized, round trampoline for our children. I was worried about safety because of some stories I had read. The reported accidents were actually about serious gymnasts and not backyard bouncing. This trampoline was probably the best "toy" we ever bought. Not only has it been a healthful addition to Dana's and Doug's lives, but it became a social center for other children. Other backyard items—from jungle gyms to sandboxes—also encourage large muscle action.

A commitment to Fat-Proofing involves a commitment to *regular* exercise and lifetime fitness. Fat-Proofing means moving more than your mouth!

As you lead your child toward making this commitment, keep these tips in mind:

- **Don't** talk about your child's body image. Say, "Exercise is fun, and it makes you feel good," not, "Exercise will make you look good" (**especially** not, "Exercise will make you prettier"). Even "Exercise will give you a better body" is the wrong approach. (Kids hear that and think, "What's wrong with the body I've got?")

- Don't nag or bribe your kids to exercise. Instead, make it so much fun they won't be able to resist.

- Help your child find enjoyable physical activities that aren't too difficult, or for that matter, embarrassing.

- Don't preach—*do*. Instead of telling your kids to exercise, join them!

- Watch out for the messages you send. If you go off for your daily walk with a frown on your face or complain while you're doing your situps, your child will wonder if exercise is that great after all. And if you shun exercise entirely, so may your child. "Do what I say, not what I do" won't work.

- Don't push your child too far. Older children and adults may grasp the "no pain, no gain" theory, but younger kids won't willingly do something that hurts. (And they shouldn't have to.)

- Don't expect your kids to be athletes. Don't expect them to be perfect. Don't expect them to be graceful. In fact, don't expect them to be *anything* but themselves.

All kids make mistakes, and many little kids are clumsy. They'll fall down (partly because they think falling down is funny). They won't be able to follow a "beat." They'll drop things. They'll step on themselves (and you). Now is the time to remind yourself how cute they are, no matter what.

- Take the need for exercise seriously, but don't *be* serious while exercising with your child. Leave room and time for giggle fits and silliness.

- Add a personal touch to "getting physical." Don't just do exercises side-by-side. Pats, strokes, hugs, and tickles are not only appropriate but required.

- Make exercise a *regular* part of your kids' lives, and yours. Once a week, just on weekends, or every third day won't be good enough. Schedule ten minutes in the morning, a half-hour after school—whatever you can fit in. Then stick to it!

- *Moderate*, habitual exercise is what leads to fitness. Low-level or sporadic exercise can actually stimulate your child's appetite and lead to overeating, while exercise that's too strenuous and demanding can lessen the appetite and cause a different set of problems.

By the way, active kids do require more calories than inactive ones, so don't be surprised if your kids eat more than they used to—without putting on excess weight. In fact, you'll have more opportunities than ever to feed them the nutrients they need!

IT'S NEVER TOO SOON TO START: EXERCISING YOUR BABY

By age 5, your child will have developed virtually *all* the primary motor skills he or she will ever have. Strength, flexibility, balance, and coordination should come early—and you can help by exercising with your baby. You can start a regular "program" as soon as the second month after birth.

Again, the benefits are many and can last far into the future. Through exercise, babies learn self-esteem and self-confidence. They become stronger and more flexible. Early body awareness can lead to a lifetime of physical fitness. And, as a bonus, the time you spend together strengthens the parent-child bond with a *nonfood connection*.

Here are some tips for exercising with baby:

- Always place the child on a clean, soft surface, such as a thick blanket or an exercise mat covered with a towel. Or try a pillow.

- Dress baby comfortably—a one-piece jumper is best, or diapers alone if the air temperature is warm enough. Don't bother with shoes or sneakers. They get in the way, and they make it harder for you to tickle baby's toes.

- When face to face with your baby, maintain eye contact—and smile! When baby is on his or her tummy, talk reassuringly. Other options: singing, saying rhymes out loud, telling your baby how much you love him or her. Auditory stimulation is important, too.

- Keep your movements gentle, steady, and smooth, not jerky. Remember that you're far stronger than your baby; hold your strength in check.

- **Never** toss your baby into the air. And **never** shake him or her; excessive shaking has been linked to brain damage. Bouncing, swinging, and tipping are okay—but again, *be gentle*.

- Pay attention to your baby's reactions. Smiles, coos, and/or a relaxed body mean that things are fine. Frowns, tears, and/or stiffness or resistance signal that it's time to stop.

It's okay for an adult to play an hour's worth of tennis or repeat a set of weight-lifting exercises to the point of exhaustion. For a baby, though, exercise sessions should be short and mildly stimulating, not tiring. Five to ten minutes is long enough, with plenty of breaks between individual exercises.

The exercises you do with your baby should be *natural* extensions of movements he or she is already making. For example: Babies like to wave their arms around, so try holding his or her hands (let baby grasp your thumbs) and *gently* raising baby's arms above baby's head, then lowering them to baby's sides, then raising and lowering them again. Then alternate—right arm up, left arm down.

Or: Try a baby "bicycle." With baby lying on his or her back, grasp baby's feet and *gently* push them up toward baby's stomach, alternating right and left.

> One excellent source of many baby exercises is *Suzy Prudden's Pregnancy and Back-To-Shape Exercise Program,* by Suzy Prudden and Jeffrey Sussman (New York: Workman Publishing Co., 1980). To order, send $7.95 postpaid to Workman Publishing Co., 1 W. 39th St., New York, NY 10018.

Grownups get to exercise with Jane Fonda and Debbie Reynolds. Why not videos for kids as well?

- *Tip Top! With Suzy Prudden* is available for two age groups, 3 to 6 and 7 to 10. Both are produced by Warner Home Video, 4000 Warner Blvd., Burbank, CA 91522. Write or call (818) 954-6000 for price information, or check with your local video sale or rental outlet.

- *Gymboree's Gymbo the Clown* and *ABC Fun Fit* starring Mary Lou Retton are both available from Lorimar. Write Lorimar Home Video, 17942 Cowan Avenue, Irvine, CA 92714, or call (800) 325-5275.

WHAT ABOUT SWIMMING?

Parents and professionals alike are divided on the subject of whether infants should be taught to swim. People tend to think that infant swimming classes are either wonderful or terrible. Babies react differently, too; some loathe the classes, some love them. Some learn to love them if the parents persist, and some are miserable no matter what their parents do.

A lot of parents take their babies to swimming classes for water-safety reasons. But Dr. James G. Garrick, director of the Center for Sports Medicine in San Francisco, claims that there is no evidence that infant swimming classes reduce the number of drownings among children.

So, what should *you* do? That's up to you—and your child. If you think swimming classes are important, then by all means try them. (Eventually your child *should* learn how to swim, and it may be easier to start earlier rather than later.)

- Don't *push* your baby if he or she really doesn't like the classes. (Warning signs: crying, stiffness, startled movements.) Your baby will end up fearing or disliking the activity—and maybe even lose trust in you.

- Don't get caught up in wanting your baby to "achieve." Simply relaxing around all that water is quite an achievement in itself.

- Use common sense. Make sure that the pool (or pond) is clean and the water temperature is sufficiently warm. Avoid sudden temperature changes. And stay in water you can stand upright in.

- Don't overdo it. One to three thirty-minute sessions per week are plenty.

- This is no time to "surprise" your baby by suddenly dipping him or her under the water. Be gentle and calm and keep your movements slow, smooth, and reassuring.

Most important: **Never leave your baby alone in or around the water, not even for a second.** In fact, don't even take your eyes off him or her. Babies have been known to drown in very little water.

You don't have to start with official swimming classes, by the way. There's a "pool" in your house—maybe you call it the bathtub. Babies can lie on their backs in shallow water, pour water over their heads, dip their faces in, splash, and kick, all skills they'll later use in swimming.

The "never leave your baby alone" rule goes for the tub, too. Doug and Dana never knew what it was like to bathe in privacy until they were 4—and then I kept the bathroom door open and stayed within earshot.

EXERCISING WITH TODDLERS AND PRESCHOOLERS

Kids this age have so much energy they almost glow. They're constantly on the move and into everything. Exercise is not only good for them—it may also divert them from other, less desirable activities (like going through your bureau drawers) by helping them to blow off steam.

Toddlers and preschoolers are capable of so many things—running, jumping, climbing, bending, stretching. They're eager to please, and they're intensely aware of the sights of the world around them. They have great imaginations and they're terrific mimics. You can use all of these characteristics to your advantage when planning exercise.

- One thing young kids *don't* have is a lengthy attention span. Avoid cramming too many different activities into a single session, and quit when they're tired (or in the mood to go on to something else).

- Turn exercises into games. Have the kids pretend they're animals, objects, or their favorite cartoon characters.

- Be encouraging and supportive, not pushy or demanding. It's okay if the session is a dramatic (or comedic) performance; it shouldn't, however, be a physical performance where the kids are expected to do everything "right."

- Be flexible. Let them run the show from time to time, deciding what to do and when.

- Allow for self-expression. Hissing, barking, making choo-choo noises, even shouting should all be permitted (unless baby brother or sister is asleep in the next room, in which case you might want to impose a ban on shouting).

- Enjoy! Tots are among the most delightful creatures on earth. They talk a mile a minute, they love to laugh, they'll try almost anything, and they're still cuddly besides. What more could you want?

If you have a spare room, a rec room, or a warm, dry area in your basement, consider designating it your "exercise room." It should have a thick, clean rug or mat for tumbling. Put an old mattress on the floor and cover it, and maybe the kids won't insist on jumping on *your* bed. Remove any and all furniture with sharp edges. Make some oversized pillows out of sturdy fabric (such as denim or corduroy) and pile them in a corner. Cut "doors" and "windows" out of big cardboard boxes. Add a minitrampoline, if you wish, but *never let a young child use it unsupervised*.

Kids don't really need a lot of special exercise equipment, as long as they have a safe space for somersaulting and stretching their legs. But if you feel like making the investment, you'll find plenty of products to choose from, including sturdy plastic indoor slides and tot-sized "jungle gyms."

KIDS' BOOKS ABOUT EXERCISE

Your local library should have some of these and others as well. Why not plan an excursion some Saturday afternoon? Spend an hour or two at the library, and allow your child to play an active part in choosing books to bring home. Then, instead of wasting Saturday evening in front of the TV, have a family exercise party!

- *Albert the Running Bear's Exercise Book,* by Barbara Isenberg and Marjorie Jaffe (New York: Clarion Books, a division of Ticknor & Fields, 1984). To order, send $4.95 postpaid to: Houghton-Mifflin, Wayside Rd., Burlington, MA 01803.

- *Calico Cat's Exercise Book,* by Donald Charles (Chicago: Children's Press, a division of Regensteiner Enterprises, 1982). To order, send $3.95 postpaid to: Children's Press, 1224 W. Van Buren St., Chicago, IL 60607.

- *Exercise—What It Is, What It Does,* by Carola S. Trier (New York: Greenwillow Books, a division of William Morrow & Co., 1982). To order, send $9.25 postpaid to: Greenwillow Books, 105 Madison Ave., New York, NY 10016.

- *Healthkins Exercise!,* by Jane B. Moncure (Elgin, IL: The Child's World, 1982). To order, send $8.40 postpaid to: The Child's World, Elgin, IL 60121.

- *Hop, Skip, & Jump,* by Lucile Jones, edited by Bobbie J. Van Dolson (Hagerstown, MD: Review & Herald Publishing Association, 1981). To order, send $3.95 postpaid to: Review & Herald Publishing Association, 55 W. Oak Ridge Drive, Hagerstown, MD 21740.

MOVING TO MUSIC

Research has shown that adults find exercise more bearable and enjoyable—and less stress-inducing—when it's accompanied by music. (It also seems to go faster.) While exercise should never be a chore for young children, it stands to reason that music can make it even more fun.

Here are some records and tapes to try during your at-home exercise sessions:

- *Fit Kids: Volume 1 for Infants* (1 month to walking)

- *Fit Kids: Volume 2* (for walking to 3 years). Includes "The Freeze Game" and ten other stretching, shaking, clapping, and rolling activities.

- *Fit Kids: Volume 3* (for ages 3 to adult)

Check your local *quality* kids' toy store. Many are starting to carry records and tapes as well as toys.

- *Diaper Gym.* This is a collection of songs and activities for babies 6 weeks to 12 months.

- *It's Toddler Time.* These movement exercises for very young children focus on body awareness and self-image. Includes a guidebook by Carol Hammett and Elaine Bueffel.

Send $10.95 postpaid for each of the above to: Kimbo Educational, PO Box 477, Long Branch, NJ 07740.

- *Wee Sing & Play.* Circle games, jump-rope rhymes, ball-bouncing rhymes, and clapping rhymes help children develop coordination and rhythm skills. Includes a words-and-music book. Send $9.95 postpaid to: Price, Stern, Sloan, 360 N. La-Cienega Blvd., Los Angeles, CA 90048.

- *Fun Fit: Workout for Kids* stars Olympic gymnast Mary Lou Retton and includes a 16-page instruction booklet. Send $6.99 postpaid to: Mosaic Records, 220 Central Park South, New York, NY 10019.

If you've got older kids at home—kids with their own record collections—ask them to make you a tape of "music to move to." (Plus, you'll learn more about the kinds of music they listen to.)

JOIN THE CROWD

If you grew up in a small town or a suburb, you probably spent many afternoons and weekends (and whole summers) free to go pretty much wherever you chose. More moms stayed at home then, ready to handle emergencies and lend an eagle eye to goings-on. It seemed safe to let kids take off on their own, knowing that plenty of neighbors with open-door policies were close at hand.

But times have changed, and parents—especially parents of city kids—are justifiably wary of allowing their children to leave the house unattended. If you live in the city, you may not even know your neighbors, and if you do it's almost a given that the moms are in the workforce, too. And we've all heard too many horror stories about kids getting snatched out of playgrounds and backyards.

Does this mean that your children must be housebound? Not at all. It *does* mean that you as a parent have to get more involved in planning and scheduling occasions when your kids can be active.

Fortunately, many communities offer exercise and fitness programs that cater to young children. These range from gymnastics-type exercises to games; some include at-home plans for between lessons.

Not only are these outings fun for kids; they also give parents the chance to meet other moms and dads who are equally dedicated to making exercise a regular part of their family lifestyle. Plus, they offer *safe* options that address children's genuine need to be active. (The alternative is letting them bounce off the walls or jump on the beds.)

- Check with your local YWCA or YMCA. Many offer a program called *Exercises for Baby and Me* for mothers, infants, and even fathers.

Children usually aren't welcome at health clubs—except in the "baby-sitting room"—but the Y is famous for its open arms. Programs include gymnasium and dance activities for preschoolers, a National Gymnastic Program at eight levels, noncompetitive or low-level competitive team sports and games, and a National Aquatics Program for teaching swimming. Some even offer training for tykes in the martial arts.

- Don't forget your municipal recreation department or park board. Find their number in the *white* pages of your telephone directory, listed under the name of your county.

- A local university with a child-development program may offer some excellent opportunities or suggestions.

The fitness craze has also resulted in franchised "kiddy health clubs," with facilities and programs designed specifically for children. Here are four you may want to look into.

GYMBOREE

Founded in California in 1975, the Gymboree program is the largest of its kind, with centers all across the United States. Based on a philosophy of parent-child sharing, it's designed to develop early-learning physical fitness, confidence, and socialization skills in kids ages 3 months to 4 years.

Each center has over forty pieces of kid-sized play equipment—from fabric tunnels for scampering through, to hollow plastic balls to roll in, and an enormous parachute to crawl under. Classes are usually offered weekly for an hour each.

Gymboree: Giving Your Child Physical, Mental, and Social Confidence Through Play, by Joan Barnes and Susan D. Astor with Umberto Tosi (New York: Doubleday-Dolphin, 1981), tells you what to expect from the program. Look for a copy in your local library.

To find out about centers and classes near you, consult your phone book, or write Gymboree Corporation, 577 Airport Blvd., Suite 400, Burlingame, CA 94010, or call (415) 579-0600.

SPORTASTIKS

Beverly Hayasaki has degrees in child psychology and development; her husband, Yoshi, has won twenty-five national gymnastic championships. Together they've founded Sportastiks, an exercise program designed for age groups ranging from toddlers to young adults.

For preschoolers, the goal of the program is recreational. Kids enjoy exercising while they learn to safely use sports equipment such as trampolines and exercise bars. Older children are taught specific gymnastics skills, and upper-level classes focus on the competitive skills needed for world-class gymnastic events.

Currently Sportastiks has fifty licensed pilot programs in twenty-three states across the country and has six franchises in operation to date. For more information, write Sportastiks, 510 S. Staley Road, Champaign, ILL 61821, or call (217) 352-4269.

PLAYORENA

According to Playorena founder and former nursery school teacher Susan Astor, "Play is a child's work." At Playorena, specially designed equipment helps children develop balance and coordination. Padded stairs, tunnels, ladders, slides, tot-sized trampolines, and "parachutes" offer opportunities for creeping, crawling, running, and jumping and, above all, for parents and children to have fun together. Fourteen-week sessions are offered for "pre-crawlers," "crawlers," "toddlers" and "runners."

Currently Playorena has franchised locations across the country. For more information, write Playorena, 125 Mineola Ave., Roslyn Heights, NY 11577, or call (516) 621-7529.

THE DAYCARE DILEMMA

Many kids today spend anywhere from six to ten hours every weekday being cared for by someone other than their parents. If you're a working mom, you can't personally supervise or participate in the exercise your child is getting during the daycare hours—but you can make sure that exercise is a regular part of each day.

- When interviewing prospective daycare providers, find out what arrangements are made for scheduled activities and free-play time.

Is there space for kids to stretch their legs, crawl, run, and climb? Is there a fenced-in yard with play equipment? If so, check it out—and look carefully at the equipment available. It should be clean, sturdy, and safe.

How much time is given to activities and free play? Ideally, kids should have an hour mid-morning and another hour in the afternoon to work off their energy reserves. They should be *outdoors* as much as possible, weather permitting. For rainy or very cold days, there should be an indoor space suitable for running, jumping, and playing group games.

- Are there special programs available that stress exercise and movement?

Many daycare centers offer lessons in dance, gymnastics, and/or swimming. Find out who's in charge; usually it's an outside provider, so ask for—and check—references. (Swimming lessons are usually given at the local Y by a qualified instructor.)

- What about field trips?

Do the kids take weekly neighborhood walks or treks to nearby parks or recreation centers? They should get out on occasion, and even a stroll through a local grocery store can be both educational and energy-releasing.

Before deciding on a daycare provider or center, you should spend a day observing what goes on. If possible, bring your child so he or she can participate. See firsthand what the kids do on their own and under direction from the teacher. They shouldn't be totally exhausted by the end of the day—but neither should they be full of pent-up energy.

Incidentally, sports at this age should be strictly *noncompetitive*. Everyone should have the chance to participate equally, and there shouldn't be any "stars." Competition will enter the picture soon enough, as your child starts primary school. For now, what's important is that he or she learn to play together with other children.

TREASURE CHEST

Many daycare centers and Family Life educational programs in schools around the country are using a program called "Treasure Chest." Designed by the American Heart Association, it provides 3-to-5-year-old children with basic health education and exercise. Kids learn how the heart works in the body and are introduced to basic health concepts, including the importance of nutrition. It's a hands-on program with brightly colored wall charts, filmstrips, a teacher's guide, a board game, and children's recipe cards.

"Treasure Chest" has proved very popular because it's easily incorporated into existing curricula. Volunteers from the American Heart Association are available to provide instruction to teachers. To find out more, contact your local American Heart Association branch—and then pass the information on to the director of your child's daycare center.

FITNESS FOR THE SCHOOL YEARS

The results of the National Children and Youth Fitness Study brought home a very important point: We can't rely on the schools to meet our kids' exercise needs. True, there are exceptions—some schools place high priority on physical fitness as well as intellectual growth—but too many neglect this essential part of our kids' education. Only *one child in three* participates in a daily program of physical education, some schools with overburdened budgets are considering dropping their PE programs, and others have no programs at all.

Is PE important? Consider that it's the *only* subject that focuses on the complex organism that houses and supports the mind. There's truth to the old saying "a strong mind in a strong body."

What can you as a parent do? You can find out about the PE program at your child's school. And if it doesn't measure up, you can take action.

PRESIDENT'S COUNCIL PERFORMANCE CHECKLIST

Yes No

☐ ☐ Physical fitness is not a part-time thing. Does your school provide at least one period per day of instruction in vigorous physical activity?

☐ ☐ Play alone won't develop physical fitness. Is a part of each physical education period devoted to activities like running, calisthenics, agility drills, and weight training?

☐ ☐ Skill in sport is a valuable social and health asset. Does your school program offer instruction in lifetime sports like tennis, swimming, golf, skiing, and jogging?

☐ ☐ Most physical problems can be alleviated if discovered early enough. Does the school give a screening test to identify those students who are weak, inflexible, overweight, or lacking in coordination?

☐ ☐ All children can improve with help. Are there special physical education programs for students with special problems, such as the retarded, the handicapped, and the underdeveloped?

☐ ☐ Testing is important to measure achievement. Are all students tested in physical fitness at least twice a year?

(Source: Physical Education: A Performance Checklist President's Council on Physical Fitness and Sports, Washington, D.C.)

- Start by requesting a thorough description of the program.

How frequently are classes scheduled, and for how long? How is the time spent—what do the kids do? What's emphasized most, competition or teamwork?

- Arrange to observe some PE classes.

Does it appear that the kids are having fun? Or is PE a bore—or a strain? Is "extra" exercise used as a punishment? (Many adults I know remember having to run additional laps around the playing field after committing some sort of infraction. They grew up *hating* gym class.)

Once you have the facts, rate your child's PE program according to the Performance Checklist prepared by the President's Council on Physical Fitness and Sports.

What if you don't like what you learn? Start by finding out what your local school code and state laws or regulations say about physical education. Then arrange a private conference with the PE teacher. Take this opportunity to voice your concerns in a nonthreatening, nonhostile way. Remember that the teacher is a trained and experienced professional; he or she will be more responsive if you treat him or her with respect.

If that doesn't get results, go to the school principal. Be specific about the concerns you have, but *don't* focus solely on your child and his or her needs (unless there's a special problem in that area). And be prepared to compromise.

If that proves insufficient, bring the matter up with your Parent/Teacher Association (PTA) or Organization (PTO). In many schools today, parents groups have clout, and you may be able to effect genuine change by working together.

Finally, if push comes to shove, talk directly to your school board or superintendent of schools. It's possible that district-wide policy changes are needed.

If your school and district are doing all they can, then you'll have to take full responsibility for your child's fitness. For additional information or help in setting up a program of vigorous physical activity for your child, write the President's Council on Physical Fitness and Sports (see following box). Start by requesting a copy of their free publication, "Youth Physical Fitness," which describes fitness programs for kids ages 4 to 18.

Incidentally, any school or youth group with a qualified physical education and/or physical fitness instructor can offer the prestigious Presidential Physical Fitness Award Program. Kids qualify by passing six tests: a sprint, an endurance run, an agility run, a standing long-jump, situps, and a test of arm and shoulder strength. Find out if your school participates in this program. If it doesn't—or if you simply want to know more about what it involves—write to the President's Council.

FIND OUT ABOUT FITNESS

The President's Council on Physical Fitness and Sports, 450 Fifth St., N.W., Suite 7103, Washington, D.C. 20001 (202-272-3421). The council provides a fitness test for students in kindergarten through 12th grade. School officials can send for a free manual that explains how to administer the test, and for certificates signed by the President for students who qualify for the President's Physical Fitness Award. In addition, schools can purchase award emblems for $1.25 each; sets of five decals cost $1.50. Forms for keeping personal fitness records as well as class and school fitness records cost 10 cents each. A "Youth Fitness Manual" giving the history of the program costs $4.50. Students can send for a free booklet called "Get Fit," which suggests exercises to develop strength, flexibility and endurance.

Know Your Body, American Health Foundation, 320 East 43rd Street, N.Y., N.Y. 10017 (212-953-1900). This comprehensive health education program for students in kindergarten through eighth grade involves 35 to 50 hours of classroom instruction over a 20-week period. Participating schools receive teachers's guides, workbooks and "health passports," forms on which records are kept for individual students. An information packet is available for $2.50; the entire program costs between $25 and $50 per student.

Feelin' Good, Fitness Finders Inc., 133 Teft Road, Spring Arbor, Mich. 49283 (517-750-1500). The Feelin' Good program, for students in kindergarten through ninth grade, involves 20-minute classroom sessions devoted to health awareness two times a week and 30-minute workouts three times a week. Fitness Finders provides two days of orientation for classroom and physical education teachers in participating schools. The annual cost of classroom materials and student workbooks is between $4 and $8 per student.

FAMILY FITNESS

From a Fat-Proofing perspective, fitness is—and ought to be—a family affair. Especially as your kids get older, you can involve them in more activities that stress togetherness and family fun while encouraging the development of body skills and overall health.

Here are some suggestions for family activities; once you get in the swing, you're sure to come up with lots of your own!

- Hikes and bike rides. Contact your state tourism department for information on the best and most interesting trails.

- Family skiing lessons.

There aren't any hills near your home? Then try cross-country skiing; it's great exercise and perfect for flat or rolling terrain.

It never snows where you live? Then go roller skating!

- Daily walks. Schedule these for after dinner, when there's a chance everyone will be around. I've found these times are perfect not only for working off calories but for talking with my kids. Set a pace that's not too slow to do any good, and not too fast to leave the little ones in the dust.

- Wrestling in the living room. If you have a nice soft carpet or rug, why not? Or move out to the backyard.

- "Beat-the-clock." Have the kids run around the house, or the block, or a tree.

- Dance. Have your kids teach you the latest steps they've learned.

- An active vacation. Plan yours to incorporate all types of physical activity—swimming, canoeing, hiking, climbing.

- Reward. A headset of one's own or a tape of a favorite musical group has been known to get many an adolescent walking or running. Why not make this a condition of purchase?

Once you form active habits with your kids, you'll feel better, look better, and probably live longer yourself.

WARNING: ADVERTISING CAN BE HAZARDOUS TO YOUR HEALTH

With fitness catching on in our culture, it's no surprise that so many advertisers are using it to get their point across. They know where the money is! Suddenly Americans are willing to pay high prices for the "right" club memberships, the "right" shoes, the "right" athletic clothing, and the "right" equipment for home use. Kiddy workout clothes are also becoming the rage.

Plus, consumers are falling prey to claims that certain foods can enhance performance, aid endurance, and so on. Let's explode some of those myths right now.

- Active people need more protein.

False! Regular exercise—not added protein—will improve physical performance.

- Active people need more vitamins and minerals.

False! The vitamin and mineral requirements of active people are about the same as those of sedentary people. Don't feed your kids supplements unless your doctor recommends them for some reason. If your kids are eating a healthful, nutritious diet, they're getting all the vitamins and minerals they need.

- Active people should eat salt tablets to replace the sodium lost through perspiration.

False! Too much salt is dangerous, and most of us already consume an excessive amount. Just drink a glass of water.

- Active people should turn to so-called "activity" or "athletes'" drinks as sources of fluid.

False! These drinks may contain large amounts of sodium and sugar. Plain water is still the best thirst quencher.

- Active people need the extra "lift" sugar provides.

False! Eating sugar may give you a rush, but it will also send you crashing. (You've probably seen the commercial where the sweaty soccer player munches on a candy bar during half-time. What the commercial doesn't tell you is that it takes twenty to thirty minutes before the energy from sugar becomes available to your muscles.)

- Active people should eat lots of meat before exercising.

False! Carbohydrates—bread, cereals, and pasta—are preferable.

Finally, do you really *need* to buy your kids special athletic clothes? Probably not. They should have loose, comfortable clothing that they can exercise in, but they don't have to have designer logos on them.

I would recommend, however, that you invest in good athletic shoes for your kids, particularly if you're planning to do a lot of running or walking. (Tots exercising indoors are better off barefoot.)

GIVE YOUR KIDS THE FITNESS TEST

If your kids are between ages 7 and 13, you can check their fitness yourself with five fitness tests developed by Dr. Charles T. Kuntzleman. Dr. Kuntzleman is an exercise physiologist in private practice at Fitness Finders, Inc., in Spring Arbor, Michigan, and national director of Living Well, Inc., in Houston, Texas. He is also the designer of a three-year "Feelin' Good" program in which 24,000 Michigan children participated.

The following is adapted from his article "How Fit Are Your Kids," *Shape*, December 1984.

TEST ONE: CARDIOVASCULAR ENDURANCE

Many physiologists believe that cardiovascular fitness is the most important kind. It's believed to reduce many of the known risk factors for heart disease, and it also boosts overall energy levels.

THE TEST

Have your child run and/or walk a mile as quickly as possible. (Measure the distance with your car odometer, or use a school running track; they're usually ¼ mile long, so your child will have to make four trips around it.)

Afterward, compare his or her time to the chart for boys or the chart for girls shown below. Find your child's time on the chart, in the column headed by his or her age; rankings are given at the left.

Exercises to improve your child's cardiovascular endurance include walking, jogging, swimming, dancing, and bicycling.

CARDIOVASCULAR TEST SCORES

BOYS

Age	7	9	11	13
Superior (95 +)	7:17	6:43	6:04	5:44
	8:06	7:17	6:50	6:11
Excellent (94–75)	8:35	7:29	7:19	6:22
	8:59	8:00	7:30	6:33
	9:18	8:22	7:48	6:42
	9:37	8:36	8:00	6:52
Good (74–50)	9:45	8:50	8:08	7:00
	10:04	9:02	8:21	7:06
	10:46	9:14	8:39	7:20
	11:10	9:30	8:56	7:20
	11:25	9:56	9:06	7:27
Fair (49–26)	11:44	10:24	9:25	7:40
	12:04	11:01	9:46	7:51
	12:44	11:25	10:10	8:02
	13:30	11:44	10:40	8:24
Poor (25–6)	14:30	13:18	12:10	10:56
	15:10	13:52	12:36	11:23
	15:27	14:22	13:16	12:20
	16:03	15:25	14:41	13:09
Very Poor (5–0)	17:44	16:42	16:56	14:55

GIRLS

Age	7	9	11	13
Superior (95 +)	7:58	7:21	7:07	6:20
	8:48	8:24	7:46	7:10
Excellent (94–75)	9:35	8:44	8:10	7:45

CARDIOVASCULAR TEST SCORES

GIRLS

Age	7	9	11	13
Excellent (94–75)	9:55	9:08	8:36	8:01
	10:27	9:31	8:57	8:12
	10:55	9:58	9:12	8:18
Good (74–50)	10:65	10:07	9:29	8:27
	11:24	10:17	9:44	8:41
	11:43	10:32	10:00	8:56
	12:03	10:56	10:16	9:14
	12:30	11:12	10:27	9:27
Fair (49–26)	12:55	11:29	10:56	9:37
	13:42	12:00	11:12	9:57
	14:05	12:20	11:29	10:12
	14:08	12:42	11:51	10:31
Poor (25–6)	14:30	13:18	12:10	10:56
	15:10	13:52	12:36	11:23
	15:27	14:22	13:16	12:20
	16:03	15:25	14:41	13:09
Very Poor (5–0)	17:44	16:42	16:56	14:55

(*SOURCE:* Lifetime Health-Related Physical Education Test Manual [*Reston, VA: American Alliance for Health, Physical Education, Recreation and Dance, 1980*])

TEST TWO: MUSCULAR STRENGTH

Muscular strength is important for supporting the back and preventing slouching, as well as for lifting and moving objects. It's also needed for athletic performance.

Exercises to improve your child's muscular strength include weight training, isometrics, isokinetics, and calisthenics.

Note: There's some question as to whether weight training is a good idea for young children. According to Larry R. Gettman, Ph.D., executive director of the Vita Center for Life Enrichment in Plano, Texas, *low-intensity* weight training won't do any harm. He recommends that beginners start with no more than 10 percent of the maximum weight they can lift at one time.

My advice is to check with your doctor before beginning a weight-training program for preadolescents.

THE TEST

Have your child perform the "No Cheating, Back Straight, Chin-to-the-Floor, Military Push-Ups" described in Kuntzleman's *The Beat Goes On* (Spring Arbor, Michigan: Arbor Press, 1980):

> Hit the deck! Face down. Get your hands directly under your shoulders. Legs straight! Now, slowly push yourself up until your arms are straight. Keep that back straight! Now, slowly return to the starting position. That's one. Now do as many as you can up to 25.

Your child's muscular strength is *good* if he or she can do 16 to 25 pushups.

Your child's muscular strength is *fair* if he or she can do 9 to 15 pushups.

Your child's muscular strength is *poor* if he or she can do 4 to 8 pushups.

TEST THREE: MUSCULAR ENDURANCE

Muscular endurance is needed to continue any activity over a length of time—including sitting with good posture. It also keeps your child from tiring too quickly during work or play.

Exercises to improve your child's muscular endurance include calisthenics, weight training, and aerobic exercises.

THE TEST

Have your child do the "Flat Belly's Favorite Exercise: The Curl-Up" described in *The Beat Goes On:*

> Lie on the floor with your knees bent and feet in front of you. Your hands should be interlaced behind your neck. Now slowly curl your-

self upward until your elbows touch your knees and then return to the starting position. Do as many as possible up to a maximum of 30.

Your child's muscular endurance is *good* if he or she can do 16 to 30 curl-ups.

Your child's muscular endurance is *fair* if he or she can do 9 to 15 curl-ups.

Your child's muscular endurance is *poor* if he or she can do 4 to 8 curl-ups.

TEST FOUR: FLEXIBILITY

Flexibility is needed to help avoid pulled and strained muscles. The more flexible your child is, the less risk that he or she will become injured as a result of physical activity.

Kids lose flexibility as they near the teenage years, so it's especially important to get them—and keep them—limber.

Exercises to improve your child's flexibility include slow, static—that means nonbouncing—stretching exercises. Each exercise should focus on a specific set of joints and/or muscles—lower back, abdomen, upper back, hamstrings, hip muscles, spine, arms.

THE TEST

You'll need a yardstick and some adhesive tape to perform this test. Have your child warm up ahead of time with some mild stretches. Then:

1. Have your child sit on the floor with his or her legs extended and heels about 5 inches apart. Put a line of tape along the floor where the heels are resting. (The heels should touch the near end of the tape.)

2. Put the yardstick on the floor between and parallel to your child's legs, with the 1-inch mark near your child's body and the 15-inch mark on the near edge of the tape line.

3. Have the child *slowly* reach with both hands as far forward as he or she can and touch the yardstick at that point. No jerking allowed! Note inch mark the child is able to reach.

4. Repeat three times, noting the inch mark each time.

Your child's flexibility is *superior* if he or she can reach 22 to 23 inches (boys) or 24 to 28 inches (girls).

Your child's flexibility is *excellent* if he or she can reach 20 to 21 inches (boys) or 21 to 23 inches (girls).

Your child's flexibility is *good* if he or she can reach 14 to 18 inches (boys) or 16 to 20 inches (girls).

Your child's flexibility is *fair* if he or she can reach 12 to 13 inches (boys) or 13 to 16 inches (girls).

Your child's flexibility is *poor* if he or she can reach 10 to 11 inches (boys) or 10 to 12 inches (girls).

TEST FIVE: BODY COMPOSITION

Is your child's body made up mostly of muscle or of fat? This test is one way to find out. (Try it on yourself. If you can pinch an inch or more, *you* need some toning up!)

THE TEST

Have your child pinch his or her upper arm above the outside of the elbow.

ELEVEN

CUTTING DOWN ON THE CULPRITS: SUGAR, SALT, AND FATS

N ow it's time to take a hard look at those everyday enemies of Fat-Proofing: sugar, salt, and fats. This trio is always hard to deal with because they make food *taste good*. It is hard to understand emotionally that foods that taste so good are not good for you. This is why we need to hear and understand the facts so we can make better-for-ourselves decisions.

THE TROUBLE WITH SUGAR

O n average, Americans consume 126.8 pounds of sugar per person every year—or a third of a pound a day. Its effects can be seen in the waistlines and thighs and stomachs so many of us lug around.

We *know* that sugar isn't good for us, yet we keep packing it in at an ever-increasing rate. Per capita consumption has gone up a pound a year for the past ten years.

We're eating more candy than ever before. According to the editor of a trade magazine for the candy industry, this upward trend is due in part to public demand for the "natural ingredients" in higher-priced candies, nuts, and fruit products.

Think for a moment about what's happened during the last few years to so-called natural snacks. Single servings of yogurt come with fruit and are sweetened with sugar to the tune of 6 teaspoons per cup. Today's granola bars are dipped in chocolate. (We've fooled ourselves for quite some time into thinking that commercial granolas are low in calories. Surprise: up to 30 percent of their weight may be in the form of sugar.) And candy by another name ("Carob Bar," "Natural Honey Bran Carob Bar") is still candy. The latest offender in your local market? Yogurt-covered raisins. These sweet treats taste just great, but yogurt has little to do with it. The main ingredient in the yogurt coating is—you guessed it—sugar, with some non-fat yogurt solids thrown in for good measure. Don't be deceived by healthful-sounding brand names or by the words *nutritious, high-protein*, or *healthful* splashed across the wrapper.

Even many medicines contain sugar. In other words, you have to watch *more* than what you eat. Sugar is used in numerous over-the-counter drugs. For example:

- Listerine Cough Drops, regular flavor, are 68 percent sugar

- Benylin Cough Syrup is 33 percent sugar

- many children's vitamins are 50 percent sugar—or more

In recent years a lot of us have been making a genuine effort to cut back on our sugar intake, usually by replacing a portion of it with saccharin or, lately, aspartame. And the sugar industry is fighting back with a series of sophisticated advertisements touting sugar as the "natural" sweetener.

Applying "natural" to most of the sugar we eat is stretching the point. Sugar may grow in the ground rather than in laboratory tanks, but by the time it reaches our sugarbowls, anything that's natural about it has been refined right out. (Plus, "natural" doesn't always mean "good for you." Salt is natural. Cholesterol is natural. Poisonous mushrooms are natural.)

We all know what sugar does to the teeth. Simply stated, tooth decay is caused by bacteria in the mouth that form sticky colonies of plaque that adhere to teeth. These bacteria convert sugars in the foods we eat into acids, and these acids dissolve tooth enamel and start the process of decay. A recent study compared the decay-causing potential of snack foods and determined that those with the highest cavity-causing potential were raisins, bananas, cake, french fries, doughnuts, cupcakes, and confectioner's sugar. Foods *least* likely to cause cavities were peanuts, gelatin dessert, corn chips, yogurt, and bologna.

What sugar does to the teeth is bad; but just what does it do to the body?

- It fills us with "empty calories"—16 per teaspoon, 48 per tablespoon—that contain virtually no useful vitamins or minerals. And when we're full of sugar, we don't eat the nutrients we need.

- There appears to be some evidence of a condition known as "sugar intolerance." Some people claim to have suffered dizziness and even temporary blindness as a result of eating sugar.

- It's easy to get "hooked" on sugar—a habit some experts equate with addiction to nicotine, caffeine, or alcohol. It may be even more insidious because it starts so much earlier in life.

Children don't start drinking coffee or beer or smoking cigarettes before they reach school age, but they do start consuming quantities of sugar—often with their parents' blessing. When we promise sweet treats in exchange for good behavior, we're helping our children get "hooked."

The signs are similar to those of other addictions: the sensation of craving, irritability when the need isn't satisfied, euphoria when it is. If you've ever responded to mid-afternoon slump by gulping a candy bar, you know what it's like. Suddenly the world looks rosier and you're full of energy.

Unfortunately, the "lift" is short-lived and is often followed by a sugar "crash"—a resurgence of the craving and the crankiness. That's because of the way sugar works once it enters the digestive system. It's absorbed very quickly, and almost immediately the blood-sugar level rises. This stimulates the pancreas to boost its production of insulin and bring the blood-sugar level back to normal. (By the way, insulin doesn't just lower blood sugar; it also stimulates the production of fat in fat cells.)

If the pancreas produces excessive amounts of insulin, hypoglycemia—a too-low level of blood sugar—may result. The signs of hypoglycemia, which strikes relatively rarely, include faintness, restlessness, headache, decreased attention span, shakiness, fatigue, and irritability. There may also be a connection between sugar intake and the onset of diabetes.

Even if you monitor your kids' intake, sugar still may account for one-third of the calories they consume each day. Much of the sugar our children eat is masked in processed foods—foods you may never suspect. There's sugar in crackers, in soups, in spaghetti sauce. Every tablespoon of ketchup contains a teaspoon of sugar. Bouillon cubes, cured meats, soups, and salad dressings have sugar in them.

If you're ever in doubt as to whether a particular packaged food contains sugar, *read the label*. Remember that the order in which ingredients are listed (which is strictly governed by federal regulations) reflects the quantities in which they're present. Whatever there's the most of is listed first, whatever there's the second-most of is listed second, and so on down to the relatively miniscule amounts of additives for preserving and coloring. In other words, if sugar is the second or third ingredient listed, watch out.

But even if you don't see the word *sugar* on a label, it may well be a main ingredient. Sugar has many aliases: corn sweetener, corn syrup, maple syrup, honey, molasses, and anything ending in "-ose"—glucose, sucrose, fructose, lactose, maltose. Some of these are processed rather than refined, but that doesn't mean they're any better for you. I first came to understand this when I put together my cookbook, *The Taming of the C.A.N.D.Y. Monster* (Bantam) in 1978. Refined sugar is our most prevalent food additive. Keep your eyes open for labels on which several types of sugar are listed; the single amounts may look insignificant, but this can be deceiving, since they may add up to a lot.

For example, the other day in the grocery store I studied the label on a box of Nabisco's Cinnamon Treats. Wheat flour was the first ingredient listed, followed by sugar, animal and vegetable shortening, and graham flour. Then came *five more* sugars—corn sweetener, honey, molasses, corn syrup, and dextrose.

How much sugar is added to the foods we buy in the grocery store?

Look down the side panel of practically any box of ready-to-eat cold cereal and you'll find some valuable information. What's listed, by grams, is the amount of "sucrose and other sugars" in one ounce of the particular cereal. Divide this number of grams by 30—the approximate number of grams in one ounce—and you have the percentage of added sugars by weight. For example:

CARBOHYDRATE INFORMATION

	Rice Krispies	
	1 oz. (28.4g)	with ¹/₂ cup whole milk
Starch and related carbohydrates	22g	22g
Sucrose and other sugars	3g	8g
Total carbohydrates	25g	30g

So, if your label lists 3 grams of sucrose and other sugars, it contains 10 percent added sugar.

$$5 \text{ grams} = 17\% \text{ sugar}$$
$$9 \text{ grams} = 30\% \text{ sugar}$$
$$12 \text{ grams} = 40\% \text{ sugar}$$

Select the gram number that is acceptable to you and then let your children decide on a good cereal choice—based on the number *they* read on the label.

Nutrition reporter Jane Brody recommends that you stick to cereals that contain less than 10 percent sugar. Some examples: General Mills' Wheaties; Kellogg's Special K; General Mills' Kix; Ralston-Purina's Chex cereals (Rice Chex, Corn Chex, Wheat Chex); General Mills' Cheerios; Nabisco's Shredded Wheat; and Quaker Oats' Puffed Wheat and Puffed Rice. She points out that most of these are brands we adults grew up with.

How can we keep our kids from getting hooked (or start them on the road to getting unhooked)? It's not easy—especially when the advertisements during so many children's programs scream **SUGAR,** and when so many of the foods their friends eat are loaded with it. But here are some Fat-Proofing tips you should find helpful:

- Replace your family sugarbowl with a "sugar shaker"—a screw-top saltshaker filled with sugar. If your kids are used to sugar on their cereal, this should help them to cut down on quantities simply because it takes a *long* time to shake out a teaspoon or two.

- The next time you go shopping, solicit your kids' cooperation in reading labels and rejecting heavily presweetened packaged foods. You may spend more time at the grocery store than you're accustomed to, but the learning experience will be worth it.

- Keep a supply of fresh fruits on hand. Replace that bowl of M&M's or Hershey's Kisses or Reese's Pieces with a bowl of whatever fruits are in season.

Your children may complain at first, but wait it out. The less refined or processed sugar they eat, the sweeter fruits will start to taste.

In many areas of the country today, you can buy all kinds of fresh fruits year-round (if you're willing to pay the price for berries flown in from New Zealand). Usually I buy whatever my local grocery store has plenty of. Sometimes, though, when it appears as if winter will never end (and in Minnesota one often gets that feeling), I'll splurge on a pint of imported strawberries or raspberries. And I can't wait for summer, when the first peaches start to appear.

At my house, we eat bushels of apples. They're great cut up into small pieces and scattered on cereal. They're tasty baked with a touch of cinnamon. Apples contain pectin, a fiber that may lower cholesterol levels in the blood. And you don't have to stick to the Red Delicious or Jonathon varieties. In Minnesota, where I live, there are several to choose from, especially in the fall—Firesides, Haralsons, Prairie Spies. Each has its own taste and texture. Try Granny Smiths in the winter, and don't be fooled by the fact that they're green. They're eminently edible.

Be creative in how you serve fruit, and your kids may be more receptive to it. Schedule an apple-tasting party for a crisp fall afternoon. Let the kids spear fresh pineapple pieces with colorful toothpicks. Serve honeydew with lime slices; squeezing lime over the melon gives it a brand-new flavor. Make a "rainbow" salad with fruits of many colors—orange cantaloupe, pink watermelon, green grapes, blueberries, red raspberries. Spread applesauce over whole-wheat pancakes instead of pouring on the syrup.

- If the fresh fruits you want aren't available, buy canned—but again, read the label.

"Packed in heavy syrup" is a red-flag warning that the contents are swimming in sugar. Look instead for fruits packed in water or their own juices, or wash the heavy syrup off before serving. Avoid dried fruits (raisins, dried apricots, figs, dates). Most of the water has been removed from these during the drying process, resulting in a far higher concentration of sugar per bite.

- For a winter pick-me-up, try frozen berries (once more, read the label and avoid the sweetened kinds).

- Another frozen favorite—green peas, straight from the bag!

- Here's a way to get your kids to eat unsweetened low-fat yogurt (it worked for me). Buy the large size, dump it into a bowl, and empty a bag of unsweetened frozen blueberries or strawberries over it. Let it sit overnight in the refrigerator. By morning the fruit will have melted, releasing much of its juice; mix it together and it's delicious (and colorful). You can even use it with cereal instead of milk by folding in some Rice Chex or Cheerios.

- Control the amount of sugar in baked goods—cookies, cakes, quick breads, pies—by preparing them yourself. You may be able to cut the sugar called for in the recipe by a fourth or even a third without noticeably affecting the taste.

In fact, you can do this with almost everything you make that's supposed to have sugar in it. Some types of herb teas (caffeine-free, of course) are delicious iced with only a hint of sugar.

- Keep a supply of "fruitsicles" in the freezer. You can buy plastic trays, complete with sticks, for this purpose. Use orange juice, unsweetened apple juice, cranberry juice, even grapefruit juice.

- Use a dash of vanilla flavoring or almond flavoring to sweeten if you've reduced the amount of sugar to a noticeable degree.

- Experiment with spices and herbs. Coriander, cinnamon, nutmeg, ginger, cardamom—any of these can make a dish taste sweeter without sugar. A vegetarian cookbook can be a good source of ideas.

- In terms of tooth decay, the amount of sugar eaten is less important than how often it's eaten—and in what form.

Chewy, sticky sweets like caramels are more cavity-producing than sodas because they linger in the mouth longer. Meanwhile, the sugar is interacting with the mouth's bacteria and producing acids that literally bore holes in the hard enamel of the teeth.

Make it a house rule that the kids must brush their teeth *every time* they consume anything with sugar in it, and they're apt to get so tired of the routine that they look for other snacks! Or insist that they follow every sugary treat with a glass of water.

- Stay away from sodas. They're nothing but sugar and flavoring— totally useless as far as nutrition goes.

Although this may take a while for your kids to accept, especially if they're soda drinkers, try buying six-packs of spring water.

Lately I've been experimenting with the flavored kinds, and some of them are quite good. There are several—lemon, lime, "citrus," even cherry and cola. To date the manufacturers haven't started adding sugar to those, so they still have zero calories (and most have zero sodium, too). It's important to keep reading your labels with water drinks, too. New York Seltzer, for one, adds fructose—a.k.a. sugar—but the package looks like similarly flavored mineral water.

What's the best way to wean your kids off a dependency on sugar? Simple: *stop buying products that contain it.* Out of sight, out of tummy. (Naturally occurring sugars—in fruits, for instance—make up only about 6 percent of the calories in our diets; 70 percent of the sugars we eat are added to or "hidden" in processed foods.) But do this gradually; making your family go "cold turkey" may cause more problems than it solves by calling attention to what you're trying to do.

Ask your friends and relatives to please stop bringing sweets when they visit. Check with your children's daycare providers or teachers to make sure that candies aren't offered as treats. And, whenever possible, serve fresh, unrefined foods rather than processed, packaged ones.

One mother I know started quietly waging a war against sugar as soon as her first child was born. Here's what she says:

> I decided early on that my son would not be a sugar addict. So we just never got in the habit of keeping sweets around the house. The sugar-bowl never sits on the table. We have fruit for snacks and dessert. I think my son is the only child I know who eats cereal without sugar. He thinks that's the way it's supposed to taste! I guess that's been the key: getting him used to the way foods taste on their own.

Of course your children will still eat some sugar—if not at home, then elsewhere. Don't get fanatical about it. Here's what another sensible mother says about how she handles the issue:

> I don't try to control what my kids eat when they visit their friends. I know they're drinking soda, eating cookies and candy, and even—help!—downing a Twinkie or two. But it's not my job to change other families' eating habits. So my kids come home full of sugar once in a while; big deal. I just point them toward their toothbrushes. However, when I learned that the gymnastics teacher at my daughter's school was handing out candies as treats after class, I put my foot down!

To satisfy a sweet tooth that won't take "no," try these substitutions:

- ½ cup of orange ice (70 calories), instead of ½ cup of chocolate ice cream (150 calories)

- 2 vanilla wafers (40 calories), instead of 2 chocolate-chip cookies (over 100 calories)

- 4 small or 2 medium-size graham crackers (55 calories), instead of 2 sandwich-type cookies (100 calories)

- 1 slice of angel-food cake, no frosting (130 calories), instead of 1 slice of frosted chocolate cake (400 calories—and a shocking *15 teaspoons* of sugar)

- 1 brownie, with nuts (90 calories), instead of 1 piece of ginger-bread (175 calories)

- 1 blueberry muffin (110 calories), instead of 1 slice of blueberry pie (285 calories)

- ¹/₂ cup of gelatin with fresh fruit added (80 calories), instead of ¹/₂ cup of vanilla pudding (140 calories)

- ¹/₂ banana blended together with 8 ounces of skim milk (about 140 calories), instead of 1 cup of chocolate milk (213 calories). Let the kids drink it while it's still foamy.

Although Fat-Proofing doesn't count calories, it pays to cut down on the "empty" ones that come in the form of sugar—if only to leave room for the healthful, nutritious foods your growing kids need.

Now let's consider the "natural" alternatives to refined white sugar. Basically, they're not what they're cracked up to be. Brown sugar is brown because it's colored with molasses, not because it's any better for you. Raw sugar may be unrefined, but it's still sugar. Honey, a pure sugar, at least is a whole food; no chemicals are used to produce it.

In general, sugar by another name is sugar just the same. It promotes tooth decay (here's where honey is worse than refined sugar, because it sticks to the teeth); it ups your calorie intake (without satisfying your hunger); and it may be connected to a number of illnesses; some researchers even relate it to heart disease. The bottom line is, the more sugar you eat, the more you want—and the more hooked you become. The world is full of "sugarholics."

Fat-Proofed children may not give up sugar altogether, but they know not to binge. They regard sugar as an occasional treat, not as an essential ingredient in their diets. And that's a healthy attitude.

A SUGAR PRIMER

Glucose (or dextrose) is naturally present in many fruits and in the starches of such vegetables as corn. It is the main blood sugar in our bodies.

Fructose, a fruit sugar, is the sweetest of sugars. In cold drinks and foods it tastes sweeter than sucrose, but at room temperature or in hot foods the taste is comparable.

Sucrose—table sugar—is the most abundant sugar in the plant kingdom and has a long history of use and refinement. It's 50 percent each fructose and glucose, chemically bonded together, and supplies about 4 calories per gram.

Raw sugar is partially refined sucrose, which still contains dirt and plant debris. Table sugar is cleaner and safer.

Brown sugar is table sugar covered with a film of molasses syrup; it's 91 to 96 percent sucrose.

Powdered sugar is table sugar ground into fine crystals. It's usually mixed with about 3 percent starch to prevent caking.

Maple sugar is made by cooking down sap from maple trees. It's almost entirely sucrose.

Honey is a natural syrup that varies in flavor and composition, depending on where the bees who make it live and what they eat, how it's processed, and how long it's stored. It is made up mainly (about 40 percent) of fructose, plus glucose, maltose, and sucrose.

Corn syrup is derived from corn starch. It's composed mainly of glucose and a variety of maltose sugars. Corn syrup is not very sweet, so it's often used in conjunction with other sugars. It has replaced sucrose in commercial brewing, soft drink, canning, and pet food production.

High fructose corn syrup (HFCS) is made from corn starch in which the fructose content has been increased by an enzymatic process. It's sweeter than conventional sugar, and less expensive than fructose. (Don't confuse this sugar with plain fructose.)

Sugar alcohols (polyols) are chemically reduced carbohydrates that include sorbitol and mannitol. These sweeteners don't contain glucose, but they have the same number of calories as other sweeteners. They are broken down more slowly and have been shown to lower dental cavity potential. These are the sugars used in many so-called sugar-free products.

WHAT ABOUT ARTIFICIAL SWEETENERS?

The fact that Americans in general have a giant sweet tooth is evident from the perpetual search for the "perfect" artificial sweetener.

Remember cyclamate? Widespread during the 1960s, it was banned by the FDA in 1970 because it was believed to be carcinogenic (cancer-causing). The furor that caused was nothing compared to what happened when the FDA tried banning saccharin, a petroleum derivative, in 1977. Consumers and scientists made such an uproar that Congress put a series of moratoriums on the ban, and saccharin is still being marketed—and studied. (It was banned in Canada.)

Products containing saccharin must now bear a "use of this product may be hazardous to your health" type warning, the same as cigarettes. But while we're cutting down on smoking as a nation, we're drinking more diet soda than ever.

Whether you drink diet soda is up to you; you're old enough to make your own choices. However, *pregnant women should avoid saccharin, and it should never be given to young children.* Some scientists believe that fetuses, infants, and toddlers may be especially susceptible to its cancer-related effects.

Also, artificial sweeteners may be one cause of diarrhea in children. Two in particular that may be troublemakers are mannitol and sorbitol.

The latest entrant in the lucrative artificial sweeteners competition is a substance called *aspartame,* which is being marketed under the names NutraSweet (when it's an additive) and Equal (when it's packaged by itself). Although aspartame was made available to the public in 1981 only after the FDA had spent a decade investigating it, the jury is still out.

In an earlier incarnation it didn't promise to have much impact on our lives because it couldn't be used in sodas or other prepared beverages; it broke down. The chemists at G. D. Searle (the original manufacturers of aspartame) fixed that, though. And now NutraSweet seems to be everywhere. Diet soda companies are shouting that they've got more NutraSweet than their competitors; powdered-chocolate-drink companies are pretending horror at the thought of using sugar (when, of course, they used it for years).

Let's leave the blare of advertising behind for a moment. The important questions are: What is aspartame? Is it safe?

In answer to the first question: Aspartame is a "small protein," a combination of two amino acids (phenylalanine and aspartic acid) that occur naturally in such foods as meat, milk, and eggs. In other words, it's not a sugar, and it's not a totally artificial substance, either, despite the fact that it's manufactured in a laboratory.

Aspartame is far sweeter than sugar—two hundred times sweeter, in fact. And while sugar contains 16 calories per teaspoon, the amount of aspartame that gives the same level of sweetness has less than 1 calorie.

In answer to the second question—is it safe?—no one knows for sure. Both the FDA and the American Medical Association say that it is. An article that appeared in the December 1984 issue of *Child Health Alert* takes a more cautious stance:

There is a basic problem with any new drug or food product; there is only limited information available on its safety when it is first introduced, and we can never have enough information to be assured it is *absolutely* safe. . . . It is only with widespread use that we become aware of less common reactions produced by a drug or food product, and it is only after decades of use that we learn of its long-term effects.

The FDA did receive a number of complaints about aspartame not long after it was introduced, and it asked the U.S. Centers for Disease Control (CDC) to look into them. The complaints—the CDC gathered nearly six hundred from all over the country—ranged from headaches to bowel trouble to allergies; one doctor linked aspartame to hyperactivity in a young patient.

The CDC concluded that the data didn't provide enough evidence that "serious, widespread, adverse health consequences" could be associated with aspartame. Since then, a Maryland mother has filed the first suit against aspartame. Claiming that her 5-year-old son suffered permanent neurological and physical damage from the substance, she is asking for a settlement of $2 million.

So where does that leave us? Again, we as adults must make up our own minds. The CDC report, along with other studies, seem to indicate that aspartame is safe for the "vast majority" of users. (The FDA cautions those with PKU—phenylketonuria—against using it because it contains a substance their bodies are unable to metabolize.)

But while we can assume some level of risk for ourselves, I do not think we should impose it on our children. I personally would recommend being conservative when giving kids products sweetened with NutraSweet. Try to keep it a limited part of your family's dietary intake.

There are two reasons why I feel this way. One, I'd like to see what the jury has to say. And two, Fat-Proofing tries to get kids out of the sweet-treats habit. Somehow it seems inconsistent to emphasize a healthy life-style on one hand and to okay the consumption of artificially sweetened stuff on the other.

Aspartame doesn't do anything *for* kids, and we don't yet know what it does *to* them.

SAY NO TO SALT

Years ago, salt was a precious commodity, essential to the preservation of food and often worth its weight in gold. (In fact, the word *salary* comes from the Latin *salarium*, or *salt money*, originally used to pay Roman soldiers). More recently, iodized salt has helped to distribute iodine throughout the population, preventing goiter.

Some salt is still essential to life. Sodium chloride—table salt—regulates the balance of water and dissolved substances outside the cells of the body. The trouble is, we're vastly overdoing our intake.

The physiological requirement for sodium is found in $1/10$ of a teaspoon of salt; the RDA, while higher (about 1 teaspoon) is still substantially lower than the $3\frac{1}{2}$ teaspoons the average American consumes daily. (Some of us eat ten to forty times the amount of salt we need each day. A single large fast-food hamburger with fries will put you over your daily quota.)

Why is too much salt bad for us? Because sodium consumption (salt is 40 percent sodium) has been linked to the hypertension (high blood pressure) hazard that affects some 34 million Americans. Studies have shown that cutting back on salt can cause a drop in blood pressure. (In one such study conducted at a London medical school, the daily salt intake of a group of patients was cut by *half a teaspoon*—from 4.4 grams a day down to 2 grams. These patients' average blood pressure fell by a significant amount.)

Most of us start consuming excessive amounts of salt from a very early age; until fairly recently, commercial baby foods contained far more salt than necessary. In infancy we learn to like the taste of salted foods, much as we learn to like the taste of sugared foods, and from that point on we're hooked.

As a Fat-Proofing parent concerned with your family's lifelong health, you must take continuing responsibility for limiting their salt consumption. Start feeding your children unsalted (or less salted) foods when they're babies; by raising them with blander tastes, you'll be giving them a healthier start. Older kids may pose more of a problem, but even with them you can take positive action.

This doesn't just mean cutting down on pickles, pretzels, and chips; plenty of other prepared foods are chock-full of salt or sodium. Canned soups and diet sodas are among the worst culprits. (Even one can of "very low sodium" diet soda contains 35 mg. of sodium.) It's important to read labels on food products, although even then you may not be getting the full story.

When you do start removing salt from your family's diet, you probably won't have to worry about whether they'll be getting enough. Many foods contain sodium naturally. But you will have to worry about whether they'll eat the "bland" foods you're suddenly presenting them with. In the beginning at least, food without salt will seem almost tasteless.

Fortunately, there are other "flavor enhancers" you can use. Try fresh-ground pepper, and start using spices—nutmeg, cinnamon, and the like—more creatively. Herbs, lemon juice, and garlic powder (*not* garlic salt!) will all make food tastier. (Some mixed-herb preparations are sold as "salt alternatives" and taste pretty good.)

> For more information on salt-free food preparation, contact your local chapter of the American Heart Association and request a copy of their publication, *Cooking Without Your Salt Shaker,* which sells for $5.00.

You may want to consider some of the commercially available salt substitutes. Be warned, however, that in cooking they can distort the flavor of foods. These substitutes usually contain potassium chloride as a partial or total replacement of sodium chloride (table salt); those who need to restrict their potassium intake for health reasons should check with their doctor first.

> To learn more about foods' sodium content, send for *Sodium Scoreboard,* a colorful poster that lists the sodium contents of some 250 everyday food items. It's available for $3.95 (unlaminated) and $7.95 (laminated) from CSPI, 1501 16th St. NW, Washington, DC 20036.

HOW—AND WHY—TO SQUEEZE FATS OUT OF YOUR FAMILY'S DIET

In *The Taming of the C.A.N.D.Y. Monster* I must admit I dealt with sugar and salt but avoided the fat issue. Many parents who painstakingly avoid giving their children sugar don't think twice about the amount of dietary fat their kids consume. Yet fats pose a far greater threat to a child's future health—and to his or her ability to maintain an ideal and healthful weight—than sugar.

To put it simply, *fats can make you fat*. Ounce for ounce, they contain more calories than carbohydrates or proteins, the other two sources of energy needed by the body. Compare an ounce of butter with an ounce of apple, for example: the butter contains 200 calories; the apple, 20.

Fats are devious because they are usually low in volume. Salad dressings (a few tablespoons) can provide more calories than a small baked potato.

Even more important than calorie content, fats have been connected to diseases of the heart and blood vessels, and to breast, colon, and other types of cancer.

Dietary fats do not create these health problems overnight. The trouble builds slowly, starting in childhood. Fatty deposits have been found building in the arteries of children ages 3 to 8. Such deposits are considered an early sign of atherosclerosis, the "hardening of the arteries" disease that causes half of all deaths in the United States. By the late teen years (ages 15 to 20), about 20 percent of our children have significant fatty deposits in their arteries. And autopsies conducted on young men (average age 22) who died in Vietnam revealed that 45 percent had coronary atherosclerosis.

Limiting your child's fat intake is one of the most healthful things you can do for him or her. Remember that Fat-Proofing means what it says—cutting down on the amount of fat your child consumes. And as fatty foods disappear from your kitchen and your table, your whole family will benefit.

WHAT ARE FATS, AND WHERE DO THEY COME FROM?

Fats are complex compounds made up of an alcohol called *glycerol* and three "fatty acids." These fatty acids give each fat its special taste and texture, making corn oil, for example, different from butter and olive oil.

Depending on which of the three fatty acids predominates, a fat is either *polyunsaturated*, *monounsaturated*, or *saturated*. What's the difference?

- Polyunsaturated fats come from vegetable sources and are usually liquid at room temperature. Safflower, sunflower, corn, and soybean oils are examples of polyunsaturated fats. They tend to lower blood cholesterol levels.

FOODS HIGH IN SATURATED FATS: A FAT-PROOFING CHECKLIST

Dairy foods

Cheddar cheese
Swiss cheese
Ice cream
Cream cheese
Whole milk

Red meats

Pork loin
Hot dog
Beef rib roast
Liverwurst
Lamb chop, well trimmed

Baked goods

Apple pie
Danish pastry
Croissant

Other

Coconut
Milk chocolate

Note: Foods with *no* saturated fat (or minimal amounts) include fruits, most vegetables, skim milk, and uncreamed cottage cheese. Foods *low* in saturated fat include herring, sardines, red salmon, and mackerel; peanut butter, almonds, sunflower seeds, and walnuts.

(*Source: Based on USDA food tables*)

- Monounsaturated fats also have vegetable origins and are liquid at room temperature. Peanut, rice, and olive oils are examples of monounsaturated fats.

- Saturated fats are usually found in foods from animal sources (meat, cheese, milk, eggs, and butter). These types of fats are usually solid at room temperature. But some vegetable foods are also surprisingly high in saturated fat, such as chocolate, coconut, and palm oils. They tend to raise blood cholesterol levels.

Fats aren't all bad. In fact, the polyunsaturated fats are essential for good health—*when consumed in moderation*. They help form the delicate membranes that line the cells and help create prostaglandins, a group of hormones that regulate blood clotting and other functions of the body.

What's important to remember is that saturated fats aren't needed by the body at all. And yet these are the kinds we Americans consume at a very high level. Part of the problem stems from the fact that saturated fats are hidden in so many of the processed foods we eat. (For example, did you know that nondairy creamers have more saturated fat than cream does? It's because they're made with coconut oil.)

In processed foods, such as cookies and crackers, the vegetable oils used are often hydrogenated, making them more saturated than they were in their original form. (Hydrogenation is a process that uses heat and pressure to convert unsaturated fats to saturated ones. It's done to keep the oil from turning rancid too quickly, thus giving the processed foods a longer "shelf life.")

The average American adult consumes 6 to 8 tablespoons of dietary fat each day. Yet, after age 2, we need only 1 tablespoon a day to stay in good health! Obviously, some major changes in our diet are called for.

FOODS HIGH IN CHOLESTEROL: A FAT-PROOFING CHECKLIST

Dairy foods

Butter
Cottage cheese (4% fat)
Cream cheese
Hard cheese
Ice cream

Fowl

Eggs (whole or yolk only)

Baked goods

Lemon meringue pie
Sponge cake

Red meats

Hot dog
Beef kidney
Beef liver

Fish

Sardines
Canned shrimp
Canned crab
Mackerel

Notes: The foods listed above contain high proportions of cholesterol relative to other foods in their groups, not to foods in other groups. In other words, while hard cheese is high in cholesterol compared to skim milk, it's low compared to beef liver.

Foods made only from plant sources—beans, vegetable margarines, grains, peanut butter, fruits, and vegetables—contain *no* cholesterol.

(*Source: Based on analyses by the U.S. Department of Agriculture*)

WHAT ABOUT CHOLESTEROL?

Cholesterol is the name for the waxy white substance that deposits itself in the arteries and can eventually lead to atherosclerosis. Some cholesterol—about 1,000 mg. a day—is made naturally in the body, primarily by the liver. But another 600 mg. gets into our blood daily through the foods we eat.

Cholesterol is found only in foods from animal sources. But the amount of cholesterol found in our blood also depends on the kinds of fat we eat. Saturated fats tend to raise blood cholesterol levels, while polyunsaturated fats tend to lower them. And monounsaturated fats seem to have no effect one way or the other.

HOW MUCH DIETARY FAT AND CHOLESTEROL SHOULD MY CHILD CONSUME?

Most doctors agree that children can benefit from a higher proportion of fat in their diets *during the first 2 years of life*. That's because their small bodies need huge amounts of calories, relatively speaking, and fats pack calories more densely than either carbohydrates or protein. A baby who has *no* polyunsaturated fats in his or her diet could develop liver abnormalities.

After age 2, however, a high-fat diet is not recommended for children. The American Heart Association advises that no more than 30 percent of a child's daily intake of calories should come from fats. (Approximately 15 percent should come from protein and the remaining 55 percent from complex carbohydrates, such as beans, cereals, and whole grains.)

Furthermore, says the American Heart Association, the fats that make up that 30 percent should be divided evenly among the three kinds: 10 percent polyunsaturated, 10 percent monounsaturated, and 10 percent saturated. (Some nutritionists would argue that the saturated-fat level should be even lower.)

According to a survey of 1,200 children age 6 to 19 years conducted by the Maryland chapters of the American Heart Association and the American Academy of Pediatrics, about 90 percent of children in the United States exceed the recommended level for total fat intake. The same percentage consumed too much saturated fat and too little polyunsaturated fat.

In addition, 75 percent of the children consumed more than the recommended amount of cholesterol. The American Heart Association advises that children limit their cholesterol intake to 100 mg. for every 1,000 calories they consume—not to exceed 300 mg. of cholesterol in a day.

It adds up surprisingly quickly; 1 egg yolk contains 252 mg. of cholesterol; 2 4-ounce hot dogs contain 112 mg.; 1 tablespoon of butter, 35 mg.; 3 ounces of chicken, dark meat, skin removed, has 77 mg.; 3 ounces of turkey, dark meat, skin removed, has 86 mg.; 1 ounce of hard cheese has 24 to 28 mg.; 1/2 cup of ice cream, 27 mg.

Furthermore, it's recommended that the blood cholesterol levels of children not be higher than 170 mg. (This translates into a cholesterol concentration of 170 mg. per 100 milliliters—or about 1/5 pint—of blood.) A recent Michigan study of 360 elementary-school children revealed that 41 percent had high blood cholesterol levels.

TIPS FOR REDUCING CHOLESTEROL AND FAT IN YOUR CHILD'S DIET

You can reduce your child's fat and cholesterol intake in a variety of ways. Some suggestions:

- Buy skim, 1-percent, or 2-percent milk rather than whole milk (which contains about 3.5 percent butterfat). Children under age 2, however, should receive whole or 2-percent milk.

- Ricotta and part-skim mozzarella cheeses are lower in fat than most others.

- Occasionally substitute beans, whole grains, and cottage cheese for meat. Or, at the very least, replace red meat (high in saturated fat) with chicken (no skin), turkey, or certain fishes (lower in all fats, including saturated fat).

- Avoid already breaded chicken, fish, and meat.

- Avoid "choice" and "prime" grades of meat, which are high in fat. Lower grades of meat are not only lower in fat; they're less expensive.

If you're worried about taste, don't be. Although higher-grade meat is reputed to taste better, a Consumers Union study revealed that a meat's grade was actually a poor indicator of its taste.

- Before cooking or serving your child meat, trim off any fat you see. It's also preferable to broil or roast all meats and fish rather than fry or stew them, because the fat can then drip off and be discarded.

- Eliminate—or at least limit—your child's consumption of hot dogs and bologna; fat makes up 80 percent of the calories in these foods. Plus, they contain sodium nitrite, a chemical that reacts with other chemicals called *amines* to produce nitrosamines, which have been linked to cancer.

If you like the convenience of hot dogs, try ones made from chicken or soybeans. You can find these in many supermarkets and health-food stores. They are actually quite tasty; many kids raised on "regular" hot dogs don't even notice the difference. And if you raise your child on these from the start, he or she will grow up believing that soybean hot dogs are the real thing!

- When a recipe calls for milk, use buttermilk instead. Don't let its name fool you—buttermilk is actually made from low-fat milk. You can now buy cans of dried buttermilk to store in your refrigerator and prepare when needed.

- When a recipe calls for sour cream, which is high in fat, try plain yogurt instead. One cup of yogurt contains only 17 mg. of cholesterol, compared to 152 mg. in a cup of sour cream. (Be sure to check yogurt labels carefully, however, for some are made with whole milk.) Look for the newer "lean creams" that reduce the fats found in sour cream.

- Avoid butter, lard, and solid vegetable shortenings when you cook or bake. Instead, use a polyunsaturated vegetable oil or margarine. But buy your margarine carefully. Look for one that has a *liquid* oil listed first on its label.

- For a buttery spread, purchase soft tub margarine made from corn, safflower, or sunflower oils.

- Limit the number of eggs your child eats. And that includes the eggs that make their way into the casseroles and other dishes and baked goods you prepare.

The yolk (that's where the problem is) of a single large egg contains between 250 and 275 mg. of cholesterol. That's already dangerously close to the daily maximum limit of 300 mg. recommended by the American Heart Association. Make an omelette using 3 egg whites and only one egg yolk.

- Buy a nonstick frying pan that doesn't need grease and use it for frying and sautéing.

- Serve single (versus two) crust pies.

- If you *must* buy processed baked goods—cakes, muffins, pastries, and the like—read their labels carefully. Avoid those that list coconut oil, palm oil, or lard, and those that just say "vegetable oil"—it could very likely be palm or coconut oil.

- Sherbet, ice milk, and low-fat frozen yogurts are all good substitutes for ice cream.

- Don't depend on fast food restaurants as a steady diet. Most of the foods served there have fat as their main source of calories. Even the shakes are often made with highly saturated coconut oil! On top of that, the foods served at fast food restaurants are usually low in iron, fiber, and several vitamins, and extremely high in sodium. Reliance on fast food establishments can only help establish unhealthful eating habits for your child. (For more on fast foods, see chapter 12).

TWELVE

MEALTIME STRATEGIES FOR THE FAT-PROOFING FAMILY

Making Fat-Proofing a part of your family's lifestyle takes some "consciousness raising" on your part. By now, however, it should be evident that a Fat-Proofed household isn't all that hard to achieve.

You *don't* have to worry about counting calories. You *don't* have to consult long, complicated lists of foods (and substitutions, or "exchanges") before deciding what your kids should eat and when. All you have to do is feed your family healthful, nutritious foods on a regular basis and make sure that they get enough exercise.

This chapter offers a wealth of ideas for the three main meals of the day, many from parents like yourself. It includes parent-tested, kid-tested recipes that reflect the Fat-Proofing philosophy. It tells you how to continue Fat-Proofing in places where you're not in control of the kitchen—restaurants. And it points the way toward other useful resources, from cookbooks to newsletters about nutrition.

BREAKFAST

Many parents report that they find breakfast the most difficult of all meals to plan. Part of this is due to our stereotyped ideas of what breakfast *is* (or should be).

Since breakfast is the first meal of the day, it should provide a third of the day's nutritional needs. But it doesn't *have* to consist of bacon and eggs, cereal and milk, or french toast and syrup. It can be peanut butter and jelly sandwiches, fish, even pizza! (See the "Pizza for Breakfast" chapter in my book *Feed Me, I'm Yours* for other suggestions!)

The problem most of us have is that breakfast must usually be fast. With parents getting ready for work and kids getting ready for school (and maybe little ones needing someone to get them ready for daycare), there just isn't time to prepare—not to mention enjoy—the breakfasts we'd like. This may be the main reason why cereal and milk have become standard operating procedure in so many families.

Over the years, the readers of my *Practical Parenting Newsletter* have submitted countless ideas for creative breakfasts. Here are some of their favorites, along with a few of my own:

- Try "Pancake Pinwheels": Make a large, skillet-sized pancake according to your favorite recipe (preferably one that uses wheat flour and little, if any, sugar). Cut off the edges to form a square. Spread with unsweetened applesauce, roll the whole thing up like a jelly roll, and cut into half-inch slices. (*Molly Melrose, Vassalboro, ME*)

- Give any cereal (dry or cooked) a boost with a sprinkling of wheat germ (toasted or raw), chopped nuts, or raisins.

- Thanks to Dr. Seuss, kids everywhere are willing to at least try eggs—if they're green! Here's an alternative to using food coloring (and a way to add vitamins and minerals): Combine alfalfa sprouts with eggs in a blender. Pour mixture into lightly oiled skillet, cover, and cook on medium heat until eggs are set. Other possibilities: parsley, a little dill weed. (*Fatima Nashatizadeh, Emporia, KS*)

- Jazz up scrambled eggs with sautéed onion, celery, and/or green pepper; bits of leftover cooked meats or vegetables; seasoned salad croutons; cottage cheese or any grated cheese; drained canned corn (sauté first); a sprinkling of wheat germ.

- Melt a low fat cheese on whole-wheat toast or halved bagels. Cheese is a good source of protein and calcium and is especially recommended for kids who aren't big milk drinkers.

- Slice bananas or pears into a dish and cover with orange juice or apple juice. (*Donna Olson, Wayzata, MN*)

- For a special treat, try quesadillas. Put sliced cheese on one of those round, flat, soft tortillas you find in the dairy case of your supermarket, slip it into the microwave for about 40 seconds, and roll up for serving.

- Keep a supply of cooked brown rice in the refrigerator. Mix a ½ cup with raisins, a dribble of honey, and a dash of cinnamon; add low-fat milk for a delicious "cereal." (Rice pudding is another terrific breakfast dish.)

WHOLE-WHEAT BAKING

Home-baked breads, whether yeast or quick, can be breakfast staples, especially if they're made with whole-wheat flour. Although the texture you end up with is somewhat coarser and heavier than white-flour breads, the added nourishment is well worth it.

If your family is used to the spongy, limp stuff that passes for white bread, whole wheat will take some getting used to. I recommend introducing it gradually. Start by substituting ½ to ¼ the white flour called for in a recipe. When your family becomes accustomed to the 50–50 mixture, begin experimenting with adding even more. You may find the resulting mixture somewhat drier than usual; if so, adjust the liquids accordingly. Or play it safe and consult a whole-foods cookbook for recipes based on whole-wheat flour.

You should be aware that whole-wheat flour has a much shorter shelf-life than white flour. Unless you plan to use the whole amount you purchase within a few weeks' time, buy in small quantities—or make room for storage in your refrigerator or freezer.

Tips to make breadmaking easier:

- Use the super-fast-action yeast that's recently appeared on your grocer's shelves; it works!

- Try some make-now, bake-later refrigerator recipes for times when your schedule is extra hectic.

- If you don't yet have a food processor and are thinking about buying one, choose a model powerful enough to knead bread. A mom I know started making all of her family's yeast breads when she bought a food processor with a 1-horsepower engine. It kneads enough dough for two loaves—in eighty seconds!

- Serve mashed potatoes with cheese. Or cottage cheese mixed with fresh fruit, sesame seeds, granola, or applesauce.

- For a "breakfast buffet," have the following sliced and ready: fresh fruits, finger veggies (carrots, green peppers, celery, zucchini), hard-boiled eggs, and whole-wheat muffins or breads. Arrange on the kitchen counter and let the kids help themselves.

In other words, almost anything goes—as long as it goes down!

Finally, if you have trouble getting your kids to sit still for breakfast (and if you have some time to spare), try what Sue Ludwil of Austin, MN, does: she reads to her daughters while they eat. "Knowing that a short story or a chapter of a book is coming," she writes, "they hurry to get dressed and ready for the day, there are no pleas for TV, and they eat good breakfasts."

LUNCH

Lunch should be a fairly light yet nutritionally sound meal. In chapter 7 I suggested several possibilities for school lunches; any and all are equally suitable for your family table.

Don't worry if your kids want a daily dose of peanut butter. Fortunately, it's good for them—and, when spread on whole-wheat bread and served with a glass of milk, it makes a protein-complete meal.

Some variations on that theme:

- For "peanut butter gravy," put a large blob of peanut butter in a blender or mixing bowl and gradually add low-fat milk, beating until the mixture is the consistency of gravy. Pour over bread for a peanut butter sandwich that doesn't stick to the roof of your mouth.

- Try "peanut butterflies." Make a peanut butter sandwich and cut it in half from corner to corner. Arrange the two triangles on a plate like "wings"—the long sides to the outsides. Place an apple quarter in the center for a "body" and two carrot strips above for "antennae."

- Make "baboon butter" with ½ cup peanut butter, 1 large ripe banana, 1 tablespoon shredded coconut, raisins, or chopped dates, and ¼ teaspoon ground cinnamon. Mashed together, it's enough for three sandwiches.

Does it matter if your peanut butter is commercial or "natural"? From a Fat-Proofing perspective, yes. They're nutritionally comparable gram for gram, but the commercial ones contain added sugar, salt, and hydrogenated oils, while the natural kinds usually contain only salt (and sometimes not even that—but if you try unsalted peanut butter, you'll understand why the plain variety is an acquired taste!).

Most supermarkets carry natural peanut butter; you may find it either in the refrigerated section or on a shelf. If it's on a shelf, you'll see oil on the top of it; pour it off or stir it, refrigerate, and it shouldn't separate again.

ALOHA LUNCH SPREAD

1 cup chopped walnuts
½ to 1 cup crushed pineapple in its own juice
1 8-ounce package cream cheese or Neufchâtel (a lower-fat form of cream cheese)

Combine ingredients and mix well. Store mixture in airtight containers in refrigerator. Use as a lunch sandwich spread, or on crackers or celery as a snack.

SUGAR-FREE CARROT-PINEAPPLE SALAD

1 package unflavored gelatin
¼ cup boiling water
1 15-ounce can pineapple in its own juice (in other words, no sugar added)
½ cup unsweetened orange juice
3 large raw carrots (approximately 4 ounces each), shredded

Sprinkle gelatin into a bowl. Add hot water and stir to dissolve. Add pineapple and orange juice; add shredded carrots; stir. Chill to set.

MACARONI SALAD

1 cup elbow macaroni
4 cups water
1/2 cup mayonnaise (or use half yogurt and half mayonnaise)
1 teaspoon lemon juice
1/2 cucumber, peeled and diced
2 hard-cooked eggs, sliced
1/2 cup diced cheese
1/2 cup diced celery
1/2 cup grated carrots

Cook macaroni in water according to package directions. Drain and chill. Combine mayonnaise (or yogurt and mayonnaise) with lemon juice. Stir veggies and mayonnaise mixture into noodles.

DINNER

If your family is like mine, dinner may be the only meal you sit down to together. And it may be the only one you spend substantial amounts of time planning and preparing.

You may have a thick file of recipes—or a cherished cookbook—you've been using for years. Now is the time to reexamine those old standbys with a Fat-Proofing eye.

- Is red meat the focus of your evening meal? Alternate with fowl or fish. Consider cutting back to three times a week for red meat—and, eventually, all meats.

Use cut-up meats in stews, soups, and casseroles rather than serving great slabs of it. Not only will this be better for your family; it will be better for your budget. When meat is an ingredient rather than a feature, you can use smaller quantities—and you don't have to buy prime cuts. And this in turn offers another advantage, especially when it comes to red meat. The higher the grade, the more fat, or "marbelization," it contains. Less expensive meats are less fatty.

- Do your favorite recipes rely heavily on salt? Try halving the amount you normally use; later, you can decrease this even more.

- Are you frying too frequently? Try stir-frying, which usually requires less oil than traditional frying. Or switch to a nonstick pan and use a vegetable spray.

One problem parents face is that of keeping dinners nutritious, interesting, and *uncomplicated*. Here are some ideas from my Practical Parenting readers:

- Keep in your refrigerator such useful staples as cooked brown rice, bulgur, and pasta.

- Top casseroles with wheat germ instead of bread crumbs. Grated cheese and wheat germ make a great topping crust. (*Elaine Wall, Jenkintown, PA*)

- When making spaghetti for fussy eaters, try using shell, bowtie, or other fancy-shaped pasta. The shapes are intriguing and easier to eat than the regular "string" kind. (*Pam Jenson, El Cajon, CA*)

SUPER SUKIYAKI

1 pound round steak, cut into thin strips
1/2 cup mushrooms (fresh are best)
2 onions, chopped
4 green onions, cut into strips
2 stalks celery, chopped
1 8-ounce can bamboo shoots
1 teaspoon soy sauce
3 tablespoons water
3 cups fresh spinach leaves, washed *thoroughly* (or they'll be gritty)
3 cups cooked brown rice

Optional:
a little vegetable oil

Brown the meat in a wok or large deep pot. If necessary, add the oil; then add all the other ingredients except the spinach and rice. When the vegetables are tender (but still crispy), add the spinach and continue stir-frying until the leaves just wilt. Serve over the rice. Serves 4.

COOKBOOKS

As you become a veteran Fat-Proofer, your home cookbook library will probably undergo some changes. Some "out with the old, in with the new" suggestions to find at (or order through) your local bookstore:

- *American Heart Association Cookbook,* 4th edition, compiled and tested by nutritionists Ruthe Eshleman and Mary Winston (New York: David McKay & Co., 1984), $15.95.

- *The New York Times New Natural Foods Cookbook,* revised edition, by Jean Hewitt (New York: Times Books, 1982), $17.95.

- *Pure & Simple: A Cookbook,* by Marian Burros (New York: Berkely, 1982), $5.95.

- *Rodale's Basic Natural Foods Cookbook,* edited by Charles Gerras and the Rodale Press staff (Emmaus, PA: Rodale Press, 1983), $21.95.

- *Jane Brody's Good Food Book,* by Jane Brody (New York: Bantam, 1987), $12.95.

PEPPERY VEAL

1 pound boneless veal, cut into small pieces
1 teaspoon paprika
1 cup bouillon (chicken, beef, or vegetable)
1 clove garlic, crushed
1/4 lemon, cut into very small pieces, seeds removed
4 green peppers, sliced, seeded, and with membranes removed

Brown the veal over medium heat. Sprinkle the paprika over the meat. Add the bouillon (don't pour directly on the meat; instead, add it to the sides of the pan). Add the crushed garlic. Lower the heat. Add the lemon pieces (do put them on the meat). Cover and simmer about 1 hour, or until tender. Ten minutes before the veal is supposed to be ready, add the peppers. Serves 4.

RAINBOW CHICKEN

1 2½-pound fryer or broiler, cut up into pieces
2 tablespoons oil
1 pound sweet potatoes, peeled and cut into slices
1 cup unsweetened pineapple juice
⅓ cup minced celery leaves
1 bay leaf, crumbled
1 large red pepper, sliced, seeded, and with membranes
    removed
1 medium-size onion, sliced
2 cups peas (fresh, thawed frozen, or, if canned, drained)

Brown the chicken in the oil and spoon off the fat when done. Add the sweet potatoes, pineapple juice, celery leaves, and bay leaf. Cover and simmer for 20 minutes, or until both the chicken and the sweet potatoes are tender. Add the red pepper, onion, and peas; cook until done but still crisp. Serves 4.

NOT FOR VEGETARIANS ONLY

Nearly 7 million Americans today are vegetarians—some for religious or moral reasons, and others simply because they like the food.

There's a lot to like about it. We meat-eaters have a hard time imagining life without turkey at Thanksgiving and the occasional filet, but the truth is that vegetarian cooking can be so varied, imaginative, and interesting that you don't even miss meat.

I know people who have been vegetarians all their lives; people who are recent "converts" due to concern for the global food supply (it takes 16 pounds of grain to yield 1 pound of meat); and people who have raised their children as vegetarians from infancy. Some of the best meals I've eaten have been at their tables—just-out-of-the-oven whole-grain breads, aromatic soups, thick stews, crispy and flavorful salads.

You don't have to swear off meat entirely to reap the benefits of vegetarian cuisine. Instead, pick up a cookbook or two and start offering your family occasional vegetarian meals. You (and they) may actually prefer them.

One of the best vegetarian cookbooks I know of is *American Wholefoods Cuisine,* by Nikki and David Goldbeck (New York: New American Library, 1983); paperback, $8.95. It's been called "the *Joy of Cooking* for the '80s," and that's a more than apt description. The more than 1,300 recipes it contains are tasty, wholesome, and easy to follow. Plus, the Goldbecks provide thorough descriptions of the whole-foods philosophy (including protein complementarity), the whole-foods pantry, and cooking techniques. This very popular cookbook should be available at your local bookstore.

Many vegetarian cookbooks (more are listed in the box on p. 224) tell you how to make the switch to a meatless lifestyle. For more information, you may want to consult a registered dietition or nutritionist. Or contact the Seventh Day Adventists, who offer classes on vegetarian cooking.

A vegetarian diet must—and can—be just as balanced as a meat-based diet. It's especially important to get sound advice if you're pregnant or lactating, or if you have infants or small children.

TABOULI SALAD

(A salad that's good with dinner, or lunch—or breakfast! Add the garbanzo beans to make this a source of complete protein.)

$1/2$ cup fine bulgur (cracked wheat)
1 cup finely chopped mild onion
1 cup finely chopped parsley
3 medium, fully ripe tomatoes, chopped
$1/3$ cup fresh lemon juice
$1/3$ cup olive oil
2 tablespoons finely snipped fresh mint, or 1 tablespoon dried
    mint

Optional:
$1/4$ cup cooked garbanzo beans
romaine lettuce
$1/2$ teaspoon salt

Pour bulgur into a bowl and cover with cold water. Soak 10 minutes and drain into a sieve or colander lined with two layers of dampened cheesecloth or a clean dishtowel. Gather the cloth and squeeze its contents firmly to extract excess water.

In a deep bowl, toss the bulgur with onion, parsley, tomatoes, lemon

juice, and garbanzo beans and salt (if desired). Just before serving, stir in oil and mint; correct seasoning. Line serving bowls or individual bowls with lettuce leaves and mound in the bulgur mixture.

SPINACH PIE

> 1 9″ or 10″ pie crust (frozen or homemade)
> 1½ pounds fresh spinach, or 2 10-ounce packages frozen
>   chopped spinach
> 5 tablespoons butter
> ½ cup chopped onion
> 1 clove garlic, crushed
> 3 tablespoons flour
> 1½ cups milk
> 1½ teaspoons salt
> ¼ teaspoon pepper
> dash of nutmeg
> 5 eggs, beaten
> 8 ounces mozzarella or Swiss cheese, shredded

Preheat oven to 350°.

Prepare the crust and flute a high edge on it. Cook the spinach, press out all water, and chop. In a skillet, melt 2 tablespoons butter and sauté onion and garlic until golden. Stir in spinach.

In a saucepan, melt the other 3 tablespoons of butter, stir in flour, and stir in milk. Stir over low heat until sauce thickens and bubbles. Stir in salt, pepper, and nutmeg. Add spinach mixture. Stir in beaten eggs and cheese until well blended. Pour into pie shell.

Bake on lower shelf of oven for 40 to 45 minutes, or until puffed and firm to the touch in the center. Let cool 10 minutes before cutting.

SCRUMPTIOUS BARLEY CASSEROLE

> 4 cups cooked barley (see below for directions)
> 3 tablespoons butter or margarine
> 1 cup chopped onions
> 2 cloves garlic, chopped
> 1 small eggplant, cubed
> 2 small zucchini, sliced

1 teaspoon dried oregano
pinch of cayenne pepper
2 cups cooked fresh tomatoes (canned are also okay)
¼ pound mild white cheese (Monterey Jack or mozzarella),
    grated

Melt butter or margarine in a heavy skillet and add onions and garlic; sauté until onions are translucent. Add cooked barley and sauté 2 more minutes. Stir in eggplant and zucchini, add seasonings, and sauté 30 seconds. Add tomatoes and simmer until vegetables are cooked yet crispy. Top with cheese and stick under broiler until bubbly.

How to cook barley: Rinse 1 cup raw barley thoroughly with cold water. Bring 4 cups of water to a boil; add barley; boil 30 to 40 minutes. Yield: 4 cups.

VEGETARIAN COOKBOOKS

■ Mollie Katzen's vegetarian cookbooks have been bestsellers for years. Find either (or both) in your local bookstore: *The Moosewood Cookbook* (Berkeley, CA: Ten Speed Press, 1979), $9.95; *The Enchanted Broccoli Forest* (Ten Speed Press, 1982), $11.95.

■ Another good source of information and recipes is *Laurel's Kitchen: A Handbook for Vegetarian Cookery and Nutrition,* by Laurel Robertson, Carol Flinders, and Bronwen Godfrey (New York: Bantam, 1978), $4.95, or (Petaluma, CA: Nilgiri Press, 1976), $11.50.

Two more popular (and easy-to-find) vegetarian cookbooks:

■ *The Vegetarian Epicure,* by Anna Thomas (New York: Vintage Books, 1972), $9.95, and *The Vegetarian Epicure Book 2,* also by Anna Thomas (New York: Knopf, 1984), $8.95.

Finally, if you're going to be cooking vegetarian a lot (or even a little), you'll probably want to invest in a food processor. It can cut preparation time in half. Here's a book that contains plenty of recipes and helpful hints:

■ *The Electric Vegetarian: Natural Cooking the Food Processor Way,* by Paula Szilard and Juliana J. Woo (Berkeley, CA: Ten Speed Press, 1982), $9.95.

ABOUT TOFU

Tofu—soybean curd—has long been a staple in many vegetarian diets. Lately it's been going "mainstream" and appearing in frozen, sherbetlike desserts. It's high in protein and low in calories, fats, and carbohydrates, contains *no* cholesterol, and is a complete vegetable protein. Because it's easy to digest, it's good for sensitive stomachs and people on milk-free diets.

It's also pretty likable (and versatile) stuff. It can be added to almost anything, as it takes on the flavor of foods with which it's combined.

- For information on how to get started bringing tofu to your family table, see *Tofu Primer: A Beginner's Book of Bean Cake Cookery*, by Juel Andersen and Sigrid Andersen (Berkeley, CA: Creative Arts Book Co.), $4.50.

- Another source of ideas on cooking with tofu: *The Tofu Cookbook*, by Kathy Bauer and Juel Andersen (Emmaus, PA: Rodale Press, 1979), $9.95.

Mollie Katzen of *Moosewood* and *Broccoli Forest* fame offers an excellent suggestion for introducing tofu to kids: let them play with it! The texture (soft and cheeselike) is fun, it oozes between the fingers, and it can be chased around the plate with a spoon. Among her recipe ideas are:

- Mash tofu with a ripe banana, mix with some honey, and top with something crunchy.

- Sneak some mashed tofu into mashed potatoes.

- Combine equal parts tofu and peanut butter and refrigerate for a fluffy sandwich spread.

Or try stirring some into a bowl of vegetable soup.

Note: Tofu has a short refrigerator life, so be sure to have a couple of uses in mind before rushing off to buy some.

TOFU HOT DISH

> butter or margarine for sautéing
> 1 pound tofu
> ¹/₂ cup chopped onion

$^1/_2$ cup chopped mushrooms
$^1/_2$ cup chopped cashew nuts
$^1/_4$ cup tamari

Optional:
$^1/_3$ cup cooked rice
$^1/_3$ to $^1/_2$ cup chopped fresh tomatoes or green pepper

Preheat oven to 350°.

Sauté the veggies and cashews. Drain the tofu (but don't squeeze out the water). Mash the tofu, add the tamari and veggies and nuts, and bake for 20 to 30 minutes. Serve over rice, if desired.

WHAT ABOUT EATING OUT?

More of us are eating out than ever before. In the 1970s Americans were consuming about a quarter of their meals away from home; in the 1980s it's twice that. Of every dollar we spend on food, thirty-seven cents goes toward food away from home.

There are several reasons for this trend. For one, there are more moms working outside the home than at any time in our past. For another, there are more two-income families who can afford to eat out. As a society, we're in a bigger hurry; grabbing a bite at a restaurant is easier and more convenient than fixing food at home. And let's not forget the influence of advertising. We're bombarded with restaurant (primarily fast food restaurant) ads on television, on the radio, on billboards, all telling us where to take the break we deserve.

I know that after a long day at the office I'm in no mood to face a cookbook, and even with the microwave (one of the great inventions of this century), fixing meals requires time I don't always have. So Doug and Dana and I often pile into the car and head for a local "family" restaurant.

Taking children out to eat is bearable at two stages in their development: when they're too young to move around on their own, and when they're old enough to sit still for a while without complaining. At the ages Doug and Dana are now, I'm reasonably sure that they won't slide under the table when I'm not looking, throw food at each other, or make socially unacceptable body noises (too often).

Of course there were several years when I couldn't take them into any restaurant, family or otherwise. I refused to be one of those parents who spend the whole meal nagging and scolding. You've overheard them (maybe you've been one yourself): "Sit up straight! Stop playing with your food! No, you can't run down the aisle. No, you can't drink the half-and-half, or eat sugar, or smear ketchup in your hair." Whose idea of fun is that? Not mine—and not any child's I know.

Eating out with kids who aren't ready for it is unwise for a number of reasons. For one, it isn't just you-and-them anymore; there are all those potentially botherable strangers around you. Your attentions are divided between caring for your kids and wondering what people nearby are thinking. Suddenly your children are no longer independent human beings but products of your parenting skills, up for judgment by the world. If they misbehave, you're the one who gets glared at.

An even better reason to wait is respect for your kids' feelings and needs. If they're used to downing their dinners in ten minutes and rushing off to play, it's not fair to make them stay in one place for an hour or longer. Naturally they're going to get antsy and bored while you sit there sipping your coffee.

But let's say your children are angelic in public, eat anything that's put in front of them, and are content to doodle on their (paper!) placemats until closing time. Does that mean you've got it made? Not if you're committed to Fat-Proofing.

No restaurant I've ever been in lists calories and ingredients on its menu. Often you simply don't know what you're getting. Plus, the menu is full of things you're trying to keep out of your house—soft drinks, fried foods, fatty meats, calorie-laden sauces, white breads. And right there on your table are plentiful supplies of sugar and salt.

So what's the answer? Fix every meal at home? We all know that's not practical. There will be days when you're too beat to turn on the oven; that doesn't mean you're a bad parent. But here are a few alternatives to eating out even when you don't feel like cooking in:

- Haul out the whole-grain crackers, cheese, peanut butter, carrot sticks, apples, and such you probably have around the house anyway, and have the kids help you make a meal out of those. Use paper plates so you don't even have any cleanup.

- Make yogurt parfaits. Let the kids help layer plain yogurt, fruit, and granola in cups or bowls.

- If your cupboards are bare, order a pizza for delivery. Almost any pizza is more nutritious than other types of fast foods. (The average slice contains 15 percent protein, 27 percent fat, and 58 percent carbohydrate).

Now for restaurants. After you've found a few that suit you (see the box on p. 229 for tips), you'll still have to wend your way through the menu maze. You won't be able to stand over the chef's/cook's shoulder, but you *can* exercise some control over what comes out of the kitchen. According to *Nutrition and Health*, the newsletter published by Columbia University's Institute of Human Nutrition, here's how:

- Skip those items described as "creamed," "in cheese sauce," "buttery," "casserole," "crispy," "pan-fried," and the like—code words for *fatty*. Choose simple dishes instead.

- Order entrees that must be prepared individually—chicken breast, fish, steak—and you can put a halt to salt before it's added. Avoid soups, since they're usually heavily salted.

- Ask for salad dressings to be served on the side so you can control the amount you use. Or request vinegar and oil and dress your own.

- Specify skim milk rather than whole, margarine rather than butter.

- Select baked potatoes (no butter, no sour cream!) instead of fried or au gratin.

- Order a la carte to fend off too much food.

- Don't be afraid to ask for what you want. Remember, you're paying the bill.

FAST FOOD FACTS

According to the U.S. Department of Agriculture, Americans spend two out of every five away-from-home food dollars in fast food restaurants. Between 1953 and 1983, the number of fast food outlets tripled—from nearly 40,000 to more than 122,000. Today they account for nearly 50 percent of all eating places in the country.

A 1978 consumer survey revealed that 90 percent of Americans (that's over 200 million people) eat fast food at least once every six months. The key words here are "at least." Most fast food consumers, in fact, eat one to three fast food meals every week. Ten percent of them eat fast food *more than five times a week*.

To me, those figures are alarming. I won't deny that Doug and Dana

A RESTAURANT SURVIVAL GUIDE
FOR PRACTICAL PARENTS

- Eat out at the kids' regular eating time—but not (if you can avoid it) a restaurant's heaviest traffic time.

- If your children are still quite young, take them to a place where they'll be welcome. It's a good sign if there are plenty of high chairs and booster chairs available.

- Try to find restaurants that place at least a token emphasis on healthful or natural foods. That's not as difficult as it used to be. A vegetarian or health-food restaurant is usually a safe bet. (Added boon: in most such places you won't have to argue about beverages. Soft drinks usually aren't available; fruit juices are abundant.) Chinese restaurants are good choices, too.

- Unless you have nerves of steel, stay away from places where the focus is on noisy entertainment rather than food.

- Teeny tables don't allow room for play while you're waiting for your food to arrive. When possible, and if your kids are past the "grabber" stage when the confines of a high chair are vital, commandeer a booth. Then get out the puzzles, Hot-Wheels cars, or crayons and coloring books you've been clever enough to bring along to make the wait more bearable for everyone.

- Is there a kids' menu? Scan it thoroughly. Too often children's menus are limited to hamburgers, hot dogs, fried chicken, and breaded fish sticks. See if it's possible to order smaller portions off the regular menu. If this isn't an option, and if the menu stresses "no substitutions," then ask for extra plates, order something everybody likes, and share.

- Follow the same Fat-Proofing rules you use at home. In other words, don't make a big deal out of whether the kids clean their plates (although paying restaurant prices makes this hard to resist). And it goes without saying that you shouldn't promise dessert as a reward for *anything*.

have consumed their share of Big Macs and Whoppers, but I hate to think that people consider fast food a staple. (So do the experts, who worry that families on budgets spend too much on fast food and may skimp on quality home-cooking ingredients and miss the nutrients from fruits, veggies, and whole grains.)

There's some food value in even the greasiest burger, but it's frequently accompanied by sugar (buns are sugared to make them toast quicker), salt (far more than you'd use at home), and fat (cheese and special sauces). And the calorie count is sky-high. A typical burger-fries-milkshake combination can approach 1,000 calories. (More, if you can believe it, than a serving of fettuccini Alfredo.)

Curious about what's in some brand-name fast foods? Here's a brief rundown to compare with what you now know about healthful eating:

- A McDonald's chocolate shake contains 383 calories, 10 grams of protein, 66 grams of carbohydrates, 9 grams of fats, and 300 mg. of sodium.

- A Burger King chocolate shake contains 340 calories, 8 grams of protein, 57 grams of carbohydrates, 10 grams of fats, and 280 mg. of sodium.

- A Wendy's Frosty contains 390 calories, 9 grams of protein, 54 grams of carbohydrates, 9 grams of fats, and 247 mg. of sodium.

Another eye-opener: Did you ever wonder why shakes aren't called milkshakes? It's because they're prepared from vegetable oils. At least they contain *some* dried-milk products.

- A McDonald's Big Mac boasts 563 calories, 26 grams of protein, 41 grams of carbohydrates, 33 grams of fats, and 1,010 mg. of sodium.

- A Burger King Whopper contains 630 calories, 26 grams of protein, 50 grams of carbohydrates, 36 grams of fats, and 990 mg. of sodium.

- A Wendy's single-with-everything has 470 calories, 26 grams of protein, 34 grams of carbohydrates, 26 grams of fats, and 774 mg. of sodium.

You thought fish was better for your kids than burgers? If it's fast food fish, think again:

- An Arthur Treacher's Fish Sandwich has 440 calories, 16 grams of protein, 39 grams of carbohydrates, 24 grams of fats, and 836 mg. of sodium.

- A McDonald's Filet-o-Fish contains 432 calories, 14 grams of protein, 37 grams of carbohydrates, 25 grams of fats, 781 mg. of sodium.

- A Burger King Whaler has 486 calories, 18 grams of protein, 64 grams of carbohydrates, 46 grams of fats, and 735 mg. of sodium.

Is chicken healthier and more nutritious? Both Kentucky Fried Chicken Original Recipe and Extra Crispy dinners are high in calories (830 and 950 respectively) and fats (46 and 54 grams). But their biggest problem is sodium. The Original Recipe dinner contains an astonishing 2,285 mg.; Extra Crispy, a slightly lower 1,915.

What about breakfast? A McDonald's Scrambled Egg Breakfast—eggs, sausage, an English muffin with butter, and hash brown potatoes—contains 1,463 mg. of sodium. And 697 calories.

Now that you know the perils and pitfalls of fast foods, are you going to keep your kids away from them until they're old enough to move out of the house? Probably not. I haven't. A meal at McDonald's or Burger King or Wendy's or Arby's or Taco Bell or Dairy Queen or Arthur Treacher's or even Kentucky Fried Chicken won't do irreparable damage. Actually, it's more harmful to make an issue out of it. After all, children want what they've been told they can't have.

My advice: Give in to their wishes from time to time. Fortunately, this doesn't necessarily mean giving up on Fat-Proofing. Despite the fact that fast food menus are limited, you can still have some effect on what your kids eat. Here's how:

- Order milk—skim, if available—rather than soft drinks (often caffeinated) or shakes. Orange or tomato juice are other options, since they add vitamins A and C (most fast food meals are short on vitamin A).

- If you can order foods cooked to your specifications, ask them to hold the pickle—and the salt. When possible, order without any condiments and add your own sparingly. If what you see is what you get, scrape off sauces.

- See if the kids will agree to substitute salad for fries; many fast food establishments now feature salad bars. But watch out for fruits in sugared syrup, sweetened bean salads, and creamed cottage cheese.

Most important, remember that the one fast food meal they eat won't be their only meal of the day. You can make up for shortages and excesses elsewhere. Or plan the next day's meals to balance things in favor of Fat-Proofing.

FAST FOOD FACTS

Want to know more about fast foods? The American Council on Science and Health has published an excellent report on the subject called "Fast Food and the American Diet." To order a copy, send $2 to:

> The American Council on Science and Health
> 47 Maple St.
> Summit, NJ 07901.

The council recommends that you write to fast food companies if you'd like complete nutrition information on their products, and the report contains addresses for the most popular chains.

Or send for (and post in your kitchen) Center for Science in the Public Interest's (CSPI's) excellent *Fast Food Eating Guide.* This large, colorful and informative poster will be a welcome addition to your family's education. Send $4.25 ppd to:

> CSPI,
> 1501 16th St. N.W.
> Washington, DC 20036

and ask for poster #94.

WHERE TO GO FOR NUTRITION INFORMATION

Do artificial food colorings cause cancer? What should you do if your baby is allergic to milk? What's the scoop on the latest "kids' diets"? How can you tell if your children are getting all the nutrients they need?

There are many sources that can give you answers to questions like these (and the thousands more you're apt to come up with now and in the future). The more information you have at hand, the better able you'll be to make the decisions that are right for your family.

Below is a listing of several such sources. (Many publications are free or very inexpensive.) And don't forget those in your own "backyard"—university extension services; local health departments; libraries; college departments of nutrition; local chapters of the American Heart Association, American Dietetic Association, and American Diabetes Association;

and area hospitals and medical centers, many of which offer courses on healthful eating and lifestyles.

- *Jane Brody's Nutrition Book* (New York: Bantam Books, 1982), $9.95. By the personal health columnist for *The New York Times*, this book is a treasure. My copy is dog-eared. Find it at your local bookstore, or write to: Bantam Books, 666 Fifth Ave., New York, NY 10103.

- The Center for Science in the Public Interest (CSPI), a food and nutrition advocacy group, has several excellent publications (some in colorful poster form). For a free catalog, write to: CSPI, 1501 W. 16th St. NW, Washington, DC 20036, or call (202) 332-9110.

CSPI also publishes a lively and readable newsletter. *Nutrition Action* (10 issues per year, $20).

- Other newsletters you may want to look into:

  - *Health and Nutrition Newsletter,* published bimonthly by the Columbia University College of Physicians and Surgeons, Subscription Dept., PO Box 8000, Patterson, NJ 12563. A 1-year subscription costs $18.
  - *The Harvard University Medical School Health Letter,* available by writing to: 79 Garden St., Cambridge, MA 02138. The price is $18 per year.
  - *Mayo Clinic Health Letter,* published monthly. A 1-year subscription costs $24. Write to: Mayo Medical Resources, Rochester, MN 55905. Or phone: (509) 284-4587.
  - The *Tufts University Diet & Nutrition Letter* is published monthly; a 1-year subscription costs $18. Write to: P.O. Box 10946, Des Moines, IA 50940.
  - *Nutrition Week,* published 50 times per year by the Community Nutrition Institute in Washington, D.C. Check your library for this one or order from 2001 S St. NW, Washington, DC 20009. A 1-year subscription costs $65.

- Keats Publishing Co. specializes in the areas of health and nutrition. Order any of the following by writing to the publisher: 27 Pine St. (Box 876), New Canaan, CT 06840, or call (203) 966-8721.

  - *Nutritional Parenting: How to Get Your Child Off Junk Foods and*

Into Healthy Eating Habits, a pamphlet by Sara Sloan (1982; $1.95).

- *Know Your Nutrition,* by Linda Clark (revised edition, 1981; $3.50).
- *The Additive Book,* by Beatrice Trum Hunter (1980; $2.25).
- *Better Food for Better Babies and Their Families,* by Gena Larson (1982; $2.25).
- *Parents' Guide to Better Nutrition for Tots to Teens,* by Emory Thurston, Ph.D. (1979; $4.95).
- *Nourishing Your Child,* by Ray Wunderlich, Jr., M.D., and Dwight K. Kalita, Ph.D. (1984; $18.95).

Keats also publishes a bimonthly newsletter, *Health News and Review;* a 1-year subscription costs $6.95.

- The American Heart Association has more than seventy-five publications on health and health-related issues, including nutrition. Many are free to the public. *Cooking Without Your Salt Shaker,* a no-salt cookbook, is available for $3.75. For more information, write or call your local American Heart Association chapter.

- Contact your local Red Cross chapter to find out whether and when it's offering the "Better Eating for Better Health" program. Developed in cooperation with the U.S. Department of Agriculture, it includes courses on what to feed babies, toddlers, 6-to-12-year-olds, adolescents, and seniors.

- The United States government is an excellent source of information on health and nutrition, and many of its publications are free. Some examples: "A Compendium on Fats," "The Confusing World of Health Foods," "Food Additives," "Nutrition and Your Health: Dietary Guidelines for Americans," "Sodium," "Sugar," "Vegetarian Diets," "Sweetness Minus Calories Equals Controversy," and "What About Nutrients in Fast Foods?" Send for a copy of the latest *Consumer Information Catalog* (published quarterly) by writing to: Consumer Information Catalogue— Pueblo, CO 81009.

- For the names of nutritionists near you, write to: Consulting Nutritionists, Public Relations Director, 2191 London Drive, Glendale Heights, IL 60139.

- Finally, if you have questions about health, nutrition, or medical treatment and need answers fast, call the ODPHP-National Health Information Center hotline. Between 9:00 A.M. and 5:00 P.M. Eastern time, you can call toll free: (800) 336-4797. In Washington, D.C., call (202) 429-9091. Or write to ODHP-NHIC, Box 1133, Washington, D.C. 20013-1133.

AFTERWORD

FAT-PROOFING:
A NEW BEGINNING

You've reached the end of the Fat-Proofing book, but the Fat-Proofing program is just beginning for you and your family.

Like anything else, it's going to have its good days and its bad days. The important thing to remember—especially on the bad days—is that Fat-Proofing doesn't happen overnight. It's a lifelong process, a lifelong commitment, and a lifelong promise to help your kids be their best and healthiest selves.

This places a lot of responsibility on you. **But** . . .

- Nobody will send you to jail for bending the rules to suit your own circumstances and your own family's needs.

- You're not perfect. Your kids aren't perfect. The Fat-Proofing program probably isn't perfect, either. The best you can do is . . . the best you can do. Relax!

- A Fat-Proofed household is no guarantee that there won't be occasional lapses—into junk-food eating, meal skipping, perhaps even periods of overweight. *This doesn't mean you're a failure.* Weather the storm and renew your efforts!

Fat-Proofing rule 4 (rewritten just for you):
"Send yourself the message—*'You're okay.'*"

There's one more benefit to Fat-Proofing you may already be aware of: It feels good to feed your family right, to watch your kids grow up strong and healthy, and to know that they're forming sound eating habits early—because of you. Congratulate yourself on giving them the best gift of all.

FOR
FURTHER
READING

Brody, Jane. *Jane Brody's Nutrition Book* (New York: Bantam Books, 1982).

_____. *Jane Brody's Good Food Book* (New York: Bantam Books, 1986).

Brown, Judith. *Nutrition for Your Pregnancy: The University of Minnesota Guide* (Minneapolis: University of Minnesota Press, 1983).

Fahey, Thomas D., Ed.D. *Good-Time Fitness for Kids* (New York: Butterick Publishing, 1979).

Goldbeck, Nikki and David. *American Wholefoods Cuisine* (New York: New American Library, 1983).

Goodwin, Mary T., and Gerry Pollen. *Creative Food Experiences for Children* (Washington, D.C.: The Center for Science in the Public Interest, 2d revised edition, 1980).

Jacobson, Michael F., Ph.D. *Nutrition Scoreboard: Your Guide to Better Eating* (New York: Avon, 1975).

Leach, Penelope. *Your Baby and Child from Birth to Age Five* (New York: Knopf, 1984).

National Board of the Young Men's Christian Associations. *The Official YMCA Fitness Program* (New York: Rawson Associates, 1984).

Natow, Annette, and Jo-Ann Heslin. *No-Nonsense Nutrition for Kids* (New York: McGraw-Hill, 1985).

Pipes, Peggy, R.D., M.P.H. *Nutrition in Infancy and Childhood* (St. Louis: C. V. Mosby, 1981).

Prudden, Suzy, and Jeffrey Sussman. *Suzy Prudden's Pregnancy & Back-to-Shape Exercise Program* (New York: Workman Publishing Co., 1980).

Satter, Ellyn, R.D. *Child of Mine: Feeding with Love and Good Sense* (Palo Alto, CA: Bull Publishing, 1983).

Silberstein, Dr. Warren P. *Helping Your Child Grow Slim* (New York: Simon and Schuster, 1982).

Whitener, Carol, and Marie Keeling. *Nutrition Education for Young Children* (Englewood Cliffs, NJ: Prentice-Hall, 1984).

Wilkinson, J.F. *Don't Raise Your Child to Be a Fat Adult* (New York: Signet, 1981).

Winick, Myron, M.D. *Growing Up Healthy* (New York: William Morrow & Company, 1982).

———. *For Mothers & Daughters: A Guide to Good Nutrition for Women* (New York: William Morrow & Company, 1983).

Wynder, Ernst L., M.D., ed. *The Book of Health: A Complete Guide to Making Health Last a Lifetime* (New York: Franklin Watts, 1981).

BOYS: BIRTH TO 36 MONTHS

PHYSICAL GROWTH
NATIONAL CENTER FOR HEALTH STATISTICS*

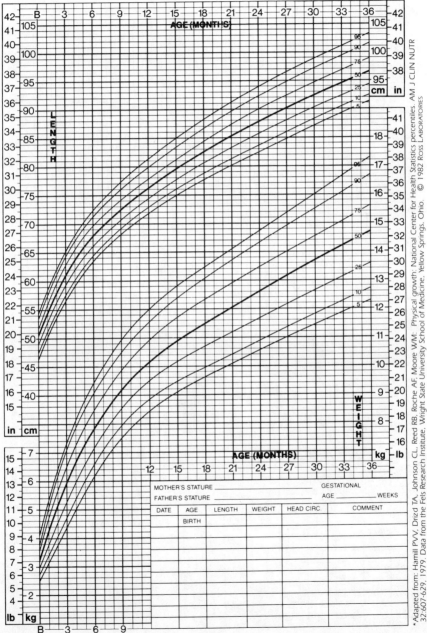

*Adapted from: Hamill PVV, Drizd TA, Johnson CL, Reed RB, Roche AF, Moore WM: Physical growth: National Center for Health Statistics percentiles. AM J CLIN NUTR 32:607-629, 1979. Data from the Fels Research Institute, Wright State University School of Medicine, Yellow Springs, Ohio. © 1982 ROSS LABORATORIES

MOTHER'S STATURE _____ GESTATIONAL
FATHER'S STATURE _____ AGE _____ WEEKS

DATE	AGE	LENGTH	WEIGHT	HEAD CIRC.	COMMENT
	BIRTH				

GIRLS: BIRTH TO 36 MONTHS
PHYSICAL GROWTH
NATIONAL CENTER FOR HEALTH STATISTICS*

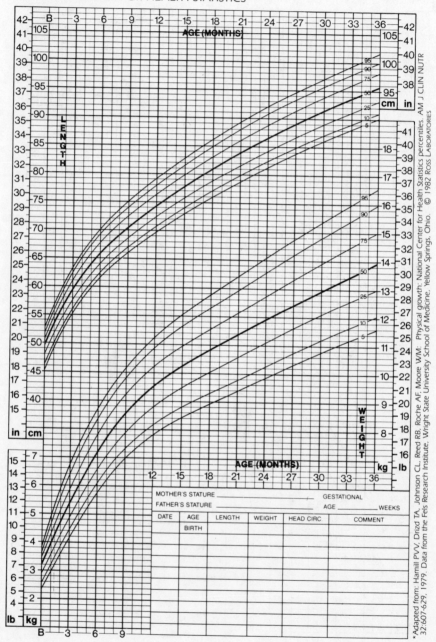

*Adapted from: Hamill PVV, Drizd TA, Johnson CL, Reed RB, Roche AF, Moore WM: Physical growth: National Center for Health Statistics percentiles. AM J CLIN NUTR 32:607-629, 1979. Data from the Fels Research Institute, Wright State University School of Medicine, Yellow Springs, Ohio. © 1982 ROSS LABORATORIES

BOYS: 2 TO 18 YEARS
PHYSICAL GROWTH
NATIONAL CENTER FOR HEALTH STATISTICS*

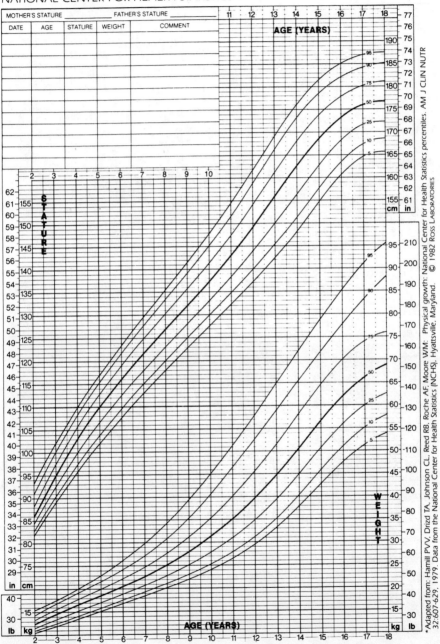

*Adapted from: Hamill PVV, Drizd TA, Johnson CL, Reed RB, Roche AF, Moore WM: Physical growth: National Center for Health Statistics percentiles. AM J CLIN NUTR 32:607-629, 1979. Data from the National Center for Health Statistics (NCHS), Hyattsville, Maryland. © 1982 ROSS LABORATORIES

GIRLS: 2 TO 18 YEARS
PHYSICAL GROWTH
NATIONAL CENTER FOR HEALTH STATISTICS*

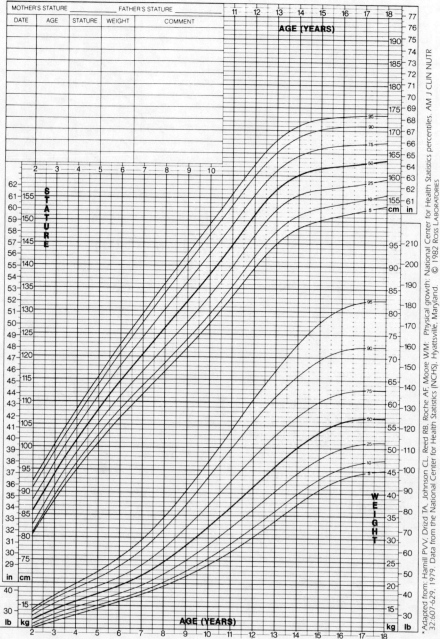

* Adapted from: Hamill PVV, Drizd TA, Johnson CL, Reed RB, Roche AF, Moore WM: Physical growth: National Center for Health Statistics percentiles. AM J CLIN NUTR 32:607-629, 1979. Data from the National Center for Health Statistics (NCHS). Hyattsville, Maryland. © 1982 ROSS LABORATORIES

Chapter Notes

CHAPTER ONE

Brody, Jane. "Helping the Overweight Child Break the Vicious Cycle of Overeating and Rejection." *The New York Times* CXXXIV (September 18, 1985): C10.

_____. "Panel Terms Obesity a Major U.S. Killer Needing Top Priority." *The New York Times* CXXXIV (February 14, 1985): 1A+.

_____. "Studies Vindicate the Obese." *Minneapolis Star & Tribune* XI (April 9, 1987): 1C+.

Clark, Matt, et al. "Why Kids Get Fat: A New Study Shows Obesity Is in the Genes." *Newsweek* 107 (February 3, 1986): 61.

"Fatter Execs Get Slimmer Paychecks." *Industry Week* 180 (January 14, 1974): 21+.

Matusewitch, Eric. "Employment Discrimination Against the Overweight." *Personnel Journal* 62 (June 1983): 446–50.

Stunkard, Albert J., M.D., ed. *Obesity*. Philadelphia: W. B. Saunders, 1980.

Waitzkin, Bonnie. "The Fat Child." *Parents* 58 (November 1983): 110–14+.

Wilkinson, J. F. *Don't Raise Your Child to Be a Fat Adult*. New York: Bobbs-Merrill, 1980.

Wishon, Phillip M., Robert Spangler, and Ben Eller. "The Myth of Baby Fat: What's So Pleasant about Plump?" *American Baby* 46 (August 1984): 51.

Zarrow, Susan. "Portly Kids Are Poor Students." *Prevention* 36 (February 1984): 13.

CHAPTER TWO

Brody, Jane. "Studies Vindicate the Obese."

Leveille, Gilbert A., Ph.D., and Dale R. Romsos, Ph.D. "Meal Eating and Obesity." *Nutrition Today* 9 (November/December 1974): 4–9.

CHAPTER THREE

Sperling, Dan. "TV Turns Kids on to Sweet Foods." *USA Today* (September 25, 1984).

CHAPTER FOUR

Brody, Jane. *Jane Brody's Nutrition Book: A Lifetime Guide to Good Eating for Better Health and Weight Control.* New York: Bantam Books, 1987.
_____. "Studies Vindicate the Obese."
Brown, Judith. *Nutrition for Your Pregnancy: The University of Minnesota Guide.* Minneapolis: University of Minnesota Press, 1983.
A Commonsense Guide to Sex, Birth and Babies. Alexandria, VA: Time-Life Books, 1982.
Satter, Ellyn, R.D. *Child of Mine: Feeding With Love and Good Sense.* Palo Alto, CA: Bull Publishing, 1983.
Shapiro, Leona, et al. "Obesity Prognosis: A Longitudinal Study of Children from the Age of 6 Months to 9 Years." *American Journal of Public Health* 74 (September 1984): 968–72.
Stunkard, Albert J., M.D., et al. "An Adoption Study of Human Obesity." *New England Journal of Medicine* 314 (January 23, 1986): 193–98.
Waitzkin, Bonnie. "The Fat Child."
Whitener, Carol, and Marie Keeling. *Nutrition Education for Young Children.* Englewood Cliffs, NJ: Prentice-Hall, 1984.
Winick, Myron, M.D. *Growing Up Healthy.* New York: William Morrow & Co., 1982.

CHAPTER FIVE

Brody, Jane. *Jane Brody's Nutrition Book.*
Brown, Judith. *Nutrition for Your Pregnancy.*
Carney, Cynthia L. "Life with a Fussy Eater." *Parents* 59 (August 1984): 60–62.
Gelman, David, et al. "The Food-Mood Link." *Newsweek* CVI (October 14, 1985): 93–94.
Goldbeck, David and Nikki. *American Wholefoods Cuisine.* New York: New American Library, 1983.
Josephson, Judith P., and Edith H. Fine. "Eating Well Early Is Not Childish." *San Diego Union* (July 26, 1984).
Natow, Annette B., and Jo-Ann Heslin. *No-Nonsense Nutrition for Kids.* New York: McGraw-Hill, 1985.
Satter, Ellyn. *Child of Mine.*
Smith, David W., M.D., ed. *The Biologic Ages of Man.* Philadelphia: W. B. Saunders, 1978.

CHAPTER SIX

Brody, Jane. *Jane Brody's Nutrition Book.*
Carney, Cynthia. "Life With a Fussy Eater."
Charlier, Marj. "Teen-Age Obesity Grows As More Kids Come Home to Empty Houses and TV." *The Wall Street Journal* LXV (July 1, 1985): 15.
Leach, Penelope. *Your Baby and Child from Birth to Age Five.* New York: Alfred A. Knopf, 1984.
Mindell, Earl. *Vitamin Bible for Your Kids.* New York: Bantam Books, 1981.
Natow and Heslin. *No-Nonsense Nutrition for Kids.*
Pipes, Peggy, R.D., M.P.H. *Nutrition in Infancy and Childhood.* St. Louis: C. V. Mosby, 1981.

CHAPTER SEVEN

American Academy of Pediatrics, Committee on Nutrition. "Prudent Life-style for Children: Dietary Fat and Cholesterol." *Pediatrics* 78 (September 1986): 521–25.
Natow and Heslin. *No-Nonsense Nutrition for Kids.*
Silberstein, Warren P., and Laurence Galton. *Helping Your Child Grow Slim.* New York: Simon & Schuster, 1982.
Tkac, Debora. "How to Slim Your Chubby Child." *Rodale's Children* (summer 1987): 46–48.
Whitener and Keeling. *Nutrition Education for Young Children.* Englewood Cliffs, NJ: Prentice Hall, 1984.

CHAPTER EIGHT

Barnard, Christiaan, and John Illman, eds. *The Body Machine.* New York: Crown, 1981.
Bayer, Alan E., and Daniel H. Baker. "Adolescent Eating Disorders: Anorexia and Bulimia." *Family Life Educator* (winter 1984).
Charlier, Marj. "Teen-Age Obesity Grows As More Kids . . ."
Edelstein, Barbara, M.D. *The Woman Doctor's Diet for Teen-Age Girls.* Englewood Cliffs, NJ: Prentice-Hall, 1980.
Jacobson, Beverly. *Anorexia Nervosa and Bulimia: Two Severe Eating Disorders.* New York: Public Affairs Pamphlets, 1985.
Kaercher, Dan. "Hypnosis: How Modern Medicine Is Using an Ancient Art." *Better Homes and Gardens* 61 (October 1983): 24–25+.
Libo, Felicia. "Bulimia." *Weight Watchers Magazine* 17 (October 1984): 14–16.
Paul, Aileen. *The Kids' Diet Cookbook.* New York: Doubleday & Co., 1980.
Winick, Myron, M.D. *For Mothers and Daughters: A Guide to Good Nutrition for Women.* New York: William Morrow & Co., 1983.

CHAPTER NINE

Clark, Jean Illsley. *Self-Esteem: A Family Affair.* Minneapolis: Winston-Seabury/Harper
& Row, 1978.

CHAPTER TEN

Kuntzleman, Charles T., Ed.D. "How Fit Are Your Kids?" *Shape* (December 1984): 49+.
"Let's Playarena." *American Baby* 46 (September 1984): 60.
National Board of the Young Men's Christian Association. *The Official YMCA Fitness Pro-
gram.* New York: Rawson Associates, 1984.
"Physical Education: A Performance Checklist." Washington, D.C.: President's Council
on Physical Fitness and Sports.
Prudden, Suzy, and Jeffrey Sussman. *Suzy Prudden's Pregnancy and Back-to-Shape Exercise
Program.* New York: Workman, 1980.

CHAPTER ELEVEN

Ahamm, Sarah. "Calls for Dietary Changes Among Children." *Pediatric News* (April 1984).
Brody, Jane. "Guiding Children to Reduce the Risks of Heart Disease." *The New York Times*
CXXVII (July 20, 1983).
_____. *Jane Brody's Nutrition Book.*
Brown, Judith. *Nutrition for Your Pregnancy.*
Clark, Matt, et al. "America's Sweet Tooth." *Newsweek* CVI (August 26, 1985): 50–56.
Fisher, Arthur. *The Healthy Heart.* Alexandria, VA: Time-Life Books, 1981.
Jacobson, Michael F., Ph.D. *Nutrition Scoreboard: Your Guide to Better Eating.* New York:
Avon, 1975.
Lecos, Chris W. "Cutting Cholesterol? Look to the Label." *FDA Consumer* (February
1984): 9–12.
Wynder, Ernst L., M.D., ed. *The Book of Health: A Complete Guide to Making Health Last a
Lifetime.* New York: Franklin Watts, 1981.

CHAPTER TWELVE

Franz, Marion J., R.D., M.S. *Fast Food Facts: Nutritive and Exchange Values for Fast-Food
Restaurants.* Minneapolis: International Diabetes Center, 1987.
Slavin, Joanne L. "Getting Nutrition Advice." *Young Families.* St. Paul: University of Min-
nesota Agricultural Extension Service, 1984.

INDEX

Vicki Lansky's warm and practical approach to parenting has helped and encouraged millions of parents. Her books, columns, and media appearances have made her one of America's leading authorities on parenting.

Vicki's first book, the now classic baby and toddler cookbook *Feed Me! I'm Yours,* was first published in 1975. Her second book, *The Taming of the C.A.N.D.Y. Monster,* was published in 1978 and became a #1 *New York Times* bestseller.

Her *Practical Parenting Newsletter* assembled tips from parents nationwide and led to the Practical Parenting series of books for new parents, as well as the Practical Parenting Read-Together series featuring KoKo Bear.

To contact the author, or to receive a flyer on her various titles, write:

> Vicki Lansky
> Practical Parenting, Dept. FP
> Deephaven, MN 55391

Or call: (800) 255-7739
                      (612) 475-3527 (in Minnesota)